TWO
CONFESSIONS

SUNY series in Latin American and Iberian Thought and Culture
Jorge J. E. Gracia and Rosemary Geisdorfer Feal, editors

TWO CONFESSIONS

MARÍA ZAMBRANO and ROSA CHACEL

Translated by NOËL VALIS and CAROL MAIER

Confession was originally published in Spanish as *La confesión: género literario y método* © 1943 María Zambrano. The English translation is made possible by permission of Fundación María Zambrano.

Confession was originally published in Spanish as *La confesión* © 1970 Rosa Chacel. The English translation is made possible by permission of Agencia Literaria Carmen Balcells, S.A.

Published by State University of New York Press, Albany

© 2015 State University of New York

All rights reserved

Printed in the United States of America

No part of this book may be used or reproduced in any manner whatsoever-without written permission. No part of this book may be stored in a retrieval system or transmitted in any form or by any means including electronic, electrostatic, magnetic tape, mechanical, photocopying, recording, or otherwise without the prior permission in writing of the publisher.

For information, contact State University of New York Press, Albany, NY
www.sunypress.edu

Production, Ryan Morris
Marketing, Fran Keneston

Library of Congress Cataloging-in-Publication Data

Two Confessions / María Zambrano and Rosa Chacel ; translated by Noël Valis and Carol Maier.
        pages cm. — (SUNY series in Latin American and Iberian Thought and Culture)
   Includes bibliographical references.
ISBN 978-1-4384-5729-1 (hc: alk paper)-978-1-4384-5730-7 (pb: alk paper)
ISBN 978-1-4384-5731-4 (e-book)
1. Spanish literature—History and criticism. 2. Confession in literature.
I. Valis, Noël Maureen, 1945- translator. II. Maier, Carol, 1943- translator.
III. Zambrano, María. Confesión: género literario y método. English
IV. Chacel, Rosa, 1898-1994. Confesión. English
   PQ6046.C64T96 2015
   860.9'353—dc23
                                                            2014034935

10 9 8 7 6 5 4 3 2 1

Contents

Introduction
Noël Valis

✲ 1 ✲

Confession
María Zambrano

✲ 13 ✲

Confession
Rosa Chacel

✲ 65 ✲

Afterword
Pieces of a Scattered Puzzle
Carol Maier

✲ 205 ✲

Annotations   229

Introduction

Noël Valis

What is confession if not an admission of failure? The essays you are about to read are doubly confessional in speaking to the subject at hand through the veil of personal failure. *Two Confessions* is the work of two remarkable women from Spain, María Zambrano and Rosa Chacel. Intellectually daring, Chacel (1898-1994) and Zambrano (1904-1991) shared a common trajectory that helps explain why both chose to focus on confession. Contemporaries and friends, they belonged to the fabled group of vanguardist writers and artists that included Lorca, Alberti, Cernuda, Buñuel, and Dalí. They were also strong supporters of the Second Republic, and exiles in Latin America after the Spanish Civil War. They were disciples of the philosopher Ortega y Gasset, but they questioned his concept of "vital reason," making their own way and creating highly original voices in different genres. Like other Spanish exiles of the time, they were marginalized and largely neglected until the transition to democracy after Franco's death in 1975.

However sweet the belated triumph of their final years, triumph was not what marked Zambrano and Chacel. The history that shaped their writings and lives came early, endured for decades, and was scarred with deep failure: the failure of the Second Republic and the trauma of the civil war in the 1930s. That failed history runs like an underground river through the essays and is part of what is confessed. Chacel underscores both the history and the failure, laden with guilt, in the preamble to her essay. After the exceptional promise of the 1920s, she says, "we felt guilty of not putting all our strength . . . in defense of life" (67). Did they do enough? Did her generation rise to meet the challenge of their circumstances, as Ortega would have said? Clearly, she is referring to the debacle of the thirties. Yet this history, as vital as it is to understanding the two essays, is really a metaphor for a more universal appreciation of confession itself, as a window into human inadequacy, human incompleteness, what in Western culture traditionally has been called original sin. For Zambrano, the self flees in "horror of being born" and falls into confusion. For Chacel, the self has become profoundly detached from the mystery of eros, an eros so all-encompassing it can only be called life.

There is a long-standing cliché that Spanish literature is lacking in the autobiographical and confessional tradition. Chacel's essay is to a significant degree a response to that view, in particular to Ortega y Gasset's remarks on the paucity of memoir. Whether we agree with Ortega depends of course on what we mean by the term *confession*. In a Catholic country, confession is penitential. But confession appears fairly early in Spanish literature, notably in the sixteenth-century picaresque novel *Lazarillo de Tormes*, in which fictional autobiographical revelations acquire a legal flavor, unsurprising in an inquisitorial society. Leopoldo Alas's 1884–1885 realist masterpiece, *La Regenta* [The Judge's Wife] (trans. *La Regenta*), is the most striking example of fictional confession, still attached to the tribunal of penance, as a driving force behind the main character and the narration itself. Chacel and Zambrano enlarge the presence and significance of confession, extending it beyond literature to life and treating writing, especially in relation to confession, as relevant and crucial to life. Indeed, confessional intimacy and autobiography are fundamental to much of their own writing. These essays exemplify that integral relationship and can both be seen as confession-texts. But are the two writers confessing the same thing?

Both essays were written in exile and are, in this sense, a product of history. Zambrano's appeared in 1943; Chacel's (written between 1964 and 1968) in 1971, with a second edition in 1980. Although there is no direct evidence that Chacel was responding to Zambrano's earlier text, we see a secret, subterranean dialogue passing between the two. In many ways, this is not surprising, given the close coincidence of intellectual formation and interests. Their relationship, while one of friendship, was at the same time filled with reticence and ambivalence. A correspondence begun in 1938 appears to have broken off by the late 1950s. In 1965, Chacel responded to a query from future novelist Ana María Moix saying that, for some unexplained reason, she had lost track of Zambrano, claiming as well that she could remember the title of only one book by her friend (Chacel, *De mar a mar* 71; see also Zubiaurre).

If we read, however, one author against, through, and alongside the other one, the resonances are striking, despite the differences of approach and emphasis. Once again, failure binds them together, here by way of a foundational figure of modern Spanish literature, the nineteenth-century realist writer Benito Pérez Galdós. I don't think we can understand these essays without considering the key role Galdós plays in shaping the vision of both confession and its relation to history, especially Spanish history, in *Two Confessions*. Galdós consumes Chacel, while, paradoxically, his name never appears in Zambrano's text. It is important to remember, however, that Zambrano wrote repeatedly on the Canary-born novelist, beginning in the 1930s all the way through to 1986 (see Mora García). Chacel views Galdós's failure to confess through the vehicle of his fiction as a failure of modern, liberal Spain. His failure is also ultimately the inability to embrace eros, which becomes a flawed understanding of reality that she extends to Spain itself.

A good deal of Chacel's essay focuses on Galdós. His canonical status today as a master of realism is taken for granted. That status, however, is relatively recent. In the 1920s and '30s, vanguardists such as Chacel rejected not only his realist aesthetics but his approach to Spanish history and society. *They* were modern; Galdós was the past. Her anti-Galdosian prejudice is generational. When civil war erupted in 1936, the view of Galdós shifted, as Republican supporters began to see in his historical novels, the *Episodios nacionales* [National Episodes], a symbol of *el pueblo*, the people, struggling to liberate themselves. Both perceptions are part of the backstory to her text and help to explain how Galdós's presumed inadequacies end up standing in for the personal and generational inadequacies to which Chacel only partially admits. I see her reading of Galdós as profoundly and brilliantly mistaken, but her misunderstanding is one of those fruitful misunderstandings that leads to further meditation and larger questions on the nature of writing, the relation between writing and life, between writing and author, between the novel and confession. If, as

Chacel argues, Galdós disappoints as a novelist insofar as he refuses to confess, then what is she saying about the novel in general? Must novels always be confessions? And if so, what should they confess?

For Chacel, what is missing in Spain and Spanish literature is eros. A person confesses, she says, "when the enormous weight of which he wants to unburden himself is not an act that he's committed, nor even a considerable number of acts, but a persistent conflict that led to all of them, a mystery that not even he himself understands and that perhaps he confesses only for the sake of hearing it told, in order to understand it. The mystery that became a conflict . . . was eros" (97). This is what she finds in the exemplary confessions of Augustine, Rousseau, and Kierkegaard, but does not see in Galdós and in Spanish literature as a whole, characterizing it as reserved and opaque when it comes to confession, with the exception of Cervantes and to some extent Unamuno. One wonders how she would have read the other master of nineteenth-century Spanish realism, Leopoldo Alas (Clarín), whose novel *La Regenta*, unappreciated in Chacel's day, is overwhelmingly confessional (and filled with the longing of eros). Augustine's confession is the universally recognized template, as both Chacel and Zambrano agree. But as Chacel writes, what we are hearing in confession is "the conflictive secret," the unresolvable tension between inner being and real life. What can ever be produced from such tension other than the admission of lack? In this sense, the ghost confessions Chacel discerns above all in Spanish writers can be observed globally. Her comments on Rousseau's "desertions," whether real, emotional, or metaphorical, make clear that he holds back when confessing, though of course we know he is holding back. He writes, "It isn't a question of saying too much or of saying lies, but of not saying everything, of silencing truths" (1:276). Can one ever confess completely? *All* confession is by nature then a failure. All confession is a specter of itself.

The failure of confession and the failure that is being confessed are at the heart of Chacel's essay. This is why Galdós is so key to her argument. She needed the absence of Galdosian confession, that is, her particular interpretation of the novelist, to propel her essay forward, to affirm the failure of confession. Chacel is at her most quixotic in her obsessive quest for the nonexistent confession in Galdós. Any traces of confession can only be found in male characters (stand-ins for the novelist?) and, most especially, in one of the heroes of his historical fiction, Monsalud, who incarnates conflict itself. In other words, where Chacel seeks confession she finds not inner conflict, but the national drama of Cain and Abel. The nineteenth-century history that Galdós brings to life is unending strife and disturbance: a Spain at war with itself, precisely the contemporary historical experience that marked the writings and lives of Chacel and Zambrano.

In this view, Galdós appears not simply to externalize the inner conflict that compels one to confess but to nationalize it. Only by briefly examining Zambrano's understanding of Galdós, however, is it possible to see how Chacel tends to box in both herself and the nineteenth-century novelist, making it nearly impossible to produce confession. And that is because the true center of her quest is ultimately unconfessable and, in that sense, unknowable. Chacel says of Galdós and Unamuno: "if they did not confess it was because they lived *unconfessable lives*" (168). The same could be said of Chacel. Zambrano too resisted the full revelation of self, but she saw something in Galdós that permitted an opening, the hope of escaping the solitude of the self. That something was the fullness of immersion in life, which in turn held the promise of communion.

Zambrano's first commentaries on Galdós appeared in the celebrated Republican wartime journal, *Hora de España*, to which Chacel also contributed, and where they undoubtedly read at least some of each other's essays. Chacel even wrote on the master of realism in *Hora de España*, characterizing his work as infused with a sacramental sense "of reciprocal and incessant communion" ("Un nombre al frente" 49). This view is actually very close to that of Zambrano, who held, in an essay published in 1939, that Spanish realism in general was "nothing less than being in love with the world, captivated by it, and therefore bound to it." She saw in realism an "equilibrium between the individual and the community. Through poetic knowledge man never separates himself from the universe, and, preserving intact his private nature, participates in everything, he belongs to the universe, to nature and to the human and even to what exists within the human, and even beyond that" (*Pensamiento y poesía* 135, 159). Galdós's characters were hungry for life, they thirsted after reality, Zambrano observed more than once (see *La España de Galdós*). They sought "the place of life."

Nowhere is this more evident than in the novelist's late masterpiece, *Misericordia* [Compassion], which is discussed in Chacel's essay.

For Zambrano, Benina, the servant who begs on the streets to save her mistress, is as a character complete and rooted in reality. Yet "free of history, it is as if she were being born at every instant." As embodied compassion, she also represents "the constant breath of creation maintaining the world.... He who lives by compassion, lives in it, caught in its orbit, connected to other creatures by this force" (*"Misericordia"* 138, 141). On another, more historical level, Benina is *el pueblo*, the Spanish people, signaling Zambrano's desperate desire for *communitas*, for the spirit of community, in an essay written as civil war raged in Spain. Chacel's view of the novel is very different. In *Confession*, she says bluntly, the theme of compassion is a cliché in Galdós's hands. She grants that he has managed to provide a richly documented figure in Benina, but clearly does not share Zambrano's sweeping, transcendent vision of the novel. One cannot help thinking that her remarks are in some ways an indirect response to Zambrano, who unlike most of the vanguardists openly embraced Galdós.

Chacel's comments on *Misericordia* reinforce her generally critical view of Galdós, which in turn drives her quest for the elusive presence of confession as a genre, albeit in a different way. Zambrano and Chacel alike associate confession with the novel. Curiously, Zambrano's essay bears the subtitle "A Literary Genre," but appears at first to speak little of the link between confession and fiction, or at least of specific novels, whereas Chacel's text concentrates heavily on the linkage, all the while *not* actually finding confession. The predominant motif in both writers once again is failure. In 1937, Zambrano argued that the novel as a genre "is submerged in failure." It is, she said, "a partial failure... revealing on the other hand a hidden sustenance. It is an historical failure, a failure in the world upon which the novel is forged" ("Reforma del entendimiento" [The Reform of Understanding] 95–96). That hidden support system is *convivencia*, which can only weakly be expressed as a living together, or *communitas*, exemplified in the relationship between Don Quixote and Sancho Panza. This is, ultimately, "the place of life," the communion of life, for Zambrano.

Zambrano's views on the novel also help explain how she sees confession. There is, she writes, a radical disjunction between the truth of reason and life, and life is confusion, a kind of scattering. (This too is what Galdós shows in his novels.) Confession serves to bridge the gap between truth and life, the gap that also points to the lack of unity of the self. One confesses to escape the self that one does not want. Confession becomes especially acute in periods of crisis, of fracture, produced in moments when culture appears to be broken. Here she observes that the novel comes closest as a genre to the confession, reflecting the pain and abandonment of life, but at the same time there are sharp differences. Only when the time of the novel is the time of life can we speak about a kind of confession. Zambrano's vanguardist aesthetics continues to see the novel and literature in general as distinct from life. (This viewpoint helps explain why she criticizes literary realism as radically false in a brief passage of *Confession*, in contradistinction to her already noted, earlier espousal of Spanish realism as a form of poetic knowledge.) Indeed, she considers the autobiographical novel a narcissistic failure, a form of perpetual adolescence revealing a failed self (see also Johnson 57). At the same time, as with Chacel, writing is never disconnected from life. Literature and life, while distinct, are also porous, the one bleeding into the other.

The trajectory of Zambrano's essay goes from Job's preconfession, or complaint, to the Augustinian act of offering himself to God, Descartes's discovery of human solitude, Rousseau's conversion of confession into the history of his solitary heart, to the later artificial paradises of Baudelaire, Rimbaud, and the surrealists, and finally to the underground man, reminiscent of Dostoyevsky's character, whose soul has gone missing. In essence, she traces through confession the eventual appearance of modern man, of what modern life is. "Modern culture," she writes, "is born lacking oneness" (46). The path she follows is like a widening fissure, blowing a large hole in the imagined integrity of the self. Confession reveals "the fragmentary character of all life . . . in that every person feels himself to be incomplete bits and pieces, no more than an outline; a piece of one's self, a fragment" (26–27). Zambrano grounds the substance of this insight in a sweeping historical awareness of the changing shape of confession. In her view, Augustine appears to be the first and the last to find the unity, or oneness, of his life—though even this statement is subject to revision, as this is the *figure* of the unity of life. All confession seeks to regain a lost paradise, but Augustine understands this to be impossible. He can only hope to find the oneness of his own being through the being of the divine.

With Descartes, she argues, thought affirms human solitariness. In a brilliant intuition, she says that Descartes's revelation is the reverse of that of Augustine, "who felt alone, a fragment among things. Descartes withdraws from things" (45). There is only consciousness. This radical solitude anticipates the crucial turn confession takes with Rousseau. The heart becomes an abyss. Even more significantly, it acquires a history. Here, Zambrano takes up once more the thread connecting confession to the novel, arguing that the outpouring of the heart's history is what allowed for the development of the modern novel—and of course for romanticism. Romanticism "makes confessions in the form of histories, turning history into confession" (48). The same can be said of the novel, demonstrating a commonality with romanticism.

Jean-Jacques not only advocated for the unique status of his own heart's history, but claimed for it a naturalness that assimilated the heart to a garden, in a word, to paradise. In underscoring the heart's originality, Rousseau "produces a life, the least imaginable kind of life, the literary life or life in literature, life in imaginary situations" (49). In essence, with Jean-Jacques, confession becomes a kind of fiction, an imaginary place. Here is the "novel" again, a personal fiction that is Jean-Jacques's life. Everything that comes after Rousseau follows a similar pattern, creating a series of artificial paradises, such as we see in Baudelaire, Rimbaud, and the surrealists. Surrealism's attempt to regain the intimate center of being ends as a confession of failure, as mere hallucination.

So we come to Zambrano's final iteration, underground man, the ultimate evolution of the Cartesian self's fundamental solitariness. This creature I take to be the endpoint to her understanding of the modern self: weighed down, larval fragments of being. The living dead. Soulless. In hell. Confession is necessary because without it we suffocate. But something has to be there, something propitious, that allows the inner reality to be confessed. What happens if that inner reality is missing or is inadequate? Paradoxically, underground man is too filled with things to properly confess. He is overloaded, jammed full, "crowded with things, with embryonic beings, hopes and longings, drafts and projects, traces and premonitions of a nameless reality" (60). In truth, he is filled with solitariness, which Zambrano figures as "faceless, anonymous beings, embittered by their halfway existence." This, she says, is hell. The Christian existentialist Nicolas Berdyaev took it further, saying that "hell belongs entirely to the subjective and not to the objective sphere; it exists in the subject and not in the object, in man and not in God.... In hell the soul is separated from everyone and from everything, completely isolated and at the same time enslaved by everything and everyone.... Hell is nothing other than complete separation from God" (268, 277). Both Zambrano and Chacel skirt around this last point in their essays, in my view, while at the same time, it is impossible to situate their writings without recognizing the spiritual imprint that shapes them.

One needs a soul to confess, not psychic facts or acts of consciousness. But modern man has erased the soul. Zambrano appears to elide the notion of soul and subject at the end of her essay, since she also talks about the disappearance of the subject. What is left is an elusive, resentful ghost. Emptiness. Despite Zambrano's asking for a "true and implacable confession" at this point, how then can confession be anything other than a shadow of itself? One is reminded of the phantom confessions Chacel finds in Spanish writers. She also observed that confession is a "spectral analysis of the will" (136). Zambrano, in turn, views confession as the pressing need to let loose the creatures inside one's being. You could say we are haunted by ghosts of our own making. In this both writers are talking about what could be called ghost confessions.

The solitary creature that is modern man is filled with phantoms, the population of solitude. Confession happens because of the pressures of this netherworld. The nightmare of existence leaves us "alienated, with no possibility of communication, as in a bad dream when we call out and no one hears us" (Zambrano 34–35). How to crawl out of this underground life? Augustine's answer was to open himself up to his fellow man, relying on their good faith in him. "When we count on the faith of others, on their belief in us," she writes, "the seal of solitariness is broken" (36). Confession ideally ends in communion, shared truth. But, like Chacel, Zambrano surveys the world as it is, filled with fratricidal war. She uses the phrase "*guerra cainita,*" while Chacel's term is "*drama cainita,*" but in either case, historically, they had in mind the Spanish Civil War. Existentially, Cain and Abel is an allegory of inner conflict. Cain was at war with himself.

Confession exists because of our divided nature, because of the war that goes on inside us, "the civil war in the heart of man," as another Republican exile, Francisco Ayala, put it (33). Doing a modern reading of Augustine, Jean-François Lyotard observed in an essay first published in 1998, "The fissure that zigzags across the confession spreads with all speed over life, over lives" (57). Zambrano, we recall, spoke of "the fragmentary character of all life"; Chacel, of the conflict that is eros and that she sees in Augustine, Rousseau, and Kierkegaard. In either case, there is something missing, something hidden, Chacel would say. Flannery O'Connor wrote, "the novelist doesn't write about people in a vacuum; he writes about people in a world where something is obviously lacking, where there is the general mystery of incompleteness and the particular tragedy of our own times to be demonstrated" (167). Confession, like the novel, underscores that incompleteness and, ultimately, the failure to attain Zambrano's unity of being or Chacel's seductive *poesis*, which may be in the end perhaps the same thing.

In any event, confession in these essays is not viewed institutionally, but, in the broadest sense of the word, historically and existentially. Unlike Foucault, neither Zambrano nor Chacel is interested in the power dynamics of confession. Foucault argued that the ritual of confession produces truth. By contrast and in a distinctly nonpostmodern way, here the individual discovers the truth about himself in confessing. What that particular truth is remains a mystery, in my view, and is in keeping not only with the complex, unrevealed personas of Zambrano and Chacel, but with the flexible nature of the essay genre used to explore confession. One of the most fascinating features of their use of the essay is their capacity to let readers see them thinking through the question of confession, the sense that nothing is fixed in stone (as befits the tentative, experimental quality of the essay form), that arguments can be undone, and yet at the same time, that style is substantial here. That is, both writers feel they have something of substance to say, what they write possesses substance, a truth and validity that ground the essays. Neither Chacel nor Zambrano espouses the view that "truth is not discovered or discerned, but rather a mere name we give to the illusion we choose to live by" (Hauerwas 73). Both also share Marilynne Robinson's defense of "the beauty and strangeness of the individual soul, that is, of the world as perceived in the course of a human life, of the mind as it exists in time" (35). Most importantly, they speak eloquently and movingly of the inner life that besets and enriches us. Or as Zambrano writes, "confession is only substantiated with the hope that what is not one's self might appear. Thus it reveals the condition of human life as floundering in contradiction and paradox" (27). In a word, to confess is to confess life itself, the life that one lives.

Works Cited

Ayala, Francisco. "Proemio." *La cabeza del cordero*. Buenos Aires: Compañía General Fabril Editora, 1962. 27–36.
Berdyaev, Nicolas. *The Destiny of Man*.1937. Trans. Natalie Duddington. London: Geoffrey Bles, 1954.
Chacel, Rosa. "Un nombre al frente: Galdós." *Hora de España* 2 (Feb. 1937): 47–50.
———. *De mar a mar. Epistolario Rosa Chacel-Ana María Moix*. Ed. Ana Rodríguez-Fischer. Barcelona: Ediciones Península, 1998.
Foucault, Michel. *The History of Sexuality. I: An Introduction*. 1976. Trans. Robert Hurley. New York: Vintage Books, 1980.
Hauerwas, Stanley. "The Kingdoms of the World." *First Things* 192 (Apr. 2009): 71–74.
Johnson, Roberta. "'Self'-Consciousness in Rosa Chacel and María Zambrano." *The Bucknell Review* 39.2 (1996): 54–72.
Lyotard, Jean-François. *The Confession of Augustine*. Trans. Richard Beardsworth. Stanford: Stanford UP, 2000.
Mora García, José Luis. "Un nombre de mujer: *Misericordia*. Galdós en la inspiración zambraniana." *María Zambrano. Raíces de la cultura española*. Madrid: Fundación Fernando Rielo, 2004. 119–46.
O'Connor, Flannery. *Mystery and Manners: Occasional Prose*.1969. Ed. Sally and Robert Fitzgerald. New York: Farrar, Straus and Giroux, 1989.
Robinson, Marilynne. *Absence of Mind. The Dispelling of Inwardness from the Modern Myth of the Self*. New Haven: Yale UP, 2010.
Rousseau, Jean-Jacques. *Les confessions*. 2 vols. Ed. Jean Guéhenno. Paris: Gallimard, 1969.
Zambrano, María. *La España de Galdós*. Barcelona: La Gaya Ciencia, 1982.
———. "*Misericordia*." *Senderos* 120–46. (Orig. *Hora de España* 21 [Sept. 1938]).

———. *Pensamiento y poesía en la vida española.* 1939. Ed. Mercedes Gómez Blesa. Madrid: Biblioteca Nueva, 2004.

———. "La reforma del entendimiento español." *Senderos* 87–104. (Orig. *Hora de España* 9 [Sept. 1937]).

———. *Senderos.* Barcelona: Anthropos, 1986.

Zubiaurre, Maite. "España, femenino plural: Escritura autobiográfica, exilio y nación en Rosa Chacel y en María Zambrano." *Letras Peninsulares* 15.2 (Fall 2002): 267–86.

Confession

María Zambrano

Translated by Noël Valis

❋ 1 ❋

Philosophy, in telling its own history, disdainfully forgets the debt to other branches of knowledge born beyond or within its borders—the debt, for example, to poetry and the novel. Philosophy would be right to ignore, and even disdain, poetry and the novel, were it not that its very existence depended on them. Philosophy, according to its own rules, does not need assumptions—or so we are led to believe—to exist ideally. But if we consider philosophy in the life of every man, philosophy needs such assumptions more than any other kind of knowledge. By comparison, religion needs no prior conditions to enter into the life of a person. Religion alone can penetrate and consume a life, utterly absorbing it. The lives of so many unlearned saints, ordinary or dissipated men who became divinely "touched," are a clear example. In contrast, philosophy needs a great number of prior conditions in the life of the philosopher. While philosophy has no life, the philosopher does, several times over. In truth, he has needed to transform himself to enter into philosophy.

Philosophy pursues truth through reason. But men do the pursuing, and as it happens, yet a man seek the truth, he can also, if need be, flee from it. Truth transforms life.

At its inception, Western philosophy did not lay out clearly the conditions and the very form of the way of life that made philosophy possible, no doubt judging it unnecessary. No doubt, when philosophy went off on its own, now detached from religion, it did not stop to consider its own reason for being, in the ordinary flow of time. Nonetheless, a life that respects existence, the mere existence of truth, is a life in which some change has occurred. That life is now transformed, converted. After all, to any truth, no matter how self-evident or great, one may respond, with indifference or bravado, "What does it matter to me?"

An ancient philosopher showed that conversion implies the willingness to seek truth, the transformation that signals surrendering oneself to life, and, thus, the religious underpinning of philosophy. Philosophy is founded on religion. Without religion, truth and reason's quest for truth are set adrift, at the mercy of any ill-conceived justification or none at all. That philosopher was Aristotle, for whom it was a given that the quest for truth is inherent in human nature. But Aristotle, who at first was so slow to speak of the need for knowledge, elsewhere felt compelled to propose a theory of the "happy life" as the proper life for the philosopher-to-be, thus making him more Platonic than Plato.

That happy life reveals the extent to which life is transformed through the act of knowledge. But, between life and truth there is a connecting link, something that Plato, though not Aristotle, demonstrates. The connecting link is love, the love that bears his name, which prepares and leads life toward truth. The nature of that love is to become all the more impassioned because truth is all the more universal and unmoved, distant and pure.

But Platonism vanished from the world long ago, at least in the form of love. The divorce between life and philosophical truth deepened until all traces of this kind of love disappeared and took refuge in mysticism. Mysticism, however, has also disappeared, at least in its most transparent, or Platonic, form.

Modern philosophy makes no claims to reforming life. Rather, philosophy tried to transform truth, by transferring to truth the reform or transformation it did not introduce into life. The many attempts to do so make up the tragic history of truth in its despair, whose evolution space does not permit us to follow in detail here and that constitutes the heart of the human drama. As the modern age advances, as we move farther away from Descartes, and mistrust, in which he showed such genius, grows, so too grows truth's despair. And in parallel fashion, life's rebelliousness. Life refused to reform, or to use the classic term, to "convert." Truth came to life, but found life more and more impenetrable. This ever-more-intolerable situation forced philosophy to consider reforming truth, given the inability to reform life.

Truth, pure and philosophical, is all the more abstract, universal. The essence of all truth is to be universal, but as soon as truth expresses and affirms a fact, a simple fact that is a nontranscendent part of life, it separates fact from life. Truth, all truth, is always transcendent with respect to life. Considered as a function of life, all truth is the transcending of life, its unfolding progression.

The most universal truths of pure reason hover over life, making contact only when life has first performed certain internal actions. The truth of philosophy, of Platonic and Aristotelian philosophy, would not be possible without the event that is narrated in the myth of the cave. Modern philosophy, which was born with Descartes, has no similar myth and has renounced the demand that life be transformed, completely ignoring that issue. Only Spinoza, philosophically peripheral to the question, devotes sufficient attention to this diminishing of life, in Book IV of the *Ethics*, on the passions, which frankly has not had much impact. Although it could be argued that philosophy has not paid explicit attention to the myth of the cave, characteristically, Platonic influence slips in anyway, in surreptitious fashion, acting quietly, like water in the physical world, as it flows, enthralls, and slowly transforms, no more visibly than mystic ecstasy.

The drama of modern culture is the initial lack of contact between the truth of reason and life. All life is more than anything a scattered swirl of confusion. In the presence of pure truth, life feels humbled. And all pure truth, rational and universal, must enchant and seduce life. In the age of bewitchment, life, rebellious and confused, must be humbled, by falling in love, which is also enchantment, wonder, and something else: submission to an order and, indeed, to accepting defeat without resentment.

Pure truth humbles life when it fails to win life. Because life is continual passion and submission. Aristotle says, understanding, the organ of truth, is "dispassionate" and life is pure passivity, insofar as it is not intellect. Life can easily feel humbled even with respect to the part of itself that operates independently under different laws and relationships. If understanding does not reform life and the truth that understanding offers does not win life, if the truth that understanding serves cannot captivate or conquer life without resentment, life revolts.

This situation appears to have determined the nature of every attempt at different "reforms of understanding" in sixteenth- and seventeenth-century Europe. The idea of the reform of understanding prospered beginning with Descartes, even though it sometimes contradicted his own thinking. In reality, this was a reform of the idea of truth that Descartes left intact in its Platonic meaning. The so-called reforms of understanding are directed against everything Platonic, against the Platonic idea of truth, against the Platonic idea of "idea," and above all, against something that Plato rarely named, but always pursued, and that his disciple, the ultra-Platonist Plotinus, was obsessed with: oneness.

The reform of understanding set out to find a scattered truth. Instead of rescuing life from this fracture, the reform became scattered through relativism; it was made to rest on relationships and from the outset on facts, simple facts. And as facts are always detached, philosophers then claimed that truth had become fractured.

And thus, the need for truth came to be replaced by the need for "sincerity," which concerns the individual and which bends and weakens truth. Truth fit less and less into that sincerity of the discoverers of relativism. They could not accept truth in their lives, and so to save life, by not reforming it, they reformed instead the traditional idea of truth.

German idealism followed a very different path. But at bottom it may be the same thing, since the "Spirit" of the idealists is *alive*, terribly alive. Nothing persists here of the Greek vision, that vision in which life was seen, contemplated, with a dispassionate eye no longer of this world. Life transferred its character to Hegel's Absolute Spirit and, in so doing, seeing its own confused nature reflected as in an enormous mirror, remained more confused than ever and, hence, more inclined to arrogance. Life and reason became prideful, mutually unchecked. Life was not illuminated by reason or reason controlled by life. Much to the contrary, life offered its driving force, all its driving force, for reason to become "total."

This situation underscores something even more momentous: that man in his modern culture, that reason, whether the relativist reason of facts or Absolute Spirit, once held with confidence, now lay confused and abandoned. Even the illiterate man could grasp an ordering truth in his life that derived from the unattainable truth of the ancient philosophers. Its trace endured over the centuries, even in the least likely places, as in Platonically inspired poetry. Even the medieval serf toiling the land was able to glean something that gave meaning to his passage on earth, something rooted in, and affirmed by, concepts that Platonic-Aristotelian, and, even Plotinian, philosophy had discovered. This aristocratic philosophy made it possible to extract a truth that the most ingenuous of men, the men who gazed at the course of the stars, the men who knew nothing of books or of constructs of the mind, could assimilate. What truth does modern reason provide men, the simple man, the everyman? As "humanism" gained purchase, the life of the simple man, who had neither time nor means to stop and find truth on his own, by his own efforts, by the agonizing effort philosophy always requires—that life was being abandoned and disdained. The growth of systems like communism must be attributed far more to this change than to economic exploitation. Life cannot bear reason when reason does not bother to respect life, when reason does not reach down to life or know how to win her love, to make life reach up toward reason.

Life—the life of man, real man in all his ignorance and confusion—was abandoned. The truth he knew was a truth that neither captivated nor captured his life. Moreover, he only understood that truth through "self-interest," which was after all not surprising. Real life, the real man of flesh and blood, either became arrogant under the influence of positivist ideology, which is the only thing to come from the failure of reason, or was humiliated. Pride and humiliation are the two notes of the modern soul's desperation, its two poles.

The European reform of understanding, the leap of philosophy in its two aspects, would not have been necessary, had confession in the Augustinian manner been achieved. Thus Kant turns out to be the most balanced and promising of philosophers today, because he was closer in his *Critique of Practical Reason* than anyone else to achieving confession. Had he probed a bit more deeply, Kant might also have given birth to modern man, this yet half-born creature. But that did not happen. And life has not achieved conversion. In the presence of reason's demands, life is humiliated. Resentment has settled into the very zone in which life needs the transparency that truth alone offers. As life cannot do without truth, it goes looking for it, but since life is not prepared to receive truth, resentment surfaces and takes over.

When life has not been transformed, it becomes confused and scattered. Those are the two notes life sounds, when left unconstrained. Rational truth proposes and, indeed, demands of life violent subjection, but offering no preparation and little compensation. "It becomes very difficult to accept the truth as is, because once accepted one must submit to it," Nietzsche said. Reason in modern philosophy is defined by its violence. On the one hand, it is the most demanding of all, and on the other—and this is what has provoked resentment more than anything else—it is inherently incapable of sustaining human hope. Plato and Aristotle demanded a hard asceticism; salvation for them turned out to be difficult but possible. They did not offer eternal life, something in any event that the men of Greek culture did not hope for. But instead of "conversion," they offered immortality. Modern reason offers nothing, but demands everything. Idealism, which offered something and was most analogous to Aristotle's theoretical position and even Plotinus's ecstasy, was even less attainable.

And thus another kind of reason had to appear, the reason that is close to life and attainable. But as it turned out, that reason left nothing of the desire for transcendence in life, snatching away even the possibility of expressing it. Soul and spirit ceased to exist, if by spirit we understand life as infinite possibility and the need (the individual need) to be born again. To be individual one needs to be born again, to be conceived once more. And so life felt humiliated in the presence of idealism, which delivered a truth but failed first to prepare life for it. That truth violently tore life asunder, and, more critically, left it adrift. Idealism obviously begins by not recognizing the need for conversion, but is itself the most violent conversion ever conceived. Idealism presupposes, yet ignores, conversion, having slashed everything subjective, everything individual, dismissing the fierce immediacy of life, but failing to show how life can cease being immediate. The transformation idealism needs is immanent—that is, it resides in the interiority of the subject and nothing more. And hence those who do not understand, or are dissatisfied with this state of things, are relegated to the status of half-men, to a degraded existence, as Heidegger, idealism's inheritor, said in the end.

But in not humiliating life, philosophy humiliates both itself and truth. How to bridge the gap, how to make life and truth understand one another, allowing life space for truth and truth to enter into life itself, transforming it where necessary but without humiliation? The strange literary genre called confession has striven to demonstrate how life can approach truth, "slipping out unobserved." This literary genre in our time has dared to fill the empty space, the now terrible abyss opened wide by the enmity between reason and life. In this sense, confession would be a redundant genre of crisis if life and truth were in harmony. But as soon as the gap or the least discord appears, confession once more becomes necessary. Hence Saint Augustine unfurled the genre with so much splendor. For it is *ancient* man, as helpless and slighted as modern man, who at last welcomes truth.

Confession as a Literary Genre

What is a confession and what does it show us? Above all, we see that as a literary genre it is distinct from poetry and the novel and even from history, the genres most like it.

The novel comes closest; like confession, it is a story. But there are two differences, which concern subject matter and time. As a result, or better said, as a precondition, there is another fundamental difference between what the novelist seeks and what is sought by the one who confesses.

What distinguishes literary genres from one another is the need on life's part that prompts them. One certainly does not write from literary need, but from life's need to express itself. In the shared, deepest origin of literary genres is life's need to express itself or the need of humans to create characters different from ourselves or to hold in our hands elusive creatures. The oldest need was the most distant from the direct expression of life. The earliest poetry, as we know, is a sacred language, which is to say, supremely objective.

The Egyptian *Book of the Dead* gives us sacred and liturgical formulas, formulas fixed and ritualized like numbers and music—pure music, albeit "the story of a soul," as the Western world would say. In this sense, the novel and confession are related and nearly contemporary, since both are expressions of individualized beings to whom a history is granted. The assumption, for both the confession and the novel, is that the individual suffers and may lose his way. The mummy that "confesses" has no history, only pure present. The mummy is already converted and glorified: a blessed one who speaks in order for the golden doors of paradise to open.

Among the Greeks, confession has no place, it cannot arise and would have felt even more disturbing than the poetry of Anacreon, that solitary breath of the irrational soul, reluctant to allow the transmutations of Platonic love. Greek confession would have been the story of the philosopher evicted from the cave, but either it did not happen or it was lost.

And when confession emerges with Augustine, it emerges whole. Are there no precedents? Apparently not, and yet something comes to mind: an unequivocal connection. It comes from a long ancestral line, from history and passion, from not being ashamed to cry out and speak of oneself, from the truth of life, from Hebraic truth. The father of confession is Job, and to say Job is equivalent to saying complaint: he is the complaint. It is Job who speaks in the first person. His words are laments that reach us at the very moment in which they were uttered, as though we were hearing them viva voce. This is confession: the word in full cry. Every confession is spoken, it is a long conversation, displacing time itself, displacing real time. It does not lead us, like the novel, to an imaginary time, to a time created by the imagination. The novel has its origins in the magic lantern, in the attic of daydreams. The novel, in its beginnings, above all in its beginnings, creates another time for us in the double sense of a mythological time—retaining the trace of myth—in the sense that it makes another time come alive in our minds, even though the mythological trace no longer exists. It is a time other than that of life. And when the novel succeeds in being the time of life—Proust, Joyce—it is really about confession, as we shall see.

Confession is substantiated in the real time of life itself, flowing from confusion and temporal immediacy. Such is its origin: it goes in search of another time, which, had it been the time of the novel, would not have to be sought, but would be found. The person who makes a confession does not seek the time of art, but some other time as real as his own. He is not satisfied with the virtual time of art. The artist, in creating, imitates divine creation and creates eternity . . . virtually. This is the game, the profound game of art. I do not know if somebody has pointed it out, but any other kind of artistic *magic* remains subordinate to this profound and supremely momentous game from which only sincerely religious art, whose time referent is that of paradise lost, is exempt. But pure art, art for art's sake, is the game of creating a time beyond the time creatable by man; it is the game for creating a time that cannot be, that can only be enjoyed, when it is enjoyed, virtually. Confession seeks not virtual time, but real time, and for that reason, because it only accepts this time, it stops precisely where that other, real time begins. This is the time that cannot be transcribed, the time that cannot be expressed or grasped, the oneness of life that no longer needs expression. Thus all art possesses something of a confession gone astray, occasionally with the same aims as confession, but going its own way, amusing itself, lingering, wasting time as a supremely human luxury. Art is the extravagance of creation, the luxury that the Creator has permitted man of a creation that is not real, but that is creation, nonetheless. Art is a game, the game of creation. Work does not separate us from reality, being embedded in it and ending in something actual and exchangeable. Art is above necessity and above facing reality—hence the seriousness of all realist art and the arrogance attached to it—it plays at believing reality and creates it virtually! This is the luxury that God in his mercy left humankind after damning it to labor and pain. After the expulsion from the enchanted garden, after the mad desire to taste the tree of knowledge, there remained the enchanted apple of art, the magic of invented time.

Poetry is the nearest thing we have to enchantment made real, and comes closest to undoing damnation. Consequently, poetry has felt the curse most, and, in that sense, all poets are *poètes maudits*. The poet also swerves from confession, either out of desperation or rash hope, in a hurry to arrive by leaping over time. But poetry sometimes succeeds and in it we have the only ecstatic moments, even if expressed approximately, as Mallarmé would say. In a successful poem, in its perfect unity, we find the next best thing to pure time, what the person writing a confession seeks.

Confession is the language of someone who has not erased his condition as a subject; it is the language of the subject as such. It is not his feelings, nor even his desires or hopes, but simply his efforts to be. Confession is an act in which the subject reveals himself, out of horror of his incomplete being and in a confused state. In writing an autobiographical novel, the novelist reveals a certain complacency of self, or at least an acceptance of his being, an acceptance of his failure, that the person carrying out a confession absolutely does not reveal. The person who self-novelizes makes real his failure, his half-created being, a recreation that implies transcendence solely in the highly risky, virtual time of art. To materialize oneself artistically is one of the most serious acts one can commit in life today, given that art is the avoidance of narcissism, and artistic objectification, by contrast, is pure narcissism. The perpetually adolescent artist who fixates, in love with himself, on his adolescence. A fatal game, in which one does not play to enjoy oneself but to die. All narcissism is a game with death.

Poetry can lapse into narcissism, confession teeters at the edge: it is a mortal risk. Slipping into narcissism, confession is incomplete, an ignoble failure, being a mere demonstration of what it is not. This is not a way forward but a tragic, grotesque hall of mirrors: a hallucinatory repetition.

Confession starts from the time that it has in hand and, while that time lasts, speaks from it, yet goes in search of a different time. Confession appears to be an action that is no longer carried out in time, but with time; it is an action about time, not virtually but in reality. Like all paths, the path leading to whatever concerns time stops.

But confession is performative in another sense, in achieving something that it wants to transmit. When we read an authentic confession, we sense that it is repeated in ourselves, and if we do not repeat it in ourselves we do not penetrate its intended secret. In that repetition we see how it is like and unlike philosophy: like philosophy, confession must be actualized. We know that to study philosophy is in reality a return to practicing philosophy. "One does not learn philosophy, one learns to philosophize," Kant said, with the authority to back it up. Philosophy, even learned, must follow the path of what one wants to learn; confession read, if it is to count, must verify what the one confessing has done. But the difference is this: here solitariness is complete and the model only an analogy, since being, the being that is sought, is not identical in the way that thought is. It is analogical; it is my being, similar to but never the same as another's being.

But if I do not perform what the author of the confession performed, reading it serves no purpose. Because confession is an action, the maximum performative action granted to words.

Confession as the Revelation of Life

Literary genres apparently develop as philosophy becomes separated from life, whether by moving away from it or being mistaken for it. In truth, life needs to reveal itself, express itself. If reason strays, life feels abandoned; if reason takes the helm, life feels asphyxiated. The challenge is to find the point of contact between life and truth.

And this point of contact is found through something achieved by life itself, something that takes place within life. Life must transform itself, by opening to truth, if only to sustain it, to accept truth prior to knowing it, a knowing that in any event is impossible to attain fully.

But in that unfolding of life there is something more than the acceptance of truth. There is the expression of life itself, the revelation of its core. When conversion is instantaneous, or when it precedes knowledge, confession is not necessary. Confession emerges from certain situations, in which life reaches maximum confusion and dissociation, because of individual and, in particular, historical circumstances. Precisely when men and women are too humiliated, when they are eaten up with resentment, when they feel only "the weight of existence," then their own lives need to be revealed. To achieve that, they perform the double movement unique to confession: the flight from self and the quest for something to sustain and clarify them.

Confession always begins with a flight from self. It comes out of desperation and rests, like every departure, on both hope and despair—despair over what is and hope that something one does not yet have might appear.

Without the depths of despair man does not emerge from his self, because the force of despair pushes him to speak about himself, something he would not otherwise do.

This despair, before it can be expressed as a confession in the way we understand confession—that is, as a flight from self and the expression of a kind of guilt, of an unwanted self—before this, despair is a complaint, a simple complaint. Hence the first confession, or preconfession, is Job's complaint.

Here we have the bare-bones situation that is part and parcel of confessing without the movement of confession itself. It is pure complaint, because Job's despair and hope are immediate. He has not yet discovered, properly speaking, interiority. His pain comes from motives in some sense external to him, as sufferings that happen to him and that make him ask questions and seek explanations. But confession does not appear because Job does not believe that anything at all depends on him. He feels himself to be nothing, dependent on the divinity: he does not believe in his own being.

He has not yet discovered his own interiority, only his naked existence in pain, anguish, and injustice. His complaint is a direct appeal to the divinity. He wants to die because no other alternative besides life and death is presented to him. He is not told there could be something else, a somewhere beyond this life, that is not death.

This complaint has been surpassed by confession, because wrapped up in confession one finds Job's complaint, only transformed. Job is in despair, but the sole option he sees is in a divine response. Job complains: about the horror of being born, the terror of certain death and of injustice. And these three complaints are summed up well when he says: "What shall I do unto thee, O thou preserver of men? Why hast thou set me as a mark against thee, so that I am a burden to myself?" And even more so in: "And where *is* now my hope? As for my hope, who shall see it?"

Thanks to that pain, we have the revelation of naked existence. Philosophy begins with either renouncing or overcoming that complaint. The philosopher is he who no longer complains. Culture, all cultures, have continued to cover up the naked existence of humankind; like clothes draped over human despair and at times, in moments of decadence, like a simple anesthetic that brings oblivion, or like the poison of drink.

Thanks to the despair that dares to seek explanations, there is this revelation of what man feels when he has nothing, when he emerges from the self: horror of being born, shame of being born; terror of dying; astonishment at the injustice of men. And thus he feels compelled to offer a remedy to such evils, or the hope of a remedy. He feels compelled to make us accept our being born, not fear death, and recognize ourselves in other men and women as the same. Without these three conversions, human life is a nightmare. This is how Job felt, finding the way out through his cry, through his complaint which was, at last, heard.

This is the hope that in truth stirred Job to complain, for without any hope at all of being heard, the complaint would not have been produced. Even the simple sigh counts on a possible interlocutor. Language, even the most irrational, lamentation itself, is born in the presence of a possible listener to receive it.

Confession also has a desperate beginning. The man tired of being a man, of being himself, confesses. There is a fleeing that at the same time wants to perpetuate what was, to perpetuate that which one flees, a wanting to express the thing in order to rid oneself of it and to become something altogether different, but at the same time letting it remain, actualizing it.

Hope of a revelation of life, hope that the three horrors will be dissolved, that life, in discovering something beyond itself, at last finds its shape and ceases being a nightmare. And thus for truth to be assimilated by life it must be verified through a conversion that makes one accept being born, feel no terror in the face of death, and remain calm in the midst of injustice. In reality, injustice always consists of the ups and downs of fortune, even when favorable, for if the contingency of pain humbles us, so too does fortune, which is equally contingent. What provokes such humbling is feeling oneself abandoned, bereft of order. It is the bitter situation that obtained at the end of the ancient world and that Lucretius forcefully captured: "If the gods exist, they do not concern themselves with us."

What Job wanted was for God to concern himself with him, to come to him with explanations. He needed divine reason more than relief from his suffering; for it is possible, through suffering itself, to anesthetize oneself with pain. But such dulling humbles us more than pain itself, and it is this, in truth, that turns life into a nightmare. Job did not ask to be released from suffering, but to escape the nightmare, to know the reason for his suffering. He asked for a revelation of life. So long as he did not have it, he despised himself, he cursed his own being. He hated his existence so much as to want it erased. "Wherefore then hast thou brought me forth out of the womb? Oh that I had given up the ghost, and no eye had seen me!" "I should have been as though I had not been; I should have been carried from the womb to the grave" (see chapters 10, 17, and 18). This total escape from the self is a true suicide who wants to wipe out the shame of birth, stave off the humiliation of death, and evade injustice.

Confession is this emerging from the self in order to take flight. One who opens the self outward does so because he does not accept how things are, life as it is given to him, because he does not accept who he is. There exists a bitter duality between something in ourselves that sees and decides, and another, another self, who, bearing our name, is experienced as a foreign foe.

So too the fragmentary character of all life is demonstrated in confession, in that every person feels himself to be incomplete bits and pieces, no more than an outline, a piece of one's self, a fragment. And with the emerging self, he seeks to push his limits, surpass them, and find, beyond those limits, perfect oneness. He hopes, like the person with his complaint, to be heard. He hopes, by expressing his own time, to perfect his shape, to acquire, in effect, the wholeness he lacks, his total shape.

These features define confession, despair of one's self, the flight from self in hopes of finding that self. Despair about feeling obscure and incomplete, and yearning to find oneness. The hope of finding that oneness makes the self come forth looking for something that will enfold it, something in which to be recognized, to be found. Hence confession presupposes hope: the hope of something beyond individual life, something like the belief, clear in some and confused in others, that truth transcends life.

Confession is only substantiated with the hope that what is not one's self might appear. Thus it reveals the condition of human life as floundering in contradiction and paradox.

Everything that confession shows us is contradictory and paradoxical: the despair of the self, the flight of the self from what one wants at once to shed and to achieve, while somehow being objective. The life of man shows that what it needs and presupposes in confession is oneness, which it lacks; it shows in the scattering of time that there must be a time without the anguish of present time. It shows that the expression of something is always like a compensatory virtual reality, and that life only expresses itself in order to be transformed.

Confession is, in effect, a method for life to free itself of paradox and succeed in becoming life. It is not the only method, though perhaps the most immediate, the most direct. And perhaps it is not sufficient, but only preparatory, a method, strictly speaking, for something that comes afterward, a method in which life shows, precisely by setting itself in motion, its essential shape and its most transcendent character.

Confession as a literary genre has not enjoyed the same good fortune in all periods. It is something peculiar and exclusive to Western culture, and within Western culture, it appears in decisive moments, moments in which culture seems to be in collapse, in which man feels defenseless and alone. These are moments of crisis, in which man, individual man, appears, his failure exposed.

Thus these confessions demonstrate the kinds of failure that our culture has promoted and something else perhaps even more important: individual desires, the profound desires concealed by art, made concrete by philosophy, faded in periods of indecision, and obscured in the fullness of ripened times. For when man lives in a matured culture, when he has found at last something concrete to inhabit, human existence in its nakedness goes into hiding.

The Confessions

First Confession: Saint Augustine

With Augustine, confession was revealed in all its plenitude and with a clarity no one has attained since. Beneath his guiding light, we can see not only what various failures of the past have said but also other, incomplete confessions of our own time, for clarity has the virtue of making us see things that cannot achieve clarity.

Augustine begins with the hostility created between himself and the divine, that is, supreme reality. Because life can turn its back on reality. This is the most typically human, the most alarming, condition of all: any other creature is faithful to its reality and lives immersed in it. All except man. This condition appears most often in utopias, those dreams of becoming one with a corresponding reality. We feel like detached beings, half born and half inserted in a reality we sense and seek.

Philosophy, the theory of knowledge, poses the problem of reality, as if reality could be found in knowledge, when in truth, reality is always understood as known before it is grasped. Religion, religions, show how man has taken for granted a reality that was not present to him and whose revelation he sought. Religion compensated in a way for the half reality of the world that is present. Even the idea of being means that we do not sufficiently grasp what we find and we need to find another reality, another reality for the mind. But the confession that is part of human interiority reveals, in turn, the quest for a complete reality. We may feel ourselves devoid of reality, even hostile to it. Confession issues from this last-named situation, feeling hostile. Anyone who has narrated the story of his life in a confessional tone begins with a moment in which he was living with his back turned on reality, buried in oblivion.

Because that hostility is felt as oblivion, as if we detached ourselves from something by forgetting it, and rushed to embrace our surroundings. In his quest for oneness, Augustine senses that he already has some grasp of it, that he remembers it from before. For life, knowing is always remembering, and all ignorance appears in the form of amnesia. Perhaps because memory is the kind of knowledge closest to life, delivering truth in the form in which life can consume it, as a temporal appropriation. The "reminiscence" of which Plato speaks may be the product of longing for a divined reality, longing for what cannot be grasped or shown. Longing for a life of oneness. So memory would be the seat of that knowledge, of that encounter with total reality, because then in reality there would be neither remembering nor forgetting, only presence.

And when we find reality, we sense that we already have some grasp of it. We could not ever cease possessing it entirely, for that would be equivalent to being absolutely nothing. "Yet how could I seek you if I no longer possessed you?"

Reality was there, but oblivious to it, our backs turned on reality, we were both decentered and confused. "Your words, Lord, clung to me within and everywhere I saw myself surrounded by you."

Though reality surrounds us, yet we must still seek it. Reality is not sufficient in itself, or perhaps reality is not there until we are prepared to receive it. Thus, the first task for Augustine is acceptance, unconditional acceptance, in an apparent reply to Job. He does not begin by asking for explanations, he does not begin with an act of reason, but of acceptance. "I do not wish to argue my case against you, for you are truth itself, nor do I wish to deceive myself, lest my own iniquity be deceived."

Modern understanding was undone through a certain kind of rationalism that seeks justification, that begins with doubt. Reality then appears to flee. Augustine, in his confession, flees from himself and accepts the reality by which he feels surrounded. The great success modern understanding has obtained in its inquiry of reality is undeniable. Reality has shed light on certain mysteries that allow modern understanding to manage reality, but has otherwise closed the door on other secrets. It would be hard to find a human being more unrealized than the one who knows how to pull all the strings and exercise great power.

For Augustine accepts reality by repudiating himself, by "casting aside iniquity." But he does so to find himself, to rescue himself.

In finding reality, we find ourselves, we enter reality, and without suggesting anything like a mystical equivalence, the fact is when we enter this discovered reality we also reveal ourselves.

Job, like the philosophers, faces reality by questioning it, by asking for explanations. He differs from them in that his questioning is not objective. He lacks the objectivity of philosophy, which is his only salvation and without which he falls into a caricature of himself and, perhaps, into an impossible existence. Job asks about himself in hopes that somebody will answer; the philosophers expect only their own answers. Job asked about himself, maddened by desperation, troubled by hope.

Augustine follows Job's line: he asks above all about himself, because he himself has become the question. Life has become impossible for him, in his wandering scattershot among creaturely things. "For love of your love, I do this remembering, with the bitterness of my heart, my past wicked ways so that you might see me, rescuing me from that dissipation in which I dwelled, divided into a thousand parts, when separated from your supreme oneness, I dissipated myself among creaturely things." He cannot find himself, as he wanders far and wide, intermingled with creaturely things, that is to say, in a useless half reality. He is an unfinished man given over to creaturely things equally lacking, unable to provide those qualities of being that are firmness and clarity. But neither can he turn inward. "The soul, therefore, is too narrow to contain itself." The soul cannot remain self-absorbed, for life means emerging from the cocoon, going beyond the insufficiencies of self, transcending. Dispersion frustrates both love and the urge to transcend.

How He Seeks to Become Visible

His way of attending to supreme reality is to make of himself an offering, hungering to be seen, "for you to see me, to rescue me." This act of offering himself to the divine gaze properly constitutes confession in Augustine. It is his reply to Job. And it is also the beginning of a path to salvation profoundly different from that of philosophy, even though Augustine is after all a philosopher. But he already philosophizes in a manner distinct from that of Plato and Plotinus, from whom he nonetheless absorbed so much. Augustine did not save himself through philosophy, but through having found himself in the kingdom of light. Entering the light, revealing oneself openly in confession, substantiates conversion. It allows us to feel detached from what we were, from the used, worn-out semblance of ourselves. When this is done, that is, by the time we really embark on the story of our past that constitutes confession, in truth confession has already achieved its end. This explains the disillusionment of so many curious readers who rush to the *Confessions* eager to lay bare scandalous incidents and scrutinize a fellow creature's inner life. Very quickly they withdraw, disappointed by not finding the expected "intimate details." And they withdraw for another reason: because a confession, in being read, obliges the reader to corroborate the confession. It obliges the reader to read within himself. The inquisitive reader wants nothing to do with this. After all, his idea was to peep through a half-opened door, to overhear someone else's secrets, throwing caution to the winds. And now he finds himself saddled with inspecting his own conscience. In literary terms, confession has very few requirements, but it does have one, for which there is no formula: to act, to lead us to perform the same act as the one confessing performs. To place ourselves, like him, in the kingdom of light.

That is the moment in which life will become clear, when the telling of sins will no longer be necessary. Augustine points this out, though even he is puzzled and asks: "But to whom do I tell these things? Certainly not to you, dear Lord, but in your presence I tell them to my own kind, to the human race, no matter how small their part who may read these pages of mine." And this is because confession takes place in the very instant in which someone discovers himself, thus verifying the movement that is the reverse of the expulsion from paradise, when Adam, ashamed, hid himself in the presence of the divine voice. Now, far from hiding himself, Augustine reveals himself, "remembering with the bitterness of my heart my past wicked ways for you to see me."

Thus is explained the shallowness of Augustine's confession, which could be faulted for a lack of sincerity. Sincerity, however, does not justify confession, rather the act does, the *action* of offering oneself wholly to the divine gaze, to the gaze that sees everything, a gaze that certainly can always see us, but that we go about avoiding. The important thing in confession is not that we are seen but that we offer ourselves to be seen, that we feel ourselves beheld, gathered up and united by that gaze.

How otherwise to explain why Augustine dwells on such a trifling thing as the childhood theft of some pears and skips over more serious things that, with malice toward none, one might assume he later committed. This theft, traces of which remain like the silky sensation of refreshing water, in laughter, the innocent laughter of a Mediterranean afternoon, the laughter of a tiny creature playing without guile, we cannot help hearing deep down inside all Augustine's faults. The love of life, play, laughter in the garden, nothing to suggest sin, were he not born for something else.

No: the telling of Augustine's faults was not necessary, the telling of his "bitter memory" that is introduced, so to speak, as if a mere "never mind," does not constitute confession itself. The confession was made as he was preparing himself to make it, because he had already performed that act which was the opposite of banishment from paradise. He had already discovered himself, the only act intuited by man—though peripheral to Church doctrine—that could erase original sin, that could signal a return to the place from which we were expelled in shame. Anyone who makes a confession is hoping to recover some lost paradise.

The Heart

But Augustine knows that the return to Paradise is not possible: there is the earth, life; his own inexhaustible heart, and all of his being, freshly born. Now is when he recognizes himself as whole; he has entered into himself. "And as for myself, my Happiness is to be united with God, for if I am not in Him, then am I not in myself" (Book VII, 17). The return to a lost paradise would nullify all this, something he never proposed. On the contrary, now he can love boundlessly, love without fear of madness. Recovered reality is supreme Oneness, which is to say that it is as much the object of his mind as the endpoint of his love. He is no longer forced into a thousand broken pieces. He has found the oneness of his life.

That kind of love forever separates Augustine's path from the path of salvation formulated or implied by philosophy. To be or not to be a philosopher is more than anything a question of love. The heart of the philosopher has been wrenched from its dispersion by the force of understanding that dispels the passions. The heart of the philosopher is more like the heart of the Eastern sage. He has led his heart to the light, he has made his heart the organ of light. "The wise man uses his heart like a mirror" (Book VII, 6, Tschuang-Tse).

The salvation of the heart appears to consist in making the heart enter into the light, converting it toward the light. Plato, when he speaks of conversion in *Phaedrus*, says that first the eyes will be transformed, then the head, and finally the entire body. This is because all paths to salvation, even that of philosophy, try to convert the heart. Confession substantiates at its core this question, this fundamental prior question. For if philosophy, as a path, is to take root, it cannot exist without somehow having conquered the heart.

Despite his Platonism, Augustine could not follow the Platonic path. His heart could not accept the transmutation of Platonic love: love that leads to the immortality of the soul, so analogous to the immortality of ideas. But he does not allow himself to be seduced by immortality. His hunger is for life. The God of philosophy, the God of being and intelligence, will not defeat him. His heart is only content with eternal life, life in which nothing is lost, nothing is renounced, true life in the kingdom of light.

The other path to the conversion of the heart, which precedes philosophy and the transmutation of Platonic love, is even more demanding. It is to empty out the heart. In modern philosophy only Spinoza was concerned with this notion. This is the path of the Eastern sage who uses the heart as a mirror, as the servant of objectivity. The same sage tells us what the method is. "Yan Hi said: 'May I know what is the fasting of the heart?' Kung-Tse (Confucius) said: 'Let your goal be Oneness! Do not listen with your ear but with your conscience; do not listen with your conscience but with your soul. The ear can do nothing but hear, the conscience can do nothing but understand. The soul must be empty and prepared to receive things. The spirit is that which can gather together emptiness. This being empty is the fasting of the heart.'" Fasting of the heart is love's conversion, in the manner of Eastern attentiveness, annihilating itself so as to leave the entire kingdom to the expected guest, to the whole of reality.

But Augustine wished to persist in his love, not to transform it. Neither the "fasting of the heart" nor Platonic love was of any use to him. He did not wish to transform love, or free himself from love. Platonic love means the conversion of love toward the universal, thus strictly ceasing to be love in converting, as the good intermediary that it is. Augustine belonged to another kind of lover distinct from those who yearn for liberation and mystical extinguishment. He did not want to recapture his heart but to enslave it entirely; he wanted only to seek the heart's true master.

He wanted not the heart as the reflected mirror of the world, but the transparent heart, the heart pierced by the light, living in the light. That living light, the mysteriously alive light of the Mediterranean, uniting all its religions, I would suggest, that religious spirit discovered what so much proliferating myth, so much mystery, of varying obscurity, craved: a revelation that in containing the light surpasses it. The religion of life in unity, which is to say, eternally alive, with eternal life and love. Augustine's truth, his God, was not one of pure thought, nor of infinite mercy, the burning bush that does not consume itself, whose light is reason; it was the supernatural oneness of life and truth. As the God of life could not overrule the heart, the heart does not pursue liberty, but lives enslaved, in rapture; the heart always lives in another. And its oneness, the oneness of life, is eternal life, not life transformed into immortality.

The oneness of love achieves its eternity and thus are dissipated once and for all the horror of being born and the horror of death, which along with injustice, constitute the nightmare of existence.

Action

The other element of the nightmare is the injustice of the world, the confusion among men: confusion, iniquity, of which Job complains so bitterly, and that is above all not being understood by other men. He complains that God has made him a stranger to his neighbors. "He hath put my brethren far from me, and mine acquaintance are verily estranged from me" (Job 19.13). "All my inward friends abhorred me; and they whom I loved are turned against me" (19.19).

In the nightmare of existence, we feel alienated, with no possibility of communication, as in a bad dream when we call out and no one hears us. From this to feeling persecuted is a small step. At the core of the European spirit of late is the persecutory mania, a persecutory mania originating less in some physical or psychic shock than in the tremendous situation of alienation, in the hermetic mantle that has settled over life.

Action then becomes impossible. Certainly action creates a reality among humans, but it cannot start from nothing, or from such complex alienation. While we are feeling alone, we cannot act. All action born of solitariness is anarchic, that is, violent and destructive. It is the typical action of modern man, perpetrated without coming to terms with himself or penetrating reality: a precipitate action, born of a dark heart. Revolutionary action in the best of cases emerges from the yearning to leave behind solitude, to find reality. The action proper to adolescence, to the age of rash hopes. And this has been our character, the character of our lives, which ought to lead us toward making our confession. After twenty centuries of Christianity and even more of philosophy, we Europeans have acted like adolescents, we surrendered ourselves to action in order to escape our solitary, festering heart, we gave in to the temptation of rushing something that was still not ripe in time, and may never be.

This is the crime that the most typical modern novel—that of Dostoyevsky—describes, a true confession of our time: the crime of wanting to assault destiny, divinity, forcing the divine to give us the desired goal, undermining our own slow efforts. The crime of evading authentic action and making an end run around the path, erasing history. Modern man, while having a greater awareness of his history, has attempted to escape history through revolutionary utopia.

Authentic action can only flow from the original I, in clarity and oneness, from the "transparent heart," whose travesty is born of a scattered heart, producing anxiety. "Unquiet is my heart." But before the eternal rest, comes action, which is anxiety transformed, anxiety converted. Transcendent.

After his confession, Augustine is not awash in anticipated happiness or an imagined Paradise. Work awaits him, authentic action: a vocation. He has by now discovered his fellow men, by discovering them within himself. In their presence, he confessed, speaking to them viva voce from the innermost depths, and when he received the truth, it was in their presence, through his fellow men. He penetrated reality. Although reality is sought in solitude and is pursued deep inside oneself, it is not found without something to counterbalance our solitude. No one finds reality for himself alone. To find reality is at once to communicate it. Indeed, it is not possible to keep a truth for oneself alone, for when truth is found, it is already a shared truth.

Throughout the *Confessions*, Augustine asks himself why he said what he said, insisting that he wanted to open his heart in the presence of all men. "But to whom do I tell these things? Certainly not to You, dear Lord, but in your presence I tell them to my own kind, to the human race, no matter how few may read these pages of mine" (Book II, 5). He also wanted to make himself transparent to other men: he told them first what it was like "when I wandered far and wide among creaturely things" and now he wants to say who he is, he wants to show them the new man, reborn: "With what fruits, my Lord, . . . with what fruits, I ask, do I confess to my fellow men before You by way of this writing, what I actually am, not what I was? For we have already seen and confided the fruits of confessing what I was. But whoever I may be in this particular time of my confessions, many who knew me want to know, but they do not know me. For if they heard something about me from others, they cannot, however, apply their ear to my heart, where I am who I am. Therefore, they want to hear by my confession what I am inside, where neither their sight nor their hearing nor their mind can penetrate. Nonetheless, they are willing to believe me, perhaps as a way to get to know me? . . . For the charity that makes them good tells them that I do not lie in my confession about myself, and my confession gives them faith in me" (Book X, 4).

When we count on the faith of others, on their belief in us, the seal of solitariness is broken. While we live in a solitary situation, all attempts at understanding among our fellow men are substantiated by appealing to explanations, by virtue of why and what for. Our fellow creature asks for an accounting, and we are obliged to give it. Without confidence, explanations do not work or unify. In life, reason only functions when it is founded on the a priori of faith, confidence, charity.

Only on the basis of this understanding, of this belief—"charity believeth all things," repeats Augustine, according to Paul (1 Cor. 13.7)—is community with others possible. And only on the basis of this community is action possible. Authentic action flows from a transparent heart and, to be effectively achieved, also must be transparent in the presence of others. To be transparent is to be believed, to be regarded with charity.

That explains why action is so often frustrated: for even action born of a pure heart can be aborted, if one's fellow men do not accept this heart. Perhaps the worst torment is to suppress action, to conceal oneself though knowing one's heart to be transparent or nearly transparent. For when others do not share transparency in the least bit, transparency produces bitterness in them. A Saint Augustine of today or of another time would have to wait perhaps, he would have to remain silent and, needless to say, not act, for he could not count on belief, on ears ardently pressed to his breast, on the charitable eagerness of his fellow men.

And that is the greatest tragedy, for if in confession one begins with solitariness, one always ends, like Augustine, with community. The truth is always shared. "Love, then, in me, the brotherly spirit, which You teach should be loved, and lament in me what is to be lamented . . . To such I will show myself: let them exalt my good deeds, sigh over my bad ones . . . and let hymns and weeping be raised in the presence of brotherly hearts, who praise You" (Book X, 5).

In sum, action is revealed above and beyond charity, above and beyond life, reaching out toward one's neighbor and receiving the neighbor's own action as he too comes forth to seek his brothers. A unique, authentic action is for this reason a "vocation," because it is a calling that comes not only from on high, but right here, alongside us, a calling from our fellow men, our brothers. Life ceases to be a nightmare when the filial bond is reestablished, when we find our Father, but also our brothers; when we can answer the tremendous question: "Am I my brother's keeper?" When the question does not even need to be asked, because we appear hand in hand, together. When rash action is not transparent to our brother and disregards his charity, no matter how pure the intentions, it unleashes violence and crime, fratricidal war.

Augustine vanquished the terror of ancient man, abandoned and brotherless. He dissolves the nightmare of existence, for he is happy to have been born: "I am a child, but my father lives eternally." He does not fear death. "When I follow You, with all my being, there will be no more pain or labor for me and my life will be a life completely filled with You" (Book X, 28). And he has found his brothers . . . Life has been made possible.

※ II ※

Peculiar to Augustine's confession is the belief that obliged him to make it. It appears in various places, but most clearly in Book X, 34, where we read: "So also the human soul, blind and languid, awkward and wretched, wishes to remain hidden, even though it does not wish anything hidden from it. So the consequences are that the soul will be revealed to the truth without truth being revealed to the soul."

This certainty quite possibly determines Augustine's singular manner of conducting himself in the matter of truth. For is it not strange that to attain truth, despite being familiar with earlier schools of thought, with their promise of ultimate and complete truth, it would occur to him to reexamine his embittered memory, to embark on a journey so different from that which the philosophers traveled?

Indeed, the philosophers started out in search of the truth without thinking that first they needed to know themselves, to discover themselves before discovering truth. We cannot put it down to their failure to meditate on the character of man. "Human nature" had been discovered and contemplated, having attained a state of pure perfection in the Stoics, who were familiar to Augustine, although it is worth pointing out how little affinity he appears to have had with them. In his peregrination through the philosophical schools, he does not ground himself in the foundations of Stoicism. But there were the Neoplatonists, who captivated him and yet could not hold him. Neoplatonism does not appear to be the most important of the ideas that he later adopted, but, rather, it was precisely this philosophical peregrination that led him to make his confession, revealing himself, speaking of himself with such a scandalous, heretical gesture toward the ancient world. Meditation on man was not unheard of in Augustine's time. Indeed, to the contrary, the Neoplatonists had made it their philosophical capstone of the happy, contemplative life, which could only be attained through philosophy.

The very same reason evidently led Augustine to go from one philosophical school to another, unable to remain permanently in any of them, the same reason that forced him to make his confession. He believed that only by discovering oneself does one end up discovering truth. Truth for the philosophers was a thing of the mind, of reason. When truth was grasped, life was radically changed. This is what Plato, Aristotle, and Plotinus tell us, as do the Stoics from the other end of the spectrum. For Plato, Aristotle, and Plotinus, this change was an annihilation, the wasting away of instinctive, psychic life, of life as passiveness, as suffering. The active intellect was the most effective reality that made the wise man who exercised it sufficient unto himself, dispassionate, eternal—in sum, a participant in the divine. "Philosophy is the most divine thing," says Aristotle. What survived of the man who went through this exercise was, properly speaking, nothing, nothing worth saving, for even Platonically defined love was a transitory god, a messenger who, having reached his terminus, ceased in his office.

The human being was thus in reality engendered by philosophical activity. Philosophical preparation for death served equally well for birth, since the immediate being in which we are immersed is of such a contradictory nature, so without substance, as though we were the mere appearance of things. "Sensation makes me other," Plato says in the *Theaetetus*, but this other is temporary. Only he who knows himself endures because he is so constituted. Yet in being, he likened himself entirely to the intelligible, becoming an object of the intelligible world. Philosophical activity was fulfilled in the instant a pure form emerged from the man of body and soul, a form incapable of suffering, immune to change, separated and freed from his very core—when the subject, ceasing forever to be a subject, passed into the objectivity of the intelligible, eternal world. This was the real reason why confession could not take place among the philosophers. Knowledge, once gained, left not a trace of the pliant life of passion in all its forms. If Augustine the African did not become one more Neoplatonist philosopher, it was because he could not accept such a devastating transformation, a veritable withering away into pure objectivity. And so he bared his heart completely. The truth that he craved had to receive him whole. It was his life transfigured, the truth of his personhood recovered, not immutable being but the one true life.

In his confession, he is transformed by finding himself: he now exists. And his being rests on a question of identity. That was and continues to be the problem. Our life plays out, scattered and dazed by desire and by time. To achieve being is only possible through oneness. The oneness of the Neoplatonists was the very oneness of intelligible being. The oneness that Augustine seeks and finds belongs properly to life, the oneness in which life recovers its shape, its living embodiment, even behind an opaque mask, as in a palimpsest.

It is not a question of identity, but of a center that otherwise confers oneness. Indeed, this notion was impossible for a classical philosopher to conceive, that there might exist some other kind of oneness distinct from identity and harmony. But let us examine the matter more closely. In truth, there are two modes of oneness that the philosophers conceived for human beings: that of the identity of being in its pure, intelligible form, the identity of the idea, and the Stoics' harmonious oneness, a oneness almost like a musical measure, in which movement is perpetual in order to sustain an apparent stasis, like a statue become a flickering flame. Proportion, harmony curbed the passions and controlled something more dramatic than any passion: the flow of time. Stoicism was the art of gathering up time in the most curious way, of which Seneca was the supreme master. Stoicism silenced something else in which evidently time is perceived: that delicate interiority, origin of the most atrocious pain, which appears to inhabit the very depths of the heart that Augustine makes transparent. A oneness like quiet music that softens and lulls can be little more than an anesthetic, a pitiful deception.

In effect, this measured oneness rested on its similarity with the primordial fire, with the Heraclitean divine into which we were to fall like a spark returning home to the hearth, a spark with no shape or image of its own, with no singularity, with no transfigured or recovered interiority.

The oneness of identity in turn rested on its entry into the intelligible world, on transformation into an object, on that which we glimpse from afar, aided by reminiscence, a reminiscence that is nostalgia and the "memory of forgetting," as Augustine would say.

Having finished his *Confessions*, having performed the act of self-revelation and self-discovery, Augustine finds none of these kinds of oneness within himself. Instead he finds a center, a depth, a limitless interiority, inhabited by a continuously inner truth as such. By simply revealing itself as an indwelling, truth has been discerned in an inaccessible, protected place, in a place untouched by suffering, where not even the terrible trace of original sin is able to cast a shadow: this well of clear, quiet water, where the reflected image does not mirror the outside but something beyond itself, an image that is not a portrait but truth, truth as such, though not all of it, visible yet unattainable while we are mantled in time. And time itself is going to be transfigured. Nothing is to be silenced, no passion is to block us, nothing that has been given us is to be annihilated. Truth lives in the inner being of man, not as an image or reflection, but as reality, even though such an immense reality can neither be seen nor imagined, nor be present to us.

The Figure of the New Man

The soul has returned to its inwardness. In the center, we find this eternal, unmoving question of identity, inside man himself, who does not tear it out to become an object of the intelligible world. The longed-for oneness is achieved in a different way; it is another kind of oneness in which life has assumed by virtue of this inner center the characteristics of true being. This oneness is authentic and it is eternal.

The subject is born and is called "I." In reality we acquire a name, a proper name. "All who turn toward God receive a proper, eternal name," the mystic Ruysbroeck said centuries later. The I is at once, and forever, I.

Without that center, the soul cannot be preserved. This is the terrible lesson that follows from philosophy, from the ideas about man it engendered, from the paths traveled to become human. The soul had to be abandoned or exhausted, although this was not always admitted. Those who were not willing to accept this tremendous transformation by Platonic or Aristotelian means, or Stoic appeasement, had to renounce salvation through philosophy. But what else was there for the person worn out by the ceaseless traffic of things, for the person asphyxiated, for mere man, in need of a path to achieve being? The humiliation had to be terrible, given the situation, given the unavoidable being of things, of nature. The man who could not achieve his own being had to feel beaten down before such things, a slave. A slave also, especially, to what was inside him, shapeless and unsupported, unstable.

This man, reborn, no longer exists naked, scattered, or self-absorbed. The pure soul in its transparency reflects an image, a being who is impressed, stamped with a shape. The mirror of life reflects in its quiet waters the very image of the supreme mystery, that of the Trinity.

In chapter 26, Book XI, of the *Civitas Dei*, Augustine speaks of the image of the Trinity in man, which, while retaining its mysterious character, forms part of that moment of certainty on which his entire work is built.

And this poses the question: Must every confession end in some kind of certainty, or evidence? Does not the new man born again from confession, any confession, now walk naked because he possesses a form and figure? In short, is he a complete man, like the man who once wandered lost or confused outside or inside himself, for *within oneself it is also possible to wander*?

Certainty

We do not yet know if the fruits of all confession are a kind of certainty. But we do know that in the beginning of any era, at the start of any crisis, certainty appears and only through certainty do we succeed. What is there in certainty?

If confession produces certainty, it surely then acquires the nature of a method. And certainty is the fruit of this method, showing the nature that truth must have, the truth by which we can live.

Because this certainty is the point when truth is a truth of mutual concern to the mind and to life. The truth of certainty asserts itself and, in asserting itself, produces assurance, certainty. It is at once firm and transparent.

Certainty is the philosophical name for something that in mysticism is called revelation. It is the unquestionable presence of a reality, an appearance. But reality is such that it produces a trace or change in the person receiving it.

Ortega y Gasset, in his study on *Ideas y creencias* [Ideas and Beliefs], affirms that reality comes to us enfolded in beliefs. "We do not live by ideas but by beliefs." But neither can we live without ideas, for if beliefs were sufficient, we would never have need to think. Belief offers us a reality, to be sure, but this reality—says Ortega—is confused. In contrast, ideas, "the children of doubt," are transparent. And this condition of being transparent to the mind is what makes us need ideas.

Beliefs, then, correspond to the spontaneous opaqueness of the human heart. A reality in which "we live, we move, and we exist" is not enough. We need this reality to be transparent, at least at some point. This is the revelation of reality that philosophy calls evidence. Greek philosophy did not appear to have needed evidence as a point of departure in the same sense as did Augustine and Descartes. Perhaps underlying evidence there was some self-transparent belief, so it seems that both certainty and inescapable doubt revealed the presence of some kind of faith.

Certainty seems to be born as a response to a more profound doubt.

Greek truth presupposes the submissiveness of life and thus has no need of confession. Confession emerges in search of a truth that will appease life, that will limit and subject life. Certainty is apparently truth in a form that life can assimilate, that shares in the qualities of beliefs and ideas. Like belief, it offers us security, and like ideas, it is transparent to the mind. And better still: it has been discovered by the mind. For it seems that the mind is only satisfied with what it alone has discovered.

But when this certainty, this belief made intelligible, emerges, it reveals something that already existed: the question of rediscovery. This is not a new truth, but a form cloaked in something already known, which now penetrates and shapes life. Before, it did not function and, since then, has once more become effective. Certainty tends to be poor, terribly poor in intellectual content. Nonetheless, it effects an unparalleled transformation of life that other kinds of thought, more rich and complex, were not capable of doing. Hence, certainty appears as the endpoint of confession, as its intellectual apex. There is something more that makes certainty resemble the fruits of a confession, and that is the transformation exercised on understanding itself, opening the spirit to confidence. The truth that appears in the evidence of certainty is the methodological point of departure for two reasons: first, because the reality that has arisen with certainty possesses a particular structure, for it is a particular reality. Second, and this may be the less visible, but most compelling reason: because the person in whom certainty has blossomed remains open to confidence.

In possessing this last-named condition, in producing an opening or expansion of the absolute depths of confidence, certainty is fruitful. Because confidence is the substratum of beliefs and the inexhaustible treasure from which they are formed. Through the evidence of certainty, this nearly asphyxiated confidence comes to light.

Can the Cartesian *cogito* be viewed as a discovery of confession? Is "methodical doubt" analogous to a confession? At first, it appears that the answer is affirmative, given that life changed. An effort to live according to this dimension of reaffirmed reason was initiated. Above all, there was a newly engendered belief in the reality that had appeared: the self. That belief, of necessity, was always at the heart of all justification: self-awareness, the singularity of one's own consciousness. In that term was encompassed reality made present through Cartesian certainty and the self would be obliged to refer to it with respect to everything doubtful. From that awareness would emanate effective reasons, and even the most rebellious and irreducible elements of reality would have to be, at least in appearance, subject to it. All reality, all objects, or with claims to being objects, would perforce seek ultimate justification in the immediacy of awareness: acts of awareness and, in its ultimate center, as the ultimate, inner oneness, the self, the self in solitude.

The emergent new man no longer feels rooted in anything. Little by little he has lost the memory of his origins and has felt increasingly more unique. A solitude that has left him alienated from family and forsaken has forced him to do something in order to feel creative, so that the action performed bears witness to his creative condition. And belief in human creation, needless to say, mirrors no less than the divine model of ex nihilo.

The new man must create in order to break the walls of this solitude, which is the space of consciousness. If Augustine's certainty discovered the image of the Trinity traced on a transparent soul, in this new encounter of man with himself, all that is mere copy, reflection, or image, is erased, leaving only human nakedness. Solitude is not a point of departure, but an arrival. Solitude is, in truth, the new certainty or what is new in this certainty. Of my existence, as of my awareness, I already knew, but the two things—become one—had hitherto endured attached to something. The revelation that I exist and think had come about in connection with something. Now the *cogito* is human solitude affirming its own existence.

It matters little that Descartes affirms everything traditional: God and the mysteries expressed in theology, reason, even the family and the existing social order. They no longer rest on the ancient foundation. Order may still be called order, but it is now a different order; the revolution is complete.

Human solitude is born. This is the mirror confession to that of Augustine, who felt alone, a fragment among things. Descartes withdraws from things. He withdraws to account for who he is and, having found that he is consciousness, he acknowledges the rich reality of the world only in the things that suit him. He will subject the world and its richness to human judgment. The new belief is transparent and firm, in its certainty, but ends up eliminating everything that cannot be reduced to that belief. The mysteries no longer count, and the very image of man in his nakedness has been erased: no longer a copy, but the original itself. What is to be the fate of this solitude revealed and professed as an inexhaustible treasure?

From Originality to the Abyss of the Heart

Cartesian solitude means that man is a unique universe, strange, nearly incommunicable. For that solitude is not the contingent solitude from which one emerges once something lost has been found again, but the underlying metaphysical solitude that fuses with one's very being.

In the ancient world, solitude is expressed in the form of a complaint. It is a rare occurrence that happens only to the melancholy, a fleeting state nothing like a "dwelling," as the precise language of the mystics subsequently characterizes it. One need only recall that the mystics make of solitude a dwelling of the soul, though not a permanent one. The mystic Abenarabí created a home out of solitude, where the soul obligingly closed in on itself, in perfect desolation, before being restored to its pure origins. Solitude, like all dwellings of the mystics, was a transitory stage. It differs from the *état d'âme*, or state of the soul, which while abused as a condition in the aftermath of romanticism, possessed reality, truly transformed the soul. For the stages along this path do not consist of mere passage through them, but of successive, unrelenting transformations.

The solitude that Descartes encountered is neither a state nor a dwelling, but the very being of man. Thus, his condition is a metaphysical discovery. The point is worth repeating: Descartes did not start from solitude. He arrived at solitude: that was his great intuition, the "new revelation."

This same revelation parallels and sustains in analogous fashion his discovery of method. The situation is very curious: certainty has gone into hiding, and the end product now has a oneness, but in inverse proportion to Augustine's certainty. Modern culture is born lacking oneness. Rather than seek the missing unity, being the child of this schism, it hides the fracture. Modern culture is the child of analysis, of a dazzling analysis practiced in the very heart of that culture. "For I am, know, and love myself," said Augustine, with deception a starting point.

Yet, this "what I am," this knowing and loving myself, forms an indissoluble unity, a priceless unity of existence, of heart and mind, which must always be the basis for any knowledge, for any "method." This is Cartesian certainty. The method and the idea that man has of himself are dissociated. Solitude is, must be, the very existence of man, who remains directionless. Thus, the seamlessness between life and knowledge is broken.

Even if we do not want this displacement, we are, in the end, obliged to accept it. The method, legitimized and stamped legal, will prevail.

Although it may appear that Descartes has managed a confession, albeit a simple confession of the mind, it is really a stunning analysis. He achieves a dissociation, having discovered the opportune moment to insert reason into life, liberating it from life. Reason advances more quickly than ever before, because of this freedom, for what is free is not man, but only his knowledge.

My whole being is isolated from all things and, with only one way to reach them, through my own knowledge, which is farther away than ever from the dwindling, abandoned world.

The supposed oneness of this man would, of necessity, be the oneness of the creator, he who creates with his reason. To know totally is to know in *status nascens*. To know things in their most intimate substance, in what they are yet to be, in their elements. And he who knows does so based on the self as the generating principle. He is the origin of his knowledge, a unique, singular being.

Nascent idealism ends up demanding a new kind of life: to live based on this originality of knowledge, to live by and in knowledge, as if knowing were, utterly and simply, existence. Life is no longer the highest form of existence, life bathed in transparency, but the reverse, the enduring transparency of knowing. For an idealist, living must be an enduring idea. Knowledge is sufficient unto itself. The "absolute" comes as an immediate aftermath.

On the other hand, that which in man is not knowledge remained alive and strong despite everything. Although more confused than ever, with access to knowledge now cut off and barely allowed the right to live, still it persisted. The originality of the heart, the originality of the individual, very soon would become visible in the same way as the mind. The individual, in his poor, confused inner sanctum, his mysterious habitations, abandoned though seemingly filled, all this is to be revealed in its originality. This originality amounts to spontaneity, for the two things are identical. The spontaneous, the painful, inflamed inner sanctum, life in its fragmentation and confusion, was the original form, which is to say, *being*, reality authenticated, whose supremacy needs no transformation, needs only to rise up, reveal itself, reclaim its rights.

Inevitably, a new kind of confession had to appear. Nothing could delay the moment in time when Jean-Jacques Rousseau, in his terrible innocence, achieved it. Possibly others, more cautious, felt some small need to do the same but did not give in to the impulse, whereas it seems that Jean-Jacques bragged about yielding to it. The originality of man in his spontaneity demands to be revealed. The originality of this world in shadow, the "abyss of the heart."

In parallel fashion, an increasingly frantic urge to seek the originality of the inner world follows the resplendent passage of idealism: to explore the solitude of every man like a mine of inexhaustible reality. On the one hand, the Idea on the march; on the other hand, the reality, unique and inexhaustible, of the heart's hallucinatory abyss.

Jean-Jacques

And thus was born the new confession of the new man. In that truthful mirror we behold his image. And, as we shall see, man gains nothing from it, it appears as an act of humility, almost of abnegation, anticipating sacrificial offerings to knowledge. A soul disgorged to human voracity, to curiosity, to malevolence, indeed the cruel gaze of men. It does not matter. The soul of the new man desires being contemplated.

This is a gesture of love. The new man offers his soul, virtually his body. Seemingly, he desires being devoured, consumed by others. "That love so honest / and longing so strange / unafraid / of the bird that tears its breast / and gives its heart as food / for love," says the wisest poetry about this pain. For love emerges unafraid, tearing apart its breast until there is no secret corner left. And with longing undiminished, love slices up its heart, in such a way that the pieces, despite the horror, cannot be refused.

But what motivates the soul of the new man? The desire to be seen. Does he perhaps already possess an image of himself? By being noticed, the new man wants to be understood by all those who in life took to disliking him.

History and Confession

The idea that "the heart has a history" allowed the splendid development of the modern novel. This is one of the underlying premises of romanticism. German romantic idealism, which at once aspires to, and fuses with, this moment of identity, whether with the self or absolute spirit, runs parallel to the history of the heart, in the process retreating from its own oneness. The identity of spirit does not include it; and human existence, as the tormented Kierkegaard saw, remains peripheral. Anguish is the heart's purity, the only purity possible and attainable if one wishes to have no history.

And thus romanticism, with the terrible innocence that characterizes it, incessantly makes confessions in the form of histories, turning history into confession. Romanticism chooses not to believe or forgets, indeed does everything possible to forget, that the history of the heart is but the means for confession to be achieved. But such forgetting is the consequence of what one believes: that the history of the heart constitutes reality. Because—and this is essential—the heart is no longer transformed into a means. To the identity of absolute spirit, the heart answers with its independently minded originality. The heart revolts and aspires to live for itself. The heart does not see itself as a mirror, does not aspire to serve anything, nor does it wish to experience the wounding transformation through which the mystics achieved the supreme liberation of the heart by negating it.

Nevertheless—and this is the high point of all things of substance in romanticism—not forgotten is what the mystics regard at once as grace and consummation: ecstasy. Far from being forgotten, ecstasy is always present in these confessions, like a secret, unconfessable longing. In ecstasy one finds freedom from history and occurrence. In ecstasy one senses something, a place, a particular place where the storyteller might gain what he seeks: to escape his own history, which is to escape from time. Such a thing does not happen, evidently, in Rousseau, except much later and after the fact.

Jean-Jacques does not seek to escape time. Indeed, he is barely aware of it. Nor has he grasped the pure perception of time. By exercising his I, he is prevented from seeing time, since he is always projected as living beyond himself, escaping all final consequences. The notably extremist and extreme model of the modern extremist soul never ventures into truly extreme places.

But who or what actually prevents Jean-Jacques from doing so, this man endowed with such an extraordinarily vivid sensibility, which constitutes the better part of his genius? A dual belief prevents him, a dual belief or two beliefs that, rather than fusing into one, intermingle in a rather confusing way: the singular belief (further elaborated though not invented by Rousseau) that the reality of the heart is its history, and another belief, whose discovery makes him giddy with enthusiasm and constitutes his immense contribution and originality—belief in the naturalness of human beings.

A Natural Heart

For in penetrating his own heart, Rousseau loses himself in it as in a garden. This is the return to the forbidden garden, the reconquest of paradise. This is what he does in reality. His commitment is founded on this act, sparked by longing—the most genuine thing in his life. And his beliefs, his dual belief in history and in naturalness, is his original theory that man is born free and everywhere finds himself in chains. His theory of man is perhaps the most strange and revealing of all such theories to have had an impact on Western culture.

The truth is, the two beliefs—that the heart has a history and consists of its history and that of the natural heart—are a single belief in the end. For the doctrine of the heart's originality produces a life, the least imaginable kind of life, the literary life or life in literature, life in imaginary situations, as a sort of a priori of the heart or of love. This situation becomes romanticism and truly characterizes that which, pervading countless minds and at last descending into travesty, is said of a man when we say he is an "idealist." This is the life of the heart become independent of all things as if the heart wanted to show off its independence or, better yet, as if, with no place worthy of containing it, the heart alone was following a phantom of its own making, its own life and passion.

The heart in its passion is at once unresisting and original. Unresisting in its originality because the more the heart clamors for passion or the more abandoned it feels, the more tethered it is seen to be to its only possession, the quality of nonresistance. Thus begins the uncertain life of the independent heart, whether rebellious or defenseless, pursuing on its own the life of insatiability. Unresistant life stands solitary, detached from all objects, and sets itself up as a principle, in the image and likeness of the self, or mingling with it. Now the heart inevitably tends toward objectification, for that is its unavoidable condition, but it does so knowing or thinking it knows that the object maintains it, that the adored idol lives at its expense. Thus, the object ends by falling into the most abject condition, disclosing everything it owes to the activity of the heart, while the heart turns more toward love than toward the object in which it is deposited. In truth, the heart turns toward itself, re-created through its own activity. For it appears impossible that the heart could act in any other manner than that of a mirror, in self-reflection, replicating its own figure, finding pleasure in its own image.

Rousseau reveals to us this process that must inevitably be expressed. There are two reasons for revealing it: because the defining feature of the life of the heart will be expression, a life that expression makes real and that is achieved through expression, as if expression were its endpoint. And even more so, because Rousseau is the first to feel it, he can do no less than hasten to communicate such good news to the entire world. It is fair to say that he does so with prodigious accuracy, with a passion so transparent it seems made of ice, in the celebrated passage where he narrates the genesis of his love for Madame d'Houdetot. That passage is surely an enduring and instant classic in the history of love, and especially in the history of those hearts who delight in the story, whose passions become their real lives. First comes a state of invented love, of self-perpetuating intoxication, then the love experienced for the woman of flesh and blood. Preceding this "state of the soul" is the most critical of all moments, an instant of reflection on his life, from which Rousseau draws this imaginary love, then real love, and finally the entanglement to which he will fall victim, the long chain of equivocations, which henceforth will forever fix the shape of his life. This new figure is like the template for the archetype of modern man: fickle, dual, even multiple, with an array of possible faces, none of them complete. He lives enfolded in, and trapped by, ambivalent, utterly ambiguous categories: victim and victimizer, pursued and pursuer, enamored and narcissistic.

The Artificial Paradise

In truth, Rousseau's confessions, this solitary life of a heart's re-created history, institute literary life, living in imaginary places, with imaginary life as the point of departure. The heart of the drama is in the episode noted above, in his romantic love for Madame d'Houdetot, to whom at another stage of his life he would scarcely have paid any attention. That is, his attention mirrors her attention, as was the rule in Rousseau's relationships with people. This is one of those rare cases in which his heart transcends the self, but this transcendence is, properly speaking, love.

It is the culmination of a life that has arrived at its center. For Rousseau has lived, as a diaspora amid the events of his life. His youth is gone now, and he is almost happy. This at least, it seems, is how he remembers his travels, or rather, his wanderings. He feels immersed in the blissful oneness of nature, in a continual "ecstasy." Later, when the responsibilities of life arrived, he avoided them. How else can we explain his unfeeling separation from his children, coming from one who so valued childhood? It is one thing to dwell on childhood, but another to accept, to welcome into his wandering life real children of flesh and blood, with their own personalities and actual needs. That presupposes coming down to earth, entering and submitting to real life. Social life, with its commitments, is thus avoided, but personal relationships—that is, life, at once unreal and intimate—are extracted from it, like a sweet liqueur. Yet in the year 1756, "in the most beautiful season of the year," something happened to his life, it seems, for the first time. Jean-Jacques was forty-four years old. Alone with himself, precisely in the idle calm and happiness of that moment, he felt dissatisfaction, the suspicion of not having found what he had sought. The now-classic passage reads: "The memory of different periods of my life led me to reflect upon the point I had reached, and I saw myself in the twilight of life, seized by sharp affliction. I believed myself nearing the end of my life's work, almost never having enjoyed practically any of the pleasures that my heart desired, never having given free rein to the vehement sentiments hidden in its depths, never having tasted, much less experienced, that intoxicating voluptuousness that I felt vigorously stirring in my soul, and that, for lack of an object, was there forever restrained, unable to do more than exhale sighs."

Dissatisfaction reveals the desiring self's desire to be, and at the same time, the absence of an object in which to invest oneself. As in Augustine, lack, absence, brings the first insight. As Rousseau was doubtless incapable of being the chaste heart that fasts when deprived of a suitable object, he threw himself immediately into acquiring one. He became intoxicated with himself, as he tells us. The evocation of the phantoms of his youth stimulated all the more the intoxication by which he saw himself possessed, though with sufficient lucidity to perceive the small distance that separated him from ridicule. The object of this infatuated state surely signifies the most abject decay: it is not an object, but a mere stimulant, and desire does not move toward the object as an end, but passes through and falls back on itself. Jean-Jacques himself, his turbulent soul, validates the enjoyment of this kind of love. Thus, he entertains himself with phantasmagorical effects, but with no intention of leaving this seal of self-enclosure. And the phantoms, as is natural, oppose no resistance to such a use. Their very nature consists in dissolving, assimilating any mirage-producing substance. But, for the same reason, the substance is soon exhausted, for as the objective reality of the love object diminishes, it is less apt to sustain the object, given its intrinsic condition of corruptibility. And thus Rousseau is obliged to replace the phantoms of memory with phantoms of his imagination: "What did I do on this occasion? No matter how little the reader knows me, he will have guessed. The impossibility of grasping real objects thrust me into the land of chimeras; and not seeing anything real that might satisfy my delirium, I distracted it with an ideal world that my fertile imagination soon filled with beings to meet my heart's desires. This remedy could not have come at a better time, or had better results. In my continual ecstasies, I became utterly intoxicated with the sweetest feelings that ever penetrated the human heart. Totally disregarding the human race, I devised perfect creatures and societies, as celestial for their virtues as for their beauty, trustworthy friends, tender and loyal, such as have never been found in this world. I became so enamored of taking up residence in the empyreal heavens, in the midst of beautiful creatures surrounding me, that I spent hours and even days oblivious to everything. And forgetting all else, I had scarcely taken a hurried morsel, when the urge to run and conceal myself in my little patch of woods at once made me anxious. Thus, just as I was departing for the enchanted world, if some unfortunate mortal arrived to detain me here on earth, I was incapable of moderating or hiding my despair. And not having mastered my emotions, I welcomed him so brusquely, I behaved like a brute. This conduct came to confirm my reputation as a misanthrope, so that it was owing to the same that might have contributed toward reserving me an entirely different reputation, had they better plumbed my heart."

Nature acted as a stimulus for the invention of an imaginary society. Such appears to be the effective end result of the natural life of Rousseau. How could he not have realized the fate that his basic idea of man as a natural being would suffer? What kind of naturalness sustains itself in the midst of nature's own beauty that is forced to appeal to the inventions of the mind? A fictional life, an image of paradise lost, an intense nostalgia for a life where reality corresponded exactly to desire, a life in which desire matched its perfect object, is a life in which reality is not the persistent counterweight to our dreams, that is, to a life without reality and, therefore, without a self as well. Taking the shape of longing as an object, the excesses of Rousseau's own heart, in a self-inflicted feeding frenzy, produced a continual and intoxicating "ecstasy."

Thus is born fictional life, the literary life. In being expressed, life finds its object. "The bird that tears its breast / and gives its heart for love" of medieval poetry has turned into the bird that feeds off its own heart. Soon a sweet love potion takes the shape of the literature of semiconfession, highly wrought poetry, romantic poetry, adorned poetry, in which the secret life of the heart is presented to be imbibed, consumed by an ever-greater craving. This is romanticism. But so long as this form of confession is not replaced by another kind of confession, literature continues, it continues to live off romanticism and to be the increasingly frustrated quest for an artificial paradise.

"Pure" poetry boldly affirms the autonomy of this space. It is concerned with other things as well, naturally, but there is also this aggressive assertion, in defense of the inner garden, of enchanted nature where all possibility is, notwithstanding, real. This is the right to supreme evasion, to flee all the contradictions of existence, to disregard everything to attain ecstasy.

Ecstasy is the confused image, indeed the mirage, of the encounter with that core of identity, where time does not pass and life, in withdrawing, relinquishes its scattered being. The soul's center, the mystics say, is the point that cannot be assimilated to anything, to no thing or event; it is freed from time, on which life cannot help but depend, a center whose intimate, indissoluble unity liberates the heart. From Rousseau's confession issues, in two directions, the quest for this literary ecstasy: first, the histories of the heart that rarely achieve ecstasy, the histories of the heart or the hearts with a history that in real life produce the stream of characters in which so many souls want to wrap themselves, eager to bore deep into their very core of being. The second path is that of poetry, purer and more demanding, closer to that intimate self-control where the life spirit achieves its transformation. Poetry consumes the mirage of the psyche, often delicately touching pure time, the object that all confession, explicitly or implicitly, pursues.

Baudelaire and Rimbaud, with their artificial paradises and hells, are the children of this "natural heart," extremists by design. Their twin poles were despair and happiness. To live was simply to feel oneself pulled in two directions, to sink into the abyss of both, which is in truth a single abyss. A surplus of the heart and intoxication of the spirit are very much like faith, a desperate faith bent on hurling both toward hell, from whose gates it never retreats.

"I have come to see as sacred the disorder of my spirit," says Rimbaud. For want of sacred order, sacred disorder. This is the cry of confession, that explains and situates the words and actions of so much modern delirium. The perpetual adolescent finds death long before finding maturity, for he destroys himself out of haste and vehemence. The image of an angel, of perfect unity, of perfect transparency, has become too visible and, seen up close, does not allow time for the transformation of the life that is only concerned with living an instant outside time, as a trade-off for absorbing time drop by drop. Haste and rapture, reckless creation, hope the moment of poetic ecstasy can free life of its weight, free us from the burden of being human.

One cannot help seeing, I think, that the last great poetic movement of our time, surrealism, is much concerned with confession. It is a clearer confession than most in our era, in which once more the literary impatiently fills the void in seeking ultimate truth, the object that the heart needs for its real sustenance. Surrealism's intent, nevertheless, appears defined with an extraordinary clarity, with a lucidity worthy of its predecessors Rimbaud and even the disavowed Baudelaire. This transparency deserves and requires special consideration.

Surrealism

"Everything leads us to believe that there exists a certain point where life and death, the real and the imaginary, the communicable and the incommunicable, the high and the low, cease to be perceived as contradictory. One seeks in vain any other motive in surrealist activity than the hope of finding that point," says André Breton in the *Second Surrealist Manifesto*.

This declared purpose intimately marries surrealism to confession. Surrealism's rebellious character, its poetic rebellion, undiluted with social struggle, further affirms this relation. Surrealism seeks this center of identity that is in man and is not a faculty or capacity, as was said earlier, or a "psychic act," to use the surrealist language of the day. The Cartesian I is the original, radical unity; but the substance of consciousness is found only in unique being. And this conception of the unity of human beings, of man the living creature, is the cause of all rebellions, increasingly violent rebellions. Confessions, whether they bear the actual name, like those of Rousseau, or whether they do not bear it, as with literature or poetry and even philosophy that aim to achieve the same thing as confession, are born, knowingly or not, as a protest against that original I. Thus, this protest is joined from the very start to confession, sometimes chaotically mixed with it. Protest is born "being against." Both somewhat confusedly believe that this "being against" is the only reason for being and lose their way, as in the case of psychoanalysis, by being opposed to the Cartesian I. Surrealism, of poetic origin, possesses a greater lucidity and, its aggressiveness notwithstanding, less violence. Because it is not a scientific method like psychoanalysis, surrealism is a more genuine confession not for its method—automatic writing—but for its quest, its ardent desire, sense of purpose, and above all, for the object it presupposes, that center alluded to earlier.

The Cartesian I excluded not only the soul, the gathering place of all things, the locus of intimacy and familiarity with the universe, but also the kind of superior oneness, the inner center that Augustine discovers and Plotinus—differences aside—transmits. This is also the transcendental I that German idealism rediscovers, the unique identity of the subject of knowledge that thinking supposes. With being, then, itself a unity, it posits the unity of the object. But this pure identity that idealism restores through rediscovery is like the Plotinian soul for those who were determined to become philosophers. It remains a benefit to philosophy that in neither case—neither that of Plotinus nor that of idealism—spreads to men who are not philosophers. And both, despite constituting a principle of life and indeed the only living thing, remain outside the life of individual man, necessitating his violent conversion. The presupposed center to which surrealism alludes is without doubt that of all poetry. It is the center as creator, where all opposites cease being opposites, because everything would be understood were we able to accede to this center in a nascent state. "A nascent creation, without memory," said Charles Péguy, a poet who was not at all surrealist. A point beyond all contradiction is a point of pure identity where thought is creative, that is, poetic, annulling "that depressing divorce between reality and dream" (Breton, *Second Surrealist Manifesto*).

But surrealism, for all its poetic character, could not help being infected by the prevailing beliefs of the time to which it belongs, the belief that the psyche is human reality. Thus, the surrealists concentrated on seeking that center, the original prime mover, through the path of the psyche. In this matter their error coincides with the error of psychoanalysis. Both rely on that which in the psyche belongs to no one, that which is seemingly outside the conscious subject, beyond the control of the self. And lo and behold, it turns out both have generally found closely analogous materials, materials that are, in effect, matter, remains, substrata of lived life and experience, sometimes taking the curious form of memory that led Jung to conceive of a collective unconscious. Surrealism and psychoanalysis alike have simply relied on the impersonal, on the very opposite of the desired unity, of becoming one with the self that at least once in our lives we hunger to taste.

Surrealism will always be valued more for what it sought than for what it achieved; more for the program than for its results. And, in common with the best of contemporary literature, more as testimony than as a fully successful body of work. Of the numerous literary testimonies of the period, surrealism is the most lucid and the most self-aware in its quest. Paradoxically, surrealism possesses too much awareness, which lays bare its character as method, as confession. This is often reluctant testimony, damaged by its own witnessing. Thus, it is a kind of broken literature, dislocated, its possibilities essentially frustrated by its own superficiality, enslaved to the psychic acts that it mirrors, unable to salvage the oneness buried beneath such acts.

We are talking about a oneness that is human and that generates the work of art. This is no doubt what those sporadic cries for a return to a "human art" mean. The humanity of art can be nothing less than the ultimate oneness of origins, found in that ultimate inner center. The creation that the work of art offers us arises from this intimate and active center, from this living, active oneness. Some works of art do not provide a path to finding this center, such as that of Proust. Another kind of "humanity" in art is always fictitious, fraudulent or crude; a radical falseness, all the more false for being "realist." Art born of such an intimate interiority finds the basis of its legitimate autonomy by not trying to supplant real life. Living through literature, the literary falsification of life, then becomes impossible. Art and real life complement each other. Art exists to offer us something that ordinary time does not give us, to offer what the time of reality denies us. Life needs art as the agent of an act that could not be achieved without art. Among the many things that modern Europeans have forgotten is the therapeutic function of art, the almost magical curative powers and genuine wonderworks of art.

The discovery of this intimate center that confession unearths does away with the misrepresentation that is human, realist art, but it also crushes the other great modern confusion, naturalism, with which realism is partly conflated, as naturalism's immediate antecedent. In truth, "realism," "humanism," and "naturalism" are simply the deviations that art suffers when it issues from a superficial self, a deviation that is seen as a matter of great urgency in the period when it is produced, but which can be said to exist in every age in which the oneness of man has been lost or terribly obscured.

The question concerning naturalism is undoubtedly one of the most profound, since it conjures up the antithesis that most influences art, of all such antitheses enunciated by André Breton: the "communicable and the incommunicable." Of all the questions that affect art, this is without doubt the greatest, given that art is above all a sign or expression, concerned with what is expressed and with the form of expression. We appear to have forgotten that everything art determines—concepts and characters, forms and desires—involves a diversity made possible by the oneness which is its underlying basis. The artist is an artist because he can plunge so deeply inside himself that he finds visions that are at the same time acts. True art erases the contradiction between act and contemplation. Art is active contemplation or contemplative activity, contemplation that engenders the work of art, out of which something is made. Therefore art erases at the same time the difference between the real and the imaginary, as well as between the natural and the artificial. In a fragment of a sacred book of China, this prodigious act is demonstrated in the clearest, most unassuming way, like water. In Master Chuang (Tschuang-Tse), we read, an artisan is asked an earnest question concerning the perfect execution of a wooden bell tower, to which he responds: "I am an artisan and have no secrets at all. Nonetheless, there is something which describes my work. As I was preparing to make the bell tower, I was very careful not to waste my energy. I fasted in order to quiet my heart. After having fasted several days, I no longer dared think about earnings or honors. After five days of fasting, I no longer dared think about praise or reproach, about talent or ineptitude. After seven days of fasting, I had by then forgotten about my body and all my limbs. Nor did I think any more about the Court of Your Highness during this time. In this way I withdrew into my art, and all the noises of the external world fell away for me. Afterward, I went to the woods to contemplate the way trees naturally grew. Once I had a real tree in my sights, I found the bell tower already finished, so that all I had to do was lay my hands on it. If I had not found the tree, I would have abandoned the project. But by having made my own nature act in harmony with the nature of the material world, people say that it is a divine work."

The Underground Men

But the solitude of the Cartesian I, by prevailing in life and incarnating the belief that the cultivated European man had of his own reality, followed other paths—one in particular that results in the kind of individual embodied in a number of brilliant men and that can be called the "underground man." Originality was his curse but also his only talent. These were tragic beings, as belief in the self made it impossible to find the inner peace that, if only fleetingly, is indispensable, above all when men are thrown frantically into the struggle for individual existence. The more original that individual existence is, the more pressing the need for that center of stillness, of confidence and calm. Immense solitude becomes an immense burden when no intimate aperture exists as a counterweight, turning into a solitude with no inner space, the worst of tragedies in which the individual perishes asphyxiated. We view the lack of space, of horizons in which to move and to inhabit, as the true condition of life for the kind of man oppressed by the terrible gift of his original, initial self. Such men are driven to suicide by the desire to exist. This is the kind of man European life has produced, in a variety of individual circumstances. They are poets, philosophers, and, above all, those unknown men and women, nameless creatures who died without yet acquiring existence, embryonic beings who have filled European life more than we realize, especially since the second half of the nineteenth century. Specters, stillborns, the twilight dead, they seem incapable of enduring one of the transformations that life demands to attain its end.

A surrealist poet helpfully evoked them in the figure of three poets. Paul Éluard says: "If Lautréamont, Baudelaire, and Rimbaud seemed full of remorse, it is because their solitude was limitless. They dream of children and brothers, and come to believe they are the dead inhabiting the dead; hence their exceptional capacity for annihilation." The truth is these poets are not the "subterranean" men who will come afterward, but something less active and more filled with sweetness. They are versions of a character from Greek tragedy, Antigone, buried alive. They are the living dead, buried in an invisible tomb, isolated from the living. The "solitary poet" phenomenon is so familiar to Europeans nowadays that we have come to believe it was always so. Nevertheless, for centuries the prevailing image was that of the poet in intimate communication with the world, as though he were the world's soul, a breath of living grace that lightens the hours, the gravity of life, and the weight of time.

Exhaling moans and cries from the depths of the grave, which is their hell, the living dead are heard incessantly, their words like screams from the abyss, shouts for help in an age less and less compassionate to the truly dead, who in the end fall silent. Hence, the fervent devotion with which their poetry is embraced by those who come to form a sort of league or brotherhood, like one of those cults to someone gone, to something or someone, in short, who needs us to survive. Hence, too, this is why their words, their cries from the pit of hell, seem like a desperate confession and work like a confession on their followers. For in the last analysis one of the functions of confession is to open a space for a reality that is in danger of asphyxiation. Thought opens a space to certain realities, freeing them from contradiction, demonstrating their objective nature. Confession conquers this space for the intimate realities that are not reducible to an object, realities that need a living support, a singular existence to sustain them, realities that reject being transformed into an object. This is the heart clamoring to live as the heart. The heart aspires to the life it properly deserves, unwilling to become something it is not, to be absorbed or dissolved by reason, for example.

The tragedy of those individuals is ultimately the absence of an inner space. Examined more closely, the first thing we sense is too much of everything. Theirs is a jam-packed world, crowded with things, with embryonic beings, hopes and longings, drafts and projects, traces and premonitions of a nameless reality, a world that borders or enters the ineffable and is no less real for being ineffable. The fact that these individuals have no space signifies not the absence of a physical space, but, rather, the absence of an adequate space. These are beings too stuffed with reality, with realities in a world that has inculcated in them a belief that prevents them from embracing those realities. They are victims, fallen prey to hallucination and constant delirium, beset by remorse for crimes they have not committed and could not commit; possessed by the vertigo of infinity, intoxicated with possibility.

Solitude, in a self without space, is congested with personages, with the individual's embryonic beings: an incongruous multiplicity of faceless, anonymous beings, embittered by their halfway existence. This seems to be hell, the hell that Rimbaud transcribed with brilliant boldness, though the privilege was not exclusively his.

Had they been able to achieve the confession they intuited, the terrible knot would have come untied, the doorway out of hell would have gently given way. Inner space would have appeared with its secret places properly prepared for everything writhing in agony that was discontented and asphyxiated. Along with, and by virtue of, that center of intimacy comes intimacy with persons and all things; intimacy with oneself. Long before the Cartesian I swept it away, there was something called a soul, which we now imagine as this inner space, as this personal kingdom, a treasure where the hidden and unexpected possibilities of every person are guarded, a secret kingdom. This space was erased and in its place appeared "psychic facts" or "acts of consciousness." All reality, no matter what kind it was, had and must even now continue to be based in and legitimated by an act of consciousness. This constitutes the legitimate, the existent, the real. It is the psychologism that followed Cartesianism, whereas the soul of antiquity, even in the most rationalist philosophy, so foreign to any kind of mysticism, Aristotle's for example, maintained that "the soul is like a hand" and that "the soul is, in some sense, all things." The soul is something, a particular place, or seat, or power, that makes contact with everything, and for this reason is the locus of intimacy, being a kind of preknowledge that makes things familiar. This is the opposite of estrangement, allowing us to be situated, to possess a sort of instinct or sense for penetrating every thing according to its nature and way of being; a skill or subtleness that suggests, in effect, the image of a hand delicately touching reality, a steady, infallible hand at once maternal and virile, a hand that is strength and insight, that the West lost a long time ago.

This place is appropriate to each and every thing or every embryo of a thing, to every thing that has no name and that offers forms of contact other than knowledge, that cannot properly speaking be called knowledge, but is as necessary as knowledge, and that in some way is the cradle of knowledge. Intellectual knowledge has been a privileged function. It was natural that in being exercised, such knowledge would become known and established. But other forms of contact exist, other relations that are not intellectual knowledge, and perhaps never could be, such as, for example, the relationship with the dead, with our own ancestors; the attendant and appropriate relationship with human beings in such a situation, with beings who are not beings in the same sense, strictly speaking, as the living, in this particular place that is ready to receive them. In reality this contact has nothing to do with beings and things, but with entering into spaces that suddenly and gently make their appearance. For this reason, one could not say therefore that religion, all religions, are something more than, or different from, acts of consciousness, or acts of faith for that matter, in which we have lately attempted to ground them. For the sense of deliverance follows from neither belief nor even love, but from those knots that come untied and those walls that silently collapse. It is intimacy with all things, with familiar things, though being familiar things is not enough, for there to be intimacy with them. We are not speaking of intellectual knowledge, or anything like it, but something that precedes and sustains intellectual knowledge and without which knowledge would float away, no matter how great its accuracy and clarity. For then distrust soon appears, a radical distrust concerning the void of lost intimacy. The reality of the objects of knowledge is called into question, without being resolved, assuming we are not dealing with objects of the mind, with objects that exhaust their existence in being thought. At stake is the reality of the things that thinking knows.

But something worse happens to the things or events not construed rationally, to the reality that is not revealed to intelligence. Such things have reality, but without being rooted in us. They possess that particular unfortunate reality of the living dead, wanderers with no place to lay their heads, for it seems that the soul is where certain things alight. The soul, evidently, by its very nature, has been given to us for this very delicate and hence indefinable task, for which it has been called sacred. The soul is indefinable and cannot be approached without risk. A risk that is all the greater for its unforeseen dimensions, the origins of which are not therefore easily ascertained. Abrogating that earlier intimacy with reality, especially in the spheres unilluminated by thought—in the spheres that have not acquired *being*—turns out to be very serious, although it does not destroy thought itself. What is surely serious are those invisible human illnesses, delirium and derangement, the nightmare into which life is transformed, in being surrounded by an opaque reality. These illnesses, ejected from their appropriate place, appear without form or figure, or leave a strange emptiness. We know nothing, or almost nothing, about this world. This is the world of wordless intimacy, where a hidden, unconscious harmony is prophesied to rule, where the root of all war must reside, where peace is not a thing of treaties or compromises, of laws or rights, but of silent harmony that, once destroyed, is ungovernable chaos, endless rebellion, discord.

This is unquestionably the discord of the living dead, their embittered presence. The living, poets such as Baudelaire and Rimbaud, philosophers such as Kierkegaard and Nietzsche, novelists such as Dostoyevsky, have been endlessly tormented in a solitude filled with phantoms, liberating themselves as art or thought opens up a place for those phantoms. Given the terribly heartless age that befell their lot, they too lived in anguish, as if pursued by the furies of ancient tragedy. And they began liberating themselves as they gave shape to the existence of their tormenters. They rejected tragedy, conquering a different kind of solitude, a solitude from which communication springs, a solitude that bears perfection within its own expanse, that sees Kierkegaard as the protagonist of "posthumous works," as the living dead he is. "Posthumous works are ruins, and ruins offer the most appropriate place of residence to the dead of this world. We dead of the world ought to cultivate the art of stamping a posthumous character on what we create; an art that consists of imitating the style of unrestraint, an insouciant, fortuitous style . . . ; an art that consists of offering a bliss that will never be present, but that always contains an element of the past." That manner of living, considering oneself as the living dead, as the protagonist of posthumous works, was the only solution, perhaps, for the man who had misplaced those realities with which nonetheless he was imbued. And it was the way to advance toward what the living dead wanted to be, toward their oneness as human beings. The all-consuming task of the living dead, of underground men, is to appropriate an alien reality, extracting from it their own being, for apparently the tragic element of tragedy is the absence of a subject, of something that remains exempt and free from destiny or the passions.

Confession thus seems to be a method for finding *who* one is, the subject to whom things happen, and as such, someone who is above the fray, freed of what happens to him. Nothing that may happen to him can invalidate or destroy him, for this kind of reality, once acquired, appears invulnerable. And the success of this point of invulnerability concerns not only pure oneness, an inner center, but also this mysterious world that must be unified by penetrating deep inside it, conquering it through intimacy, and serving it through an enslavement that ends in liberty. Perhaps only philosophy is capable of settling the conflict, supposing the lack of intimacy to affect uniquely the reality of things. But the worst thing is to be a stranger to oneself, to have lost or never to have possessed intimacy with oneself, to walk about alienated, a stranger in one's own house.

The insertion of this inner center, if that is what it really is, makes the world of delirium acquire a form and an order, because the embittered, aching heart is at once fashioned from someone, from a being who takes hold of the heart. But there is something more: from that being shines a light, in which this inner world becomes visible, true. The subject, who is now a subject, possesses this world, although no violent domination is implied, for the inner world does not obey in this manner. This form of possession lacks commands or orders, because it is intent on uniting that which in being united forms a single being.

Does not the terrifying face of the present time unquestionably offer us this figure of a world without a subject, where the subject has disappeared, where the self wanders like a lost king without subjects or territory, where the person responsible, the person with identity and a presence of his own, does not exist anywhere? A world that precedes being, in which the psychic possesses the demoniacal existence of an unattainable yet diluted multiplicity; a world from which the forms have fled, leaving only the ungraspable, embittered phantom, phantom and emptiness. Is the world not in need of a true and implacable confession?

Confession

Rosa Chacel

Translated by Carol Maier

To Concha Albornoz

The roads traveled together

—Rosa

Preamble

When this book was written some fifteen years ago, I defined its purpose as an attempt to answer a question posed by Ortega: Why are there so few memoirs, and even fewer confessions, in Spanish literature? Now, after such a long time, the question seems to coincide less with reality; memoirs, most of them autobiographies, a few confessions, are beginning to appear in a veritable swarm. To suggest, at least, even if it's not possible to define, an appropriate route for studying both phenomena—why there were none before and why they are appearing now—I want to stress here at the outset the fundamental condition or consistency of all confessions.

"The most dramatic of history's greatest confessions," I wrote in the first line, "are those inspired by a feeling of guilt." The most dramatic prove to be the most true, in other words, the most consistent with their reason for being, with their motive or cause; therefore, their profusion—I'm tempted to say their production—or their lack must indicate either a superabundance or a dwindling or exhaustion of raw material.

Among the many quotations that I've included from Kierkegaard, one of them seems the most directly related to this topic: "To dare to be completely oneself, to dare to actualize an individual, not just any individual, but this one, isolated before God, alone in the immensity of his effort and his responsibility, such is Christian heroism." For one individual to dare self-actualization is to assume the offense of having been born—"man's greatest offense" before God, of whom he is image and likeness. Now a young writer says that "The man of today believes that he does not believe in God," a perfect definition of our most deeply rooted belief. Still, there is guilt. Sometimes we touch truth beyond belief—not a truth that either destroys or corroborates guilt, but a truth that coexists with everything: with its opposites as well as its affinities. Truth that can arise only as fulminate, poetic imposition. I felt it one day in the La Plata zoo, a day in late spring, summer bursting in a gust of calm (I'm well aware that this does nothing to support any thesis, but if I were to forget it, if I made no mention of its value as a real event, I would omit the exemplary nature of an overwhelming experience). One day, in the La Plata zoo, at sundown, it stopped me in my tracks—an ecstasy that left me incapable of taking another step—the contemplation of terror. . . . Terror was the breath of that garden. There was a small rose garden, a bed of flaming roses—the fleshiest, the ones most likely to seem alive—and they were open, so serene, so prepared to spend the night in that state of vigilance, without shying away, without seeking to defend their carnality, their mortality. ("The fleeting winged halo I now see smiling, I fear soon withered.") Indeed, those roses did not seem to fear anything. The swallows, though, were seething with terror, screaming furiously among the wisteria vines, fighting to secure a safe place, disputing the highest, most isolated branches, dislodging their occupants in whom terror was a shared scream, a venting, an expression of their smallness. The other creatures, the most powerful, the fiercest, all trembled and hid in their refuges; they sensed sleep lowering their eyelids and they refused to give in. They growled a little to show their half-extinguished ferocity, to threaten and also to implore, to make their anguish visible by appealing for pity. Having taken refuge in their lairs, they held their babies close—those were the most frightened, the ones that carried the babies on their backs like a maternal excrescence—anteater, weasel—and they walked from one side to the other without finding a safe place. We men (with deep affection I recall my friends, students in La Plata, who accompanied me so often during that very difficult period, with infinite sadness, I recall the ones definitively departed), we men, the humans walked there, seeing, breathing in their terror and we felt profoundly guilty . . . of what I don't know, although yes, I do know . . . We felt guilty of not putting all our strength—all our ferocity of watchful lions, all our strength of bison or elephants, a strength strong enough to rip branches from trees—in defense of life. We, humans, with our minds stronger than any irrational force, wandered aimlessly about, among them and they were afraid of us . . . with reason.

Well, enough poetry, I want to recall other moments when guilt was germinating. No, no, guilt doesn't germinate slowly, it opens in one's conscience—way down deep, where it's barely discernible—as when a flower blooms and fills the air with scent. Its seeds, though, are planted gradually, and accumulate craftily, not altering the pace of one's conscious actions; one lives untroubled, incubating them. More than untroubled, certain, with an innovative smugness—the innovator like the conservative, both of them holding tight to the certainty of his personal determination—fulfilling himself because—I'll correct myself again—the seeds produced aren't things with parasitical lives. No, we ourselves are the seeds, each one accumulating his I-ness, packed to incalculable degrees of density. That's what was happening in those days, those days called the twenties, a numerical naming that today marks their qualitatively exceptional nature. *Un chien andalou* opened and we were all dazzled, happy to find ourselves in that situation—because that's what was happening, *we were in that*—and each of us responded in his own way. There were many who responded by assenting, yielding, without understanding much of anything—or understanding what they needed to understand—others, by wanting to understand more. I, among the latter.

I, with the greatest enthusiasm and, above all, believing that I saw such unfathomable depth in all that, such an inexhaustible wealth of suggestions, of previously unsuspected information, I was afraid of coming out with some paltry or harebrained judgment and I wrote to Buñuel. I admired Buñuel enormously, but he did not intimidate me, he was one of the young men of my time, a few years younger than I and I told him, with my earnest, self-assured frankness, that I would like to talk with him, thinking that perhaps he would be able to explain a few things about certain parts that I might not have interpreted correctly. Buñuel responded, which I did consider a kindness, limiting himself to a superficial explanation, telling me—unfortunately, I did not save the letter, which today would be very valuable, but I do have a clear memory of its contents, in which he breezily expounded. "This," the quote is approximate, "means nothing more than an incitement to crime and rape." I felt deeply offended because that offhand remark showed that he considered me sufficiently cowed to be frightened by such words and I wrote to him again, saying that he had not impressed me and that, in spite of those very interesting topics, I was still determined to speak with him. I don't know if there was further correspondence between us, but he did come to see me. He came, greeted me with a respectful click of his heels and everything, and we talked for a long time. Cordially? No. Hostilely? Not that either: we played our respective roles like a pair of idiots, like the two poorly mannered children we were, each in our own way. He very much wanted to win and he won quickly, deserving his triumph. I went into eclipse—something that goes into eclipse remains hidden behind a body that hides its brilliance, I never had any brilliance, no one eclipsed me: I shed my light in silence, slightly splattered by praise from a few prestigious minds. With my unguarded smarty-pants or perhaps smart frankness—my ancestral types were those universally created paradigms of the stubborn woman; with my simplicity and certainty, I was full of confidence. In myself, in my personality, in my values? No, in my vocation, which greatly surpassed what's called professional vocation.

Mine was a vital, essential vocation, to which I had consecrated myself when I was very young, following another ecstasy as irrational as the one that would move me fifty years later as I witnessed the frightened life of beasts. The irrational aspect of that first vision, I must note—it took possession of my mind, my soul's three potentialities (the event is sufficiently explained in my autobiography) with an invasive strength great enough to fill the entire space and to ensure that the enemy would never gain entry—clearly concerned the essential enemy. I'm afraid that is not clear, but I can't condense it further, I'm afraid that I could not prevent it from becoming tedious, from emphatic prosopopeia. I'm afraid to speak clearly—constrained by the fear that rushes in, cutting off one's voice as it utters the name of the beloved being—I'm afraid to say clearly that just as the beasts' terror made me see—sight of the evidence itself, life—presence anguished by the burden of existence—in the same way, seeing Apollo—as I've written elsewhere—I saw man's life freed from anguish by Apollonian law—as I've written elsewhere—that is to say, I saw man, the human, exactly as he should be, exactly as he must be. To that seeing I devoted myself, I embraced that vocation in the first years of my life. The only thing unusual about that, of course, is the brazen way that I explain it. Others have probably lived it just as intensely, others more timidly, others with an academic preparation strong enough to explain it more authoritatively. Be that as it may, a few of us, cloaked in the habit we'd endorsed—one as indelible as the grain or texture of our own skin—circulated amidst the advancing chaos. Ah! Also, of course, without opposing that chaos: watching it politely, like researchers, without getting involved.

For the same reasons—the date, again, sometime in the twenties—when the translation of the *Chants of Maldoror* appeared, I said, categorically: it makes me want to throw up! I said that and, naturally, I paid the consequences, I remained sidelined. About the same time, a little later, I read Freud with a passion. In Freud, the greatest impurities of the human soul were saved by law—research, science or its ambition, whatever is born in the purity of study—one could contemplate them without repugnance, then . . . I won't linger on what happened next, I want to speak about now. And now we speak with a verbal brazenness devoid of any reticence. Now, Sade, who in Freud's hands was an exuberant, labyrinthine topic, has invaded aesthetics and ethics. The children of our century delight in the divine marquis's refinements, which not even soccer's awesome power could sanitize. Meanwhile, the Apollonians—since there are some, there definitely are—we limit ourselves to saying, the divine marquis, to put it bluntly, was a nauseating guy.

Now we're living in a time when memories and confessions are starting to spring up, which shows that guilt lurks beneath every contemporary conscience. Do I seem to divide our current world between the perverse or the chaotic and the righteous, the unblemished, letting all guilt fall on the former? That would be ridiculous! For some time I've been planning to repeat a famous title, *J'Accuse*, and take the liberty of adopting that very winning and worthy approach, adding a subtitle, *Good people*, because it is them—among whom I count myself—that I want to accuse, profoundly. The evil—on a previous occasion I already adopted that division with respect to young people—good and evil—because it's very real, in its simplicity. The wicked, in our age, are stupendous, they've broken every historical record. The good, on the other hand, what have they done? Are they content to live with what they haven't done, because of not having done it? No, they don't live—we don't live—content, because we've not been able to do something overwhelming. Something seductive, tempting, which is the only thing that counts. We're not capable of tempting with the *Good*: that's the problem. We try, some of us, to preach—a way like any other to waste time. We've not managed to arouse our age, we've not been able to play up to it, to stupefy it with irresistible wooing until we had it tamed, until we had it wishing for seed. That's what is now hovering over our conscience, we feel as guilty as the worst of them and we would like to come up with some quick fix, but something that's been prodigally torn apart for years can't be stitched together in a minute. So the only thing we can do now is ask for confession.

—Madrid, 1979

The most dramatic of history's greatest confessions are those inspired by a feeling of guilt. My goal here is to study the three confessions I consider most important, those of Saint Augustine, Rousseau, and Kierkegaard, because the last two had such a decisive influence on the Spanish writers I want to analyze: Cervantes, Benito Pérez Galdós, and Miguel de Unamuno. Of course the strongest influence has been on the two who lived into the twentieth century; Cervantes stands apart. This entire meditation will be filled with asides, parentheses, and digressions, because it's impossible to generalize—even if it were possible, I would not want to, nor would I have the necessary resources—about things as individual as confessions: those gas escapes leaked from a conscience.

Cervantes stands apart, and this is what prompted me to study confession. Spanish literature suffers from a lack of confessions (as José Ortega y Gasset pointed out some time ago), and I believe Cervantes to be the only one who gave us a true, authentic, and pure confession. I can also say that Augustine stands apart, because he bears no direct relation to any of the Spanish authors in my study. But even if his confession bears no explicit relation to those I will analyze— rather, to those I will assume exist, seeking them in their hideouts, from which they are determined not to emerge—Augustine's confession does bear such a close relation to what I consider the archetypal confession that I find it impossible to ignore. In addition, his confession springs from the most violent and authentic feeling of guilt. The truth of this feeling lies in the direct relation that exists between his guilt—what he considers to be that—and his real, actual, life. Not in his actions, which have no decisive value in confession, but in the tension or tone of his conscience in relation to life.

So Augustine and Kierkegaard completely fulfill the requirement of a feeling of guilt, but Rousseau? If I could say that Rousseau lacked feeling, the question would be settled, but that's not exactly the case. Rousseau confessed not because his conscience tormented him but to find all manner of excuses for it. Does that mean the feeling of guilt did not exist in him? I think it's rather that *conscience*, a faculty both mental and psychic, was suffocated in him by his powerful *consciousness*, the rational discernment, the ability to fabricate covers, hats, shells, for what the world calls guilt. Not just to conceal guilt but to take one swift stroke of his racket and send rebounding everything facing it on the court. Consequently, Rousseau appears in this study principally because traces of his work are evident in Spain's writers at the beginning of the twentieth century; also, because another of my fundamental requirements for confession is particular to him.

Confession can be defined as one's *last will*. If it's not that it's not confession; it's what we generally call *memoirs*. There is not an abundance of memoirs in Spanish literature either; we usually find that form of discourse in the pleasurable genre of narrative, because there is no greater pleasure than recollecting—even great pain or great horror: *recollection is the possibility we're given of retailed resurrection*. A modest resurrection to be sure, but such a positive confirmation of our very *being*. And narrating is positively a form of *power*. We narrate and we relive and reconstruct for another something that other has not lived, has not *been*. Confession does not consist in reliving or reconstructing; it consists in manifesting what never disappeared in the past, what never ceased to live because it was consubstantial with the life of the confessant.

If I say that confession is one's *last will*, this definition has two meanings, one *temporal*, one *essential*. The first involves the urgency we feel today to know about the lives of others. *The feeling of danger is the constant of current life.* People always knew that any time is a good time to die, but today they *know* because they *feel* it. And, like all sensations, once known, that feeling is cultivated and savored; people acquire a taste for its exquisite quality and they gorge themselves, often. No one is willing to let escape an occasion to know what a man's like, once that man *is*. There's a fear that as people *pass* they might escape from us without paying us their tribute, a fear that our age will have *passed* before they've managed to speak, and because of that constant fear, *we ask for confession*. This is the *temporal* meaning. The *essential* meaning lies in the adjective—*last*. The will that confesses represents the self—"the more will there is, the more self"—and the more will derives from the self's ultimacy, the more representative of the self it is. So this concept of *last will* indicates will assayed in its *ultimate* truth, in the *ultimate depth of one's selfness. In Augustine and Kierkegaard, that will seeks in confession the freedom of communication, in Rousseau what it seeks is imposition.* Behind his will there are no pressing *ultimacies*, because in his unstable being he never manages to see the *ultimate* depth of any distinct category: only in his ability to attract can one find something obvious and *ultimate*—although devious.

In addition to the relation these confessions might have to the larger topic of my study—in reality, the relation is not to the confessions themselves but to the subjects of whom those confessions are the *ultimate* essence—I use these examples because I find none of higher quality. After Augustine's, I don't believe there were other great confessions until Rousseau. The one that Saint Theresa gave her confessor as a story of her life resembles an accusation more than a confession. Augustine accused himself as rigorously or more, diving stubbornly into the depth of his guilt, Saint Theresa covers herself with the harshest of insults, but does not set before us the evidence of what's hidden beneath them: we never learn if her faults are really faults or if they're adolescent apprehensions. In any case, her confession is obviously prompted more by the duty to provide an account than by the uncontrollable urge to confess.

Before Kierkegaard's confession there is Chateaubriand's, which influenced Galdós and is voluntarily and manifestly, a confession, while Kierkegaard's does not bear that name. There is no doubt, though, that every word of Kierkegaard is confession and, with respect to the influence of Chateaubriand—which I will discuss later—I don't believe it can be called influence; perhaps impression, emulation. It never occurred to me to include Chateaubriand in this introduction because there is much of the memoir in his confession.

Memory—as phenomenon, power, the most valuable faculty of mind and soul—is multifaceted, it acts in incalculable ways. According to one's nature—a thing of the soul, I've said—memory settles in one quality or another. In some, it accumulates external sorts of data, whether weighty or trivial, whether emotive or quite speculative; in others, it probes only within itself—for every fact, every experience, emotion, or analysis memory seeks the very beginning—the beginning of those facts and memory's own beginning—this is the memory that produces confession. And of course the various categories and qualities do not always appear clearly delimited, without any mix or infiltration. They are frequently found furthering each other and iridescing in mutual interpenetration. All great literature of the nineteenth century or, better, all literature since the nineteenth century, consists of memoirs and confessions.

※ ※ ※

Turning to the novel, the French novel can be taken as a good example of balanced reflection, as an interweaving of nuances or a harmony of elements. The Russian novel—in Dostoyevsky, its most eminent representative—can be taken as an example of unswerving direction: excavation, descendent molehill. During the first quarter of this century, Dostoyevsky's singularity of focus is what gave him a fascinating power, a pull greater than that of other, perhaps even more perfect novelists, because we all longed for him to pull us with him to wherever he was headed. The Spanish novel—can it be taken? Yes it can, although with effort, because it interests me a great deal—in its best-known representative, Galdós, as an additional example of unswerving direction, although the opposite one; observation, accumulation of facts and characters, psychological precision more detailed than profound: an evident lack of everything that can be called confession.

I feel very tempted to take the Spanish novel in its entirety, but that would mean a study of incalculable length. At present it would be more valuable to indicate the high points that demonstrate the singularity of the Spanish novel in the context of my topic, in the body of European literature that spans the period between the nineteenth and twentieth centuries. Singularity is something that generally attracts attention, but there is also the possibility that attention will not feel attracted by someone who demonstrates his singularity by *not attracting*. One might say that no one *pays* attention to him, because that's what people say, but attention is not at all precarious: attention *is given* as *participation*; the one who receives attention is nourished by it, and the one who does not receive attention because he doesn't ask for it—just as the one who doesn't cry doesn't suckle—grows up in silence. In Spanish literature, few have known how to cry—to clamor, we could say—but those few are the greatest. I will begin with the greatest of them all.

The first—first and foremost—Spanish novel does not consist in external observation. Does it consist in excavation? Not entirely, but definitely in an interiority sui generis, of unabashed spatial ambition, in other words, an ambition for depth that is not directed inward but that attempts to extend its interiority over everything that exists—and does not exist—the breath from its depth blurring the mirror of reality.

This is the closest to confession that has been made in Spain. An indirect form of confession—the *Quixote*—different or, rather, opposite to that in Cervantes's other novels, from which the Galdosian branch sprang.

On several previous occasions I have commented on "El sentido del tiempo en Quevedo" [The Sense of Time in Quevedo], Manuel Durán's excellent essay, because it contains a highly accurate vision of the drama that for centuries has afflicted the Spanish novel. "The lack of confidence in himself and in man in general," Durán says about Quevedo, ". . . made epic production impossible for him. The epic is based on faith in the hero, which in turn is faith in man. The novel and the epic require a harmony between solitude and society . . . one of the first symptoms of a weakening belief in man's worth is man's withdrawal into himself, the appreciation of the most subtle nuances of his personal experience and consequently his expression in lyric poetry. . . . It follows from this that when he—Quevedo—tried to express himself literally in an 'objectified' medium, he turned to phantasmagoric sorts of endeavors. It was certainly not the first time that such a phenomenon occurred in Spain or in Europe, but it was an occurrence inseparable from a profound crisis working on a sensitive nature."

In those paragraphs Durán studies Quevedo, the poet, but his observation about Quevedo's conflict with the novel seems equally definitive if applied to Spain's three greatest novelists—Cervantes, Galdós, and Unamuno. The "harmony between solitude and society" disintegrated in an obvious divorce. Quevedo, unable to achieve that harmony, centered in his solitude—his poetry; for Cervantes and Unamuno, the divorce took a form other than solitude. Cervantes was unsure of his poetry, Unamuno's confidence in his was great, and Galdós, neither sure nor unsure, did not look to poetry for harmony, because he was unaware of poetry's absence from the ambience of his prose. (I'm not assuming an unarguable absence of poetry in Galdós's work, in the part of his work that chronicles an obviously prosaic reality, because it is precisely in that reality where the poetic exists beneath the surface and irradiates in a tactile way; consequently, it is not impossible to come on it suddenly—frequently in the *Episodios nacionales* [National Episodes], on rare occasions in the other novels. However, when Galdós turns to his phantasmagorical endeavors, poetry is not absent, it is mistreated to the point of being unrecognizable.)

Cervantes, however, avoided the conflict once and for all by choosing the path of solitude—the closed sphere of one person, his—and achieved poetry, surrendering to it by way of confession. The *Quixote* is *confession*—undoubtedly indirect—and it is *last* will because it sprang from a *conclusion: in order to believe and to love you must be mad.* It is this that Cervantes confessed *terminally*; it is here that he arrived, after having passed through horrible tests, which *left him at this* and, of course this was what he wanted to leave us. His *last will* consists in affirming his disbelief. For this, he created an archetype of faith and nobility, collecting in it every human excellence, omitting only reason, and he sent that archetype into the world to be kicked about. We must not forget that the world surrounding Don Quixote is the same world that surrounded Cervantes. In other words, Cervantes confesses in *Don Quixote* to having lived that world and gives us a harsh view of it to show us that living in such a world, one *inevitably loses his faith or his reason.*

Cervantes scholars, I assume, have gone to great lengths to point out and confirm, probably with conclusive documentation, the facts of his life that are represented or alluded to indirectly in the *Quixote.* My assertions are a purely personal interpretation, to which I'm led by the meaning of what I'm in search of here.

After that confession of Cervantes, the genre disappeared, and during the eighteenth and nineteenth centuries, when it proliferated throughout Europe like a plant native to the period, in Spain there was nary a sprout. It sprang up nowhere and on no occasion, not even—as the "Astete" commands—"at least once a year, or before, if one expects mortal danger." The fact is that Spain did not want to *commune*, and the nation's love of life was so weak there was no fear that mortal danger might be waiting. Of course the only Spaniard who lived with this danger hanging over his head, *Unamuno*—between the two centuries, and more in the twentieth than the nineteenth—*made his work an unabashed and uncommon confession.* His creation, as he himself explained, was an effort at *personification.* Bearing in mind the very precise definition of *person* offered by Julián Marías, *the person* is the key to Unamuno's aesthetics of the novel, and Unamuno *personified* each moment of his I, giving it full rein to demonstrate its freedom.

This process on Unamuno's part has been analyzed exhaustively in Ricardo Gullón's *Autobiografías de Unamuno* [Unamuno's

Autobiographies], to which I will return later, in which all of Unamuno's fundamental themes are studied thoroughly. Personification, linked so closely to survival, led Gullón to write: "When Unamuno contemplated his reflections, he considered himself saved—ay, relatively saved!—from death. He surrendered to those reflections, desiring the inevitable contradiction, to make them autonomous and Unamunize them to the marrow. Cervantes, whom Unamuno so admired, and Galdós, with whom he was so obsessed, took a different stance, one inspired by the conviction that the novelist must be self-denying and must sacrifice himself to his character, remaining in the shadows in order to give the character freedom of movement, without restraints. Galdós put bits of his soul in his characters, but he forced himself to preserve the individuality of each one, and to remain outside the novel. Unamuno did not accept that marginal situation because his purpose when he wrote was, above all, to create himself."

I believe that the stance Gullón finds in Cervantes is embodied in his *Novelas ejemplares* [Exemplary Novels]. It might seem that the method followed in those novels also governs the composition of the *Quixote*, but my hunch is that what truly reveals the novel to be a confession is indemnity. Don Quixote was never once regarded, observed, or interpreted through external facts or images: he was engendered in the silence of immediacy. In his personal integrity, he breathes—insuperably in manner and degree—what I call the *last will* of a *person* in solitude. Consequently, having decided to study the work of Spain's greatest novelists, as I develop my subject, the *Quixote* is the only work of Cervantes I will consider, since the *Quixote* is exceptional not solely because of its excellence but also because of its single note, the unique clamor that constitutes the confession.

In the work of Galdós no one character stands out—I was about to say stands up—because he has the essential poetic intensity necessary either to be universal and timeless, like Don Quixote, or to disseminate problems, existential tension, pathos, and insomnia, like Unamuno's *persons*. I understand Unamuno's obsession with Galdós because I'm obsessed with him too. Moreover, I believe that one must be obsessed with Galdós. I believe that any Spanish writer who has a true vocation must enter the jungle of Galdós's prose with a machete, because it is *our jungle*. And I believe that it must be entered in an ambiguous way very difficult to achieve: it must be entered *with love and with no mercy*.

Galdós must be forgiven nothing. If his greatness had not been well proved on certain pages—obviously there are many—of the *Episodios*, obsession would be unnecessary: Galdós would be a writer who pleased some and not others. But the heights achieved in the *Episodios* emerge from a novelistic world that has lacked both sufficient energy and life to fill the minds of several generations. None of his characters live with us in the way that any one of their European contemporaries lives, and this is true not only of the geniuses but also of a Daudet, a Gautier. Many people argue that the critics are to blame, because they haven't known how to guide the reader, but that's not the issue. Even when wounding, the pain caused us by Galdós's characters does not ask to be preserved in loving memory. I will try to explain this further on.

Although I must limit myself to my three examples in order to study the place confession occupies in the Spanish novel, I cannot but include a brief digression and point to a testimony that, although it is not novelistic, is of enormous importance: José Ortega y Gasset's opposition to confession and the memoir, which he explained in his essay about the novel and in the prologue to the first edition of his *Obras completas* [Complete Works]. Ortega states very clearly that he does not want to recollect or to make confessions, that he has neither the need nor the desire to do so. It could not be more clear. Although . . . no, it's not so clear: what he says is in itself a confession, because Ortega does not speak against either confessions or memoirs, quite the contrary, he clearly demonstrates his admiration for the great memoirs and for the abundance of life stories with which French literature overflows. Only when it comes to him, when he's asked or pressed to confess, does he say, like a capricious child, "Not me, not me, I don't want to" (when speaking about memoirs what always comes out, whether in affirmation or denial, is the voice of the child). In this not wanting, he shows us his entire person and, obviously, his entire philosophy. Included here is the digression, which could be condensed in an Ortegan phrase that Ortega never uttered: "I will never make a confession of my circumstance, consequently, I will never make my confession."

It's true that confession involves two practical difficulties, in addition to many others. The first is the impossibility of writing one's own biography without at the same time writing that of his fellow man. Rigorous sincerity with respect to one's own faults, sins, or passions demands that one indicate with equal rigor those of the people who shared or provoked them. Tolerance or benevolence toward others is false when we describe our own lives, if we did not practice them when we were alive. The other difficulty implies clarity on the part of the one who confesses and the opinion of the one who listens to him. In other words, the one who confesses in this literary form, which is a way of novelizing oneself, offers his novel or confession as an example, as a "way of knowing"; consequently, although we can't say that it "follows the sure path of science," at least it tries to walk that path, which means being or, rather, having to be discussed, refuted, and even unmasked, something that, if one truly tried to appear sincere, would amount to being destroyed. Those are the two difficulties. I will hold in abeyance, for the moment, the writers who did not want to confess.

In Augustine's *Confessions* the power of truth in the sphere of intelligence proves itself on its own, because the book, from beginning to end, is the self-accusation of a penitent who assumes analytical rigor without needing to be coerced. In Rousseau's *Confessions* the situation of the *I* in regard to the *Other* is imposed in an exemplary way. This is a form of confession in which predominates a game of capture, a flirtation, coquetry, a dare, and an entreaty. In Kierkegaard's work, confession can be studied indirectly and limitlessly. Being, or seeming to be, the most elaborate, his confession includes almost no opinions of the author about himself. Indirectness, in itself already a search, tends to create the exact equivalence and, being a mask that to a certain extent makes the author unpunishable, he tends to be merciless with himself—with a self whose suffering he can treat as though it belonged to someone else.

Years ago—exactly forty years—I wrote, defending the I in the novel, "it's repulsive that someone would have said 'poor Jean-Jacques' about himself. It's begging for another's compassion, becoming Jean-Jacques, in other words, what this represents for others and trading it for wealth, for the suggestive intensity of the name that no one can give us." At that time, my natural intolerance totally repudiated Jean-Jacques. Today I can look at his devilish talent calmly and evaluate it fairly. But that leitmotiv—"Poor Jean-Jacques," "Austere Jean-Jacques," "Jean-Jacques was incapable of being a man without feeling," and the still astonishing "I will continue to show faithfully what Jean-Jacques Rousseau was, did, and thought, without explaining or justifying the singularities of his feelings and his ideas, or discovering if others have thought as *he* did." I've emphasized *he*, because I wonder if a man can give us the secret of his I if he speaks of himself *in the third person* as he confesses. Could he himself even really possess that secret? Was he truly evaluating, defending, or risking it? It would be better to say that he was elaborating it. He was analyzing it, of course, but to manufacture it, to make it presentable. That does not exactly suggest artifice, however, but the genuine way of his *I* being *possible*, in view of the *other*.

If Augustine "anticipated the great Romantic discovery that consists in having the person who is supposedly speaking coincide with the real man who writes" (Ortega), Rousseau worked comfortably with that technique, confident that he knew how to offer what everyone wanted. His confession is valuable because all the components are included and organized, and doses of *responsibility* are prescribed with clever wit. It is with this step that Rousseau advanced toward the modern world.

In his preface to the *Confessions*, Mauriac defines this advance in *method* bequeathed by Rousseau to future generations so they would not find confession so difficult. His first stage was to "establish the extent to which our actions deserve blame where society bears the burden." The strong persuasive force in that *stage* is more efficient than all the rational wisdom in the *Social Contract*. Being social, the *Contract* is something plural and public: the rest is what concerns each individual in the solitude of his conscience. "This master of falsehood and pride," Mauriac argues, "finds among us his true disciples. . . . We know him because we are one with his conscience." I don't subscribe to that *we*, but I realize or, rather, I believe that our conscience—that of us all, of our age—has been radically affected by his *method*. Of course Mauriac alludes with that *we* to the leaders of the current intelligentsia—Proust, Gide, and so many others, to those whom we can't help but consider *us*. Our addiction to that leads us to admit easily that *no one is free of guilt*—a Christian principle that has been transformed into the extreme conclusion that *we are all criminals*.

At first glance, that conclusion seems contrite, but no, it's clumsy. If we modestly say *we're all sinners*, I recognize that the phrase is worn out from use, but if we become convinced that *we're all criminals*, even if we're included in that *all*, we will end up feeling inclined to disdain *everyone* and, of course, to fear *everyone*. Consequently, we will try to avoid, deceive, surprise, or trap *everyone*. "Rousseau," Mauriac tells us, "may be the father of the modern world, but it is first of all the modern world that has vomited forth Rousseau," and if it's certainly true that the modern world deserved him, it's true that he knew how to settle the score. The strange thing is that he himself participated in the darkest sin of the world in which he lived, immeasurable hypocrisy. The transmutation—secularization, rationalization—of Christianity was occurring in Rousseau's century, the last—until now—but in Rousseau's voice it acquired a comically sacrilegious accent—if it's possible to join those two terms. When Rousseau prepares to tell the Supreme Being, aloud, what he has done and to ask that He gather all of his peers to hear his confessions, he ends by saying: "Let each one in turn reveal his heart at the feet of your throne with the same sincerity, then a single one say to you, if he dares, that I was better than that man there." The sentence is so ridiculous that it denounces the imposture of the man trying to take cover behind the defense of the adulterous woman. But since here the adulterer—adulterer of the spirit—is he himself, his self-defense has the plebeian stridence of the mouthy servant. Mauriac's effort, even though he acknowledges that this is the guiltiest of Rousseau's sentences, to grant a certain courage to Rousseau's Christianizing action, in contrast to Voltaire's sterility, serves to no avail; they are sermons of scant interest today.

The Christianity of our day beats most vitally—its beats not marking the regular rhythm of a *possible* life but pounding convulsively against a reality difficult to inhabit—in Kierkegaard, as I mentioned above, although that other Christianity does persist in our day. *Other*, here, seems an absurd term, but it's not as absurd as it seems. In my opinion, to say *other* is much more exact than to say a part, a branch, or a facet, which would seem to indicate heretical or reformist sects. If I say *other* Christianity—in reference to whichever of them—I mean a distinct inflorescence, a rare presence of the *same*. That *other*, then, that persists is the one that experiencing a seemingly destructive rationalization managed to modify profound zones of conscience, in which the new morality, the new idea of man was germinating. For the moment, though, what I'm trying to talk about is not that other but the one debated in Kierkegaard: pure passion, conflict, enigma.

Confessions are undoubtedly a Christian product—post-Christian or anti-Christian—whose defining stance is their particular position with respect to guilt. Augustine's confessions are a bold effort to separate himself from guilt, cloaking himself in his yearning for salvation, like "a man who wears the tatters of his mortality wrapped around him, who wears the stigma of his sin on himself." The defining stance of Rousseau's confessions, expressed in the sentence quoted above, is that of a man who presents himself in the company of others, demanding that he be compared to them and revealing his own guilt as an example of everyone's guilt. In the case of Kierkegaard's confession, it is difficult to select the most representative paragraph, since his guilt is reiterated on each and every page; I will use this one from *Sickness unto Death*: "To dare to be completely oneself, to dare to actualize an individual, not just any one, but this one, isolated before God, alone in the immensity of his effort and his responsibility, such is Christian heroism." In other words, the guilt that Kierkegaard confesses is the guilt of having been born.

Each of them, in accordance with his personal position, confronts the two difficulties that I mentioned above. The first—revealing the secret—secret not because of concealment, but secret as enigma or key—of those who collaborated in the secret itself. The method followed by Augustine is the same as that employed by Rousseau: an account of illustrative events, the person in his world, acts, thoughts, and passions. Kierkegaard's method is totally different. Kierkegaard also seeks comparison, not with his contemporaries or his colleagues but, rather, with extreme, culminating types: only with those types that can be paradigms of the *event of his life*, because in his life there is only one event.

Augustine coincides with Kierkegaard in the acceptance of the initial circumstance of his fate. The condition—condition, not situation—of being sons is decisive in the childhood of all three. Augustine, given his mother's strong presence in his life, begins by evoking the image of his earliest childhood: "Because then the only things I knew how to do were nurse and be calmed by lullabies and presents, complain about my bodily discomforts, and nothing else." But the bond that began by consisting in a climate of tenderness and praise, becomes an imperious spiritual guide when he reaches puberty.

Rousseau, who lost his mother shortly after his birth, preserved from his earliest years the memory of the woman who cared for him, overcoming the deplorable health with which he had come into the world, but he soon entered the paternal orbit and was initiated by his father into the exercise of the intellect: shared readings, long evenings about fictional tales at first, then about history books, Bossuet's sermons, etc.

Kierkegaard also began to exercise his spirit at his father's side, but not so much with books as led and swept along by his father on ineffable excursions created by his magisterial mind. For Augustine and Kierkegaard, the condition of being sons consists in the fact that until the end of their days they preserved an awareness of their paternal origin. Paternal for Augustine no less than Kierkegaard, because his mother converted her maternity into paternity, so she could follow him on his masculine trajectory. Rousseau soon lost the traces of his father or, rather, the traces were erased in him. He gradually entered a world in which both what he was or what he continued to be were useless to him. He prepared to be the son of his works, although without maintaining filial loyalty to them either, without ever admitting that *today* he was the son of his *yesterday*. In other words, without ever presenting himself as son and, of course, never as father.

Here there seems to be a slight coincidence between Augustine and Rousseau. Rousseau's unspeakable behavior toward his children is well known; Augustine's behavior toward his son was something inhuman at the beginning, but in his case it was more a consequence of his entire moral order: his son was illegitimate, a son of sin. When Augustine finally considered his spiritual being, he lavished him with paternal attention, because the paternal condition in Augustine, as in all men with great virility, grand, true virility, which is to say *manliness*, was superabundant, fecund, infinitely lavish. Kierkegaard never experienced fatherhood—he may not have had any experience—for him too eros was charged with paternity. Suffice it to recall that the ultimate comparison he chose for the *event of his life* was that of Abraham sacrificing Isaac.

The only secret belonging to someone else that Augustine reveals in his *Confessions* is his mother's, since in truth, she was the only *person placed before him*. He makes us see his friends, so important in his affective life, more as they were for him, in his love, than as they were for themselves, in their own lives. And the woman with whom he shared his childhood he submerges in anonymity, erases, sacrifices in life and death.

Monica's secret is brought to light by the unsurpassable writer, by the amiable psychologist who nevertheless does not know—could he really not have known?—the ultimate truth hidden behind her clearly visible virtue. Monica's personality is defined in the *Confessions* when Augustine tells about the time in the public baths when his father noticed that his son had reached puberty and goes to inform her of the happy event. That revelation prompted a sort of metamorphosis in Monica. At that moment she realized that her mission was over, a realization possible because she knew her son's nature. I say *nature* not because she knew his healthy animality and his childhood, which had been sensual from the very beginning. She knew his entire nature, his *person*, in which his most trivial inclinations to his greatest potentialities were nourished by eros, as by a sap. At that moment, Monica realized that her sphere would be invaded by woman, that inevitably there would appear a being with the right or the ability to take over what, until recently, she had governed, possessed to a certain extent. Of course she knew that modifying his nature would be impossible and, moreover, it would not be desirable. She decided then, making a vital decision—not with a determination seized because of that impossibility, but with a decision similar to that of a woman throwing herself headfirst into the water, in other words, one entering another element—she decided to invade that sphere and close off all access to it. Monica had unquestionably been a Christian since childhood and she had always tried to inculcate her faith into her husband and son, but until that moment her faith had not prevented her from exercising her feminine, maternal role. At that point she realized that to prevail she had to change, that to continue being what she most wanted to be, she had to be what she most wanted to be in a different way. She took the reins then, conferred on herself an authority that Augustine's father was no doubt unable to wield, a masculine, strictly spiritual authority: "She made every effort to see that You, my God, were my father, rather than he." I said above that Augustine was perhaps unaware of the ultimate truth hidden behind Monica's ostensible virtue, which is not to deny her virtue but to suppose that there was another, not ostensible, virtue. An explanation of that I will leave for the analysis of my second point, when I will try to show the doubtful, debatable, uncertain element in every presentation—in every confession, which always implies presence.

Rousseau, on the other hand, reveals numerous secrets in his *Confessions* and, I repeat, not because he brazenly recounts intimate details about one person or another. He reveals because he uncovers, denudes, profiles people from his world—rather, a world that he wanted to make his, into which he peered with unsurpassable eagerness and perception. Rousseau experienced no personal influence; he did, however, experience a colossal pressure capable of crushing anyone who does not possess, as he did, a like measure of strength and malleability. The pressure exerted by his world centered him and helped him to evolve. It neither solidified nor hardened him because he needed fluidity, not solidness, and he had no need of hardness because he carried so much negation within that it made him sufficiently impenetrable. Others appear in his confessions as real as he himself—exactly as they are in themselves and not for the purpose of his love, although he speaks of that love constantly. His love, including his love for himself, is not very convincing, which is why he continually escaped his reality, broke every chain—a very important point for all three confessants, to which I will return later. In fact, in the case of his two most fulfilled loves, those of Mme de Warens and Thérèse le Vasseur, it would be hard to degrade love more. With Mme de Warens, one of the most wretchedly abysmal types of femininity bequeathed to us by literature, Rousseau enacts the maternal comedy. On his part, there is not much of the farce in that performance: there is regression to or, rather, liberation from his infantile impulses. Mme de Warens is Maman for him, because he can enter her chamber feeling that he's at an age when it's still all right to wet the bed. Something similar happens with Thérèse le Vasseur, whom he names *Tante*—during his childhood illness, he was raised and cared for by an aunt—but her he transforms into a household servant who is constantly changing his diapers.

Rousseau's concept of carnal sin was not dramatic, like that of Augustine and Kierkegaard, but rational because of his early religious formation, and experiential because of his deplorable experiences. His century was the century of license, ornamented with hypocritical ideality. The unbridgeable distance between his sublime notion of love and its material fulfillment consisted primarily of its physical irregularity. None of the relationships in the *Confessions* begun in a scenario of increasing passion reaches climax—not even those of a simply pleasant nature—for instance, the adventure with the Venetian courtesan.

The precocious excitement caused by Mlle Lambercier's spankings—we would call them bare-bottomed—suggests a sexuality cross-eyed and crippled, in other words, irremediably warped, at an early age. Add to this his illness, and it's obvious that at no moment in his life could he have full access to physical love and that, consequently, every direct path to love was unknown to him. I find Mauriac's supposition about the origin of Rousseau's children very pertinent—that perhaps they were not his, which would explain, in part, his monstrous behavior toward them. "There is no crime," Mauriac says about Rousseau, "to which an impotent man would not admit in order to disguise his misfortune"; and about Thérèse le Vasseur, "It appears that this woman, practically an idiot, has the right to demand everything, that she can expect recompense from him. Can we not imagine Rousseau allowing himself to go along with that fiction, out of vanity, out of false shame, without realizing, at first, the terrible burden he was taking on, in the face of a world that had yet to know him?" This is all very credible and reveals the colossal importance that impotence was able to assume in Rousseau's life. Of course, with respect to the episode—one has to call it something—concerning his abandoning his children, the thought that he knew for certain that they were not his can lead us to feel some compassion for the unfortunate man who entangles himself in a morass to conceal his sad case.

Except that compassion, once you think about it for a moment, evaporates because even if there is no reason for the bonds of blood to restrain Rousseau from his inhuman act, his paternity, in other words, his spiritual responsibility with respect to the children of others—the men of the future—is not simply negated by coldheartedness, or the lack of charity or even of common sense: it is adulterated, corrupted by an inept assertion difficult to understand in a man whose life is the exercise of his mind. After sending off his five children—whether his own or presumed to be so—one after the other, he says, "I believed that I was acting as a citizen and a father; and I considered myself a member of Plato's republic." In other words, he sends the five unfortunates to perish in a wretched foundling home, and to the children of others, to the youth of his and future centuries he offers as nourishment a counterfeit image of the Platonic republic. Incapable of defending the indefensible, he twists and degrades the meaning of a sublime creation, dressed up Grecian style, in percaline. The feeling of social and physical inferiority was a very deep wound in Rousseau, but at the same time he was confident of the superiority that gave him his strong power of seduction, rather, his charm. He knew that the line about paternity would get him visibility. The fact that its truth did not correspond to the model he endorsed was unimportant because his truth did not exist: he had no other truth than the one he presented and represented. The loner, the savage, the natural man has, in reality, at least three lives, and he confesses all three, but the I that inhabits them is neither naked nor whole in any of them. We easily deduce that multiplicity from his confession, but we never manage to learn who it is that speaks of poor Jean-Jacques.

Who is the man that maintains such a close relationship with Mme de Francueil, with Mme de Chenonceaux? Is it the same man who resolves his intimate life with a nearly abnormal woman, who fills his house with her miserable relatives? Is it the same man who plots imaginary, passion-filled love affairs on his solitary walks? All three are Jean-Jacques, but which is Jean-Jacques? Jean-Jacques is the man who puts his five little ones of doubtful parentage into a foundling home, incriminating society in his action: "It's the estate of the rich," he tells Mme de Francueil in a letter, "it's your estate that steals from mine the bread of my children." Is this the same man who fashions his Émile—Spartan and doltish, savage, natural, and physically and intellectually retarded—on his lauded solitary walks? Rousseau's several lives, independent and incommunicado, transpire in both the amorous and the paternal spheres. And in the social sphere they transpire the same way: his obscure origin, with dramatic experiences of humiliation early in life, his access to society (not without difficulty, but with obvious success) give birth, on his solitary walks, to the creation of a *Contract*, like a being or natural child entirely his. It's essential to note that in this context of his ideas there is much greater coherence among his three lives. The thread of his personal history that runs through them is less diffuse; you can tell who the speaker is in that history because from the beginning the speaker, with his *power*, possesses a wealth of intelligence that won't fail him at the opportune moment. This makes the sections in his *Confessions* that develop ideas or observations social in nature solid and clear, characteristics associated more with the genre we call *memoirs*: they have neither the atmosphere nor the trembling of the *Confessions*. Consequently, I will refrain from commenting on them.

Kierkegaard also had several lives, but *the same thing happened in all of them*. That is to say, Kierkegaard was stopped before something that *did not happen*, even if he lived a thousand lives, even if he changed his face, his race: whether a child or a patriarch, whether a policeman or a shepherd or a high-fashion designer—he was always himself, Kierkegaard. And in truth he changed faces so many times for the same reason that Rousseau traversed, one after the other, his various positions, but the difference lies in Kierkegaard's refusal to accept the name given him by others: only he and God knew his name. This doesn't mean that he was indifferent to others, the world around him. His love was centered on a real being and on reality. "When he uttered the word 'reality,' referring to philosophy's relation to reality, the child of my thought leapt happily as if in Elizabeth's womb," he said, after hearing Schelling's second lesson. And his despair, like his love, was real: it was never prompted by resentment about a level difficult to reach. Difficult, rather, impossible to reach applied to him in only one category, one so common that almost all men attain it, "being a husband." His mind was of course too limpid and rigorous to allow him to degrade from resentment what he really and truly desired. Convincing himself that he did not want it would have been a solution, but never one that Kierkegaard could accept. On the contrary, he was determined to travel throughout the human world, trying to discern from one man to another, and another, how it's possible to attain *that*.

There is, as I mentioned earlier, a noteworthy coincidence among those three spirits who have so little else in common, one that all three confess without concealing its significance: their escape from, desertion, and breaking of the most sacred ties. That Augustine confesses this, full of contrition, accusing himself mercilessly, only signifies that the moment of accounting for his actions is now on an entirely different plane, but in truth he really did live his escape, with both daring and cruelty. He went from Carthage to Rome against his mother's will, with her following him to the coast and grabbing hold of him to prevent him from leaving, but he convinced her that he was there waiting for the wind to change so that he could see off a friend. Since she refused to return home without him, he convinced her, he says, "with great difficulty" to spend the night in a chapel near the ship and "that very night I left clandestinely as she was praying and weeping." Those are his words.

Rousseau recounts a more chronic desertion. He escapes from the arms of Mme de Warens, an act of indescribable ingratitude, although a relationship so turbulent hardly deserved a better end. He escapes from the workshop where he is serving his apprenticeship and escapes, or sneaks off, with his friend Le Maître, who suffers an epileptic fit as they're walking along the street. Rousseau screams, people rush to the scene, and Rousseau silently slips away in the crowd, not to return.

Kierkegaard also deserted: he broke his engagement with Regine Olsen. He tore himself from her with a decisive act of freedom, but he did not escape; on the contrary, he stayed, in the presence of that action or, rather, in that action, absorbed, immersed in it. You could say he was free *within* his action. As he wrote in his journal in the penultimate year of his life: "When my father died, Sibbern told me, 'Now you will never get your theology degree,' and precisely because of that, I passed. If my father had remained alive, I would never have gotten it. When I broke my promise, Peter told me you're lost. Nevertheless, it's obvious that in truth I've managed to amount to something, it was taking that step that made me accomplish that."

We could contrast the fugitive behavior of each one of them with their own thoughts, as they themselves expressed them. In Augustine's account, for example, his escape was a truce. As he says, it is similar "to the way people stretch when they try to wake up but sink again into sleep, defeated by sleep's profound tenacity." "I had no answer to give You when You said to me: Get up, sleeper, rise from the dead and Christ will help you; and even though You made me see everywhere I looked that You were speaking the truth and I was convinced of it, I had no response but slow, sleepy words—Soon. Right Away. Let me be a little longer." In that prayer, in that bargaining with earthly time, Augustine struggles with God, but not with his mother. She grabs his tunic and won't give an inch. Since neither entreaty nor force does any good with her, he resorts to cunning: "And I lied to my mother, to that mother! And I sneaked away." But he escapes only *a little*, he spends, enjoys, consumes a small portion of his mortal time, and despite his great desire and love for Him, *at the same time* he gradually kills Him until finally achieving everlasting freedom.

Rousseau's desertions, rather, desertion in Rousseau—although there are several, they all boil down to one long desertion—which is in him as a component of his personal makeup, is his constant. Rousseau absents himself, because he cannot be here, or there, or even more distant. And *he is not here* because he *is not*. Jean-Jacques escapes when he's played his part only halfway, as if he suddenly forgot his lines or said to himself: no, it's not this; on to something else. And he never gets to that real something. Alone, on his walks, which are the workshop where he formulates and polishes something he tries to offer as truth, there is no play, so he doesn't sense that he's meandering off the stage, and therefore achieves on his walks the continuity of a work undoubtedly worth staging. In his solitude he peoples the room with imaginary beings and adjusts their *poses* to the taste of a public created for his own taste—for which he has the key. In his solitude he acts with the ease of an actor in rehearsal, without the costume but sensing in the comfort of his everyday attire the greatness that his real mantle will give him (we must not forget the Armenian robe that Rousseau was forced to wear to hide his ailments). On those walks he is alone, but *not there*, because he himself is his own creation, a creature not weighed down by things material, since, unlike Augustine, he is not bound by any ties of the flesh. He has no knowledge of the body's warm drowsiness and he wanders completely unburdened, since his denials cannot ballast the ascent of a strictly mental I. This might seem to be an ideal system for finding oneself, but his escape provides no salvation: it's simply a move to a region inaccessible to others from which it's possible to correct, *in one's mind*, the design of the real world. However, despite the loftiness of Jean-Jacques's refuge, the atmosphere is not purified of his turbulent experiences. The world he formulates is undermined by the nastiest deceit. Preparing his Émile for marriage, he offers the following sermon: "Before tasting the pleasures of life, you already exhausted happiness, there is nothing beyond what you have felt. The felicity of the senses is fleeting; the habitual state of the heart always loses. You have enjoyed more through hope than you will ever enjoy in reality. The imagination that wards off what one desires abandons it in possession." So that even in his demiurgic solitude, in which he can contemplate himself in his creation, Rousseau is assaulted by the memory of his sad bedchamber, where a deficient wife tends to the lowly tasks of conjugal life.

There is no need to contrast Kierkegaard's flight with any event or idea. Augustine and Rousseau reveal the vicissitudes they experience from the deficiency or tyranny of the flesh, with no beating around the bush—their tone and meaning differ, but the important thing is that revealing. Kierkegaard does not speak of such things, even less in relation to himself. Augustine speaks of them, first with abhorrence, and then with the modesty his attitude toward them requires. Rousseau exposes them with no modesty at all, and when he finds it inappropriate for them to be seen, he simply lies or deforms them. Kierkegaard can adopt neither of those systems. He does not loathe the demands of the flesh, because for him they are inseparable from the demands of eros. He never has recourse to immodesty because that would lead him to give away his secret, and he does not have recourse to deceit because he could never cover his lies in a dignified way. Consequently, the only method left to him is supertruth, that is, poetic truth. To speak of his ultimate truth he never speaks of himself: he looks for equations of his own selfhood. He creates neither characters nor personas—he puts himself in the lives of others. This does not mean disguise, though, because he does not invade those lives like the hermit crab that inhabits a dead shell, he deposits himself in them like a seed and, feeding on their essences, he develops in possibility.

Drawing a comparison among such different natures reveals that they do have something in common: they are strong-willed pugilists. Rousseau and Kierkegaard suffer from an affliction whose effects are similar to a certain extent, but the nature of their malady is not the same. Does the difference in the moral and intellectual result consist in their differing spiritual orientation—we could say magnetization—or is it determined by the difference in their respective pathologies? It's very hard to be certain, but it's not so hard to study the process followed by the phenomenon and its consequences. Rousseau suffered his affliction from childhood; painful remedies, an ugly suffering that he could not attend to in public, that left residual traces on his clothing, etc. Based on that, a psychoanalytic study could discover the series of falsehoods about the erotic aspect of his adolescence that he develops in his *Confessions*. Having revealed the unhealthy tendency of his childish escapades, he states that at sixteen his restlessness tormented him precisely because of his innocence. "My inflamed blood filled my head incessantly with young girls and women but, not sensing the actual point, I made peculiar use of them, following my fantasies without knowing what else to do." However, in that state of innocence he spent his time exposing himself in the gardens and plazas of Turin. Is this comedy, a barefaced lie? Yes, it is, but that's not all it is.

From Rousseau's earliest years something fundamental in him was split in two: his impulses, what he called his restlessness, which manifested itself physically in the sphere concerning evil; and his imagination, which was free and powerful. In order not to assume the reality of his defect, he invented his innocence. This explains why the pages of *Émile* reflect a lack of knowledge that anyone who has observed childish eroticism even minimally would find unbelievable. Rousseau asserts there that if we did not awaken children's imaginations, they would never have any impure intentions, and he tries to silence their curiosity by responding to their questions with a description of some horrible scene. If the child asks where children come from, the mother should give him some crude, hair-raising answer; that will keep mystery's seductiveness at bay. "At first the idea of a natural need known to the child banishes the idea of things that work mysteriously. The accessory ideas of pain and death throw a veil of sadness that deadens the imagination and curbs curiosity; everything focuses the spirit on the consequences of childbirth, not on its causes. The infirmities of human nature, of disgusting objects, of images of suffering, such is the enlightenment to which this response leads, providing the repugnance that it inspires allows the child to want enlightenment. How will the restlessness of desire manage to materialize in conversations directed in this way? And yet you see that the truth has not been altered, and that there has been no need to abuse his pupil but rather to instruct him."

That sort of infanticidal executioner has governed the education of children for several generations in both Europe and America, and what's worse, with several successes so undeniable they can't be revoked. If it were only a question of sexual aberration, though, it would be defined simply as pathological, but that's not the case; Rousseau's morals as a whole, his position with respect to science, to culture, to all human effort consists in exaggeratedly exalting the natural in order to deprecate and slander man's power. "Oh, man, enclose your existence within yourself, and you will no longer be miserable.... Your liberty, your power, extend only as far as your natural forces and no farther; everything else is nothing but slavery, illusion, prestige."

Within himself, Kierkegaard knew that the enemy lies in the ideal. Reality appeared to him neither corrupt nor false but perfect and desirable. His physical reality, his body, was neither disabled nor lame, even though he was rather thin and frail: drama, catastrophe originated in an intangible, inaccessible sphere, where his passion burst forth, with the ambition to be omnipotent: "If I find so little happiness in life it's because when a thought occurs to me it's born with such energy, with a form so supernatural, that it actually leaves me crippled: this ideal anticipation is so far from transfiguring my existence that I emerge quite powerless to find a correspondence for it, my nerves having been too shaken to remain within the experience."

In short, those two consciousnesses with respect to unattained power—or possibility—lived in conflict in quite different ways. Rousseau denigrated the powerful—at the same time that he courted them; he worked marvels of cleverness to strip man of his ambition, to inculcate in him the feeling of impotence that he complains of himself. He obviously formulated his claim to justice and his accusations and anathemas against the powerful more skillfully than most of his contemporaries, but no less obvious is the absence of either compassion or true respect in his inclination toward the simple and humble. It will suffice to recall his words as he lists Émile's virtues: "He gives little money away, knowing that, in general, it is not put to good use." His ability to wound the soul of his—and future—centuries with the frustration he bore in his body was extraordinary. Kierkegaard knew that others possessed the power he lacked, but human injustice had nothing to do with that. He also knew that his failure did not originate in any fault or lack but rather from something like an error or deviation caused by the disproportionate nature of his impulses, like something that escapes from its flow and becomes lost in the sand, like a force whose dispersal he could not arrest, so he desperately concentrated his entire spirit on attaining the thing that gives strength: faith.

It would seem that if the malady afflicting these two men represents a colossal conflict, the opposite condition would lead to peace and plenitude. Augustine, however, suffered as much as or more than they did, from the opposite malady. We can't say that his conflict was more insoluble than theirs, but it is more difficult to explain because Augustine set out to create the schism precisely where his entire being—his personal way of being, his genuine consistency—opposed it. What best characterized his person was unity. More than harmony, we find in him something akin to a principle of wholeness. Maybe it would be more precise to say that in him we find *inception*. His nature, his person, is based on or constituted by eros. And his problem—using that term only in the sense of practical difficulty—consisted in breaking off a branch of that whole. Eros is arborescent in structure; in other words its medullary virtue spreads and branches out limitlessly and, in a superabundant life, nothing can stop that spreading. The only way to counter its luxuriant growth is by pruning, stripping it of the sprouts considered *defective* so that the sap will intensify in the central branch, in the stem itself.

In that laborious task Augustine struggled with himself until he reached thirty. If we ask why, we will get various unobjectionable answers, but there will always be an unknown that provokes perplexity, we will always be asking something that is very difficult to explain: With what? With what psychic organ, with what faculty or power, did he carry out that task, which was as painful as it was complicated?

I explained that I chose these three men to point them out as strong-willed pugilists: unarmed fighters in hand-to-hand combat with *nothingness* or with the *all*. Rousseau's struggle is cunning struggle, Kierkegaard's is struggle to the death, Augustine's victorious struggle. The modernity that Ortega finds in Augustine involves an amazing technical anticipation, but besides the fact that he himself is the person who speaks, what he confesses, what he places beneath the lens of his analysis is anticipatory in a way even more inspired. In Augustine we find Freud, Bergson, Gide. When he writes "because in your eyes no one is free of sin, not even the child born only a day ago on this earth," it might seem that he's alluding to original sin, but that's not quite it. Rather, it's a particular knowledge, the product of external and internal observation, free of all prejudice. "So that the feebleness of the childish limbs is innocent, but the childish mind is not. I once knew a very small child who was already jealous; he could not talk yet, but he had paled, his gaze dark, his bitter little eyes fixed on a competitor for the breast." I don't want to linger here adding excerpts from brilliant chapters about memory and time, but I would be remiss not to point out a few of Augustine's many violent self-accusations. "What would I not have been capable of, having come to love gratuitous sin? . . . And what affection was it affecting my soul on that occasion? Certainly a very ugly one. Woe to me who harbored it. But what affection was it? Who understands sins? It was a sort of laughter tickling my heart." Is this proposal to *understand* nothing less than one's sins not profoundly anticipatory? In fact, Augustine's tendency to yearn for knowledge consists in a blind—and mute, that is, inexpressible—knowledge of the principle from which his own sins spring. He knows—with terror—the unity of *that*, in which those sins teem, intermingled with every *virtue*—power—with everything good—with the good—and he expresses this in terms that say more than he himself realizes. It's a *laughter* that *tickles* his *heart*. So that the place where the deed occurs is the *heart*, seat of *love*; its perceptible effect is a *tickle*, that is, a pleasure, and the thing itself—the sin—*is*, in so far as affect, a *laugh*. Laughter is a voice of *happiness*, and what happiness means to Augustine is well known: exultant plenitude.

The more we meditate on the weight borne by *laughter* in that sentence, the more we're reminded of Bergson. (Having promised in his title to study laughter, curiously, he studies only the comic, something entirely different. His study became very famous, despite being the most superficial of his works.) And the more we meditate on the similarity between the two appearances of "laughter," the more its content unfolds and branches out. The "will to power" *plays* in that word—*plays*, as performance and as game—with pleasing levity, since *laughter* always involves, if not the comic, the *joke*. Laughter, voice of happiness, celebrates—also in two senses, *fêtes* and *performs*—the affirmation of the I. In it the I is shouted—you can't say *it shouts*, since it's an alogical voice: it doesn't say anything, *it is said*—and in that affirming—of Christian heroism and original sin, according to Kierkegaard—there is a pleasure almost bordering on tenderness, there is something akin to a *concession*—offering and license—that the I makes to itself. Augustine insists on making very clear that the pleasure he and his friends obtained from what they stole was evil and that they knew it beforehand: "I loved nothing, then, but theft itself, and I spoke the truth, since theft is nothing," and he goes on to examine what he did love. From the beginning he recognizes that he would not have acted alone: "since on that occasion I loved the company of the people I stole with." But that doesn't satisfy him: the fact that he loved the company of his friends seems both obvious and contingent, because it's also possible to imagine that he would have stolen in the company of someone he did not love. He must continue his analysis, he needs to go over it a thousand times until he finds the pregnant word, the word able to explode in seeds sprung to the wind in a cloud of pappi. He repeats that his motive in that incident of the theft was not to enjoy what he stole: had that been what he wanted, he would have committed the robbery alone. As he says, "by myself I could also have . . . committed that crime, which would have allowed me to experience pleasure on my own, without that *brushing against the intention* of my accomplices scratching the itch of my greed."

The key is there in those four words, which I've italicized because he understands only contacts. Such, for him, is the presence of the *other*: not an opinion that compels or deforms the very image of one's conscience—not a presence from which one accepts whatever more or less appropriate name it wants to give us. At the end of Book II, Augustine tries to close with a moral, which is merely a poetic paradox: "Oh, friendship too unfriendly! Inscrutable seducer of the soul, eagerness to harm through jest and play, appetite for another's ill, lacking desire or self-interest . . . hearing: 'Let's go? Let's do it!' And feeling ashamed not to be shameless." If only we could say that such *feeling* ashamed *not to be* shameless is the positive element of sin, since in any case it is a *feeling* and a *wanting to be*. But Augustine cannot stop being analytical, not even in his metaphors. He is such a colossal writer that even though his words try to imprison truth in a tight knot, they make it flash and emit its essence. They say that friendship is a sweet enemy, the inscrutable seduction of the soul, therefore desired, pursued to the abyss.

※ ※ ※

I believe this is an appropriate point to explain the purpose of these digressions. The rich, alluring nature of the material covered thus far tempts me to continue, but I need to close the circle. The three exemplary confessions that I've discussed briefly show that man confesses when the enormous weight of which he wants to unburden himself is not an act that he's committed, nor even a considerable number of acts, but a persistent conflict that led to all of them, a mystery that not even he himself understands and that perhaps he confesses only for the sake of hearing it told, to understand it.

The mystery that became a conflict in these three exceptional minds was eros. Countless experiences weathered, countless problems solved with rational skill: these three superabundant lives went through everything without getting lost on ill-chosen paths, finding themselves in the labyrinth only when their consciences tried to confront eros. It's not that simple, though. If it were, the question might seem one of successfully fortifying eros against the attack of reason, but their effort at examination did not end up before a closed door at a particular moment. Rather, the most obvious events of their lives, their most well-defined character traits, are nothing but poignant signs of *the only thing that matters*.

I will not attempt a personal definition of eros but calculate its possibilities very briefly. Human love between the sexes. Human love in which sex is of no account or in which sex is surpassed—by sublimating or degrading it. Human love that ignores its own interest, its own pleasure, or its own good—charity. Love blind to everything human and placed before God in contemplation. Love as a phenomenon sensed in its incalculable registers: desire, pleasure, ecstasy. Love as efficient power, generative impulse, creation. Also, needless to say, each one of those possibilities ramified infinitely and all of them tangled together like a hedge of blackberry bushes: a spiny intricacy surrounding mystery. Because mystery is *one*: perhaps nothing more than life. And life is what every *one* of us *desires*—is one's *desiring*, thus one's love. The I, which knows itself to be unique, knows too that within itself lies the common mystery—common to all the different I's. The I experiences that mystery as an effort struggling to act and tries to insufflate it with force—will. But of course both that violent force and that weak effort are will. Life is will, which at times will combats and at times assists. And since both the assistance and the combat are agony, the only thing man can do is cry out, confess.

❋ ❋ ❋

Now it is relevant to ask why there are no—or almost no—*confessions* in Spanish literature.

Among the things that are not going well in Spain—and have not been for centuries—the one going least well is eros. I will try to study this in the three great Spaniards I mentioned at the beginning.

I want to stress that the *Quixote* is Cervantes's *confession*. To explain this, it is first necessary to locate the conflict. The *Quixote* is a chaste book. The *Quixote*, not Don Quixote. If its chasteness were a question of the character, it could be considered a character trait, but it's not limited to that; chasteness extends throughout the entire book. Sancho is equally chaste. The other, contingent couples in the novel are not, but that's not what's important, because those couples represent love idealized harmoniously with the spirit of the hero. Sancho, though, who is Don Quixote's counterpoint, who quite frequently makes incursions into the basest areas of matter, never even comes close to having a lascivious idea. Sancho wants to eat when he's hungry, sleep when he's tired, and evacuate when the need presses. No other desire makes him lose his composure; he never demands satisfaction or relaxation in the matter of sex. The *Quixote*, in a word, is a chaste book because Cervantes's eros does not enter into conflict—either positive or negative—with the flesh.

Ramiro de Maeztu some time ago defined don Quixote as "love"—a supremely exact definition. The *fêlure*—a term that has been applied appropriately in the case of Baudelaire—of Cervantes's soul occurred in the world of love, but love with respect to *charity* and *faith*. In captivity, where he began to know helplessness, and then in repatriation, where he established it as an inexorable reality, is where Cervantes's temper, his disposition, lost its *integrity*. This is why I use the term *fêlure*, suggestive of the *cracked* vase or bell, which can no longer emit a note, because that tone of a cracked bell is the tone that Cervantes turned into irony. If Cervantes had opted for resentment, there would have been at least one poisonous line in his book; there is not. There are many cruel lines, unspeakably cruel. Cruelly, Cervantes becomes enraged with himself, in his character. If Don Quixote were a character that Cervantes had observed, with whom he had had either close or distant dealings, who would have been able to inspire in him such bloody ridicule, such constant failure and error, it's almost impossible that he would not have seen in him some trace of human weakness. No one like Don Quixote or anyone who resembled him has ever existed on this earth. Where Don Quixote existed is in the soul of Cervantes, who revived him to prove that he had ceased to exist.

It's impossible, after all these years, to have a clear idea of Cervantes's moral being. Documents that tell us what he did or failed to do show nothing. In any case, it's inconceivable that a man who lived the life of his century, with tasks, comings and goings, needs and obligations, would wander among his contemporaries and have Don Quixote's purity. But even though that's inconceivable, it's certain that Cervantes *conceived* that purity and that faith. When and to what extent is unimportant: perhaps it was only an instant, which continued to resonate in his mind like the note of his youth, which could not sound again. And Cervantes's rancor was not wasted on cursing his century, with regard to which he knew he was impotent, which he feared—like all his contemporaries, both within and outside of Spain. His rancor polarized at a moment, his, that consisted in the possibility of *loving, believing, erring,* of being *deceived*. From another plane, the plane of maturity, Cervantes perceived the *error* of *his being*—being of an instant but nevertheless eternal—as a *deception*. From his *undeception* he sees his *self-deception* and he trains in vengeance, making the *being* that *was* live. In fact, making him live extendedly—only in time is there suffering—the life he himself left, beating him up, kicking him painstakingly and pitilessly. (Some time ago I heard one of the harshest critics of the Spanish spirit—Spanish language, literature—say, "I like Don Quixote a lot, but I don't like his adventures," and I had to agree. The situations in which Don Quixote finds himself are extremely coarse, it's true, and since then I've been thinking about the reason for that coarseness. Valuable advice, that of critics who set us on the trail of our own secrets by simply pointing a finger.)

Cervantes turned to that coarse ridicule because that's why he created Don Quixote—so he would get what he deserved, so he would pay for that *faith*, that *love*, that *integrity*. That's why he conceived of him as lost in advance, already *cracked*, or *cracked in the head*, so that at every moment he sounds like some useless old crock from which the real *slowly seeps*. Cervantes was not content with launching his creation into the world, with exposing him to mistreatment by others: he mistreated him himself—a fundamental characteristic of Spanish pride—so that no one could believe that he *believed*.

Don Quixote's universality shows that he truly existed in the soul of his creator, and it also marks Cervantes as one of the precursors. Like Augustine, Rousseau, and Kierkegaard, Cervantes announced the man already coming along the path: the man who laughs at his own faith. Because the purpose of *Don Quixote*'s comicality was not to make the reader laugh. No, it was the author—or, as Unamuno would say, it was Cervantes the man—who was laughing at himself, the one mocking himself. That's why he highlighted Don Quixote's uniqueness. What he presented as an oddity was not really the profession or practice of chivalry—although that's how it might be expressed—but the image of the spirit that inspired chivalry. The *figure* of Don Quixote is something like the *sign* of its *nature*, like the *cipher* of its *significance*. In other words, his characteristics speak of something vital: a human formula that tends to give generously of itself without receiving—without demanding or expecting—more than glory and honor as nourishment. (I said that I found the definition of Don Quixote as "love" to be very accurate and it undoubtedly is, but of Spanish love, since those notions of *honor* and *glory* summarize the typical Spanish position with respect to the *other*, consequently, a very particular love.) The fact is that Don Quixote is nothing but *love*. Don Quixote's love, giving everything, asks only *honor*. He never has an appetite for real, tangible qualities, only for the loftiness he assumes in everything and everyone, in which he believes his own loftiness reverberates. In other words, he assumes that everyone is capable of giving him the honor he deserves. And it is this that Cervantes showed with a character both whole and absolute but also *sick in the head*. The ridicule, the dissonance, the false note in the middle of the concert as the result of any action—the galley slaves, the horsewhipped boy—everything that, with its reality, contests Don Quixote's senseless purpose—the supernatural action of the balm one would expect to prompt vomiting; Sancho's fear and his inability to move away from his partner in the dark because he believes in him, because beside him he's not afraid, but (impossible to confer more *honor* on a man than that confidence in his *power*) also his inability to contain the weakness of his flesh. Yes, Don Quixote's adventures are undoubtedly ugly, but that's not by chance. It's because that excrement is what Cervantes threw, deliberately, over his *moment of love and faith*. It was his own excrement.

In my discussion of Cervantes's *confession* I've suggested that the *Quixote* is a *popular* book in the highest—that is, the broadest—sense of the word, and it's a popular book because it was made *with the speech of Cervantes's people*. The *Quixote*, carrying the metaphor to the extreme, is a curse—the most common curse in the speech of the Spanish people. Here I will need to linger a little to analyze that genuineness, which, because it is genuine, is participable, since—according to Unamuno— we can give only what is *ours*. I can best analyze by comparing the two—let's call them excremental curses—most prevalent in the new realism, the French and the Spanish (the French is quite well known, the Spanish, strangely spelled, of course, is now turning up in excellent French novels, but the important thing is that it has crossed the border). The difference is notable and extremely profound. The French imprecation implies a value judgment. In Cambronne's response, it means "Take this as an answer," in other words, "What you've proposed to me is worthless." The same is true when a curse is uttered in a situation, conflict, or presence whose contact or acceptance is repellent and prompts disdain: the word, uttered as an interjection, either by itself or repeated, is a definition. The Spanish curse defines nothing, it's not based on the value or lack of value of the thing being execrated. On the contrary, it's usually uttered against a situation or person, specifying his name; and when it's said that way, vaguely, ". . . on ten," its reach is incalculable, because if that ten increases in a geometric progression, not even the imagination can place limits on it. (I've cloaked the meaning of the phrase, which is clearly blasphemous, in the greatest possible triviality.) The Spanish curse, then, is not based on a noun but a verb: it's pure action. The curser attempts an offense against the object of his anger and tries to stain him with the dejecta from his own cache.

My insistence on analyzing this Spanish verbal expression might seem excessive, but it's not: rather, its sin is the opposite. I'll let it rest here, though, because to get to the bottom of it and consider the serious nature of its content, I would need to engage in an extended psychological analysis of the entire Spanish tradition, which would divert me from my real topic. With what I *have* said, I've only wanted to suggest what Cervantes tried to stain in the *Quixote*. To stain it, of course, he had to create it, that is, he had to show it. However, he did not proceed from a preliminary demonstration of its sublime side; from the beginning he mixed it with the grotesque, without permitting the sublime to outdo the grotesque or to come out even moderately unscathed. To the sublime side of Don Quixote, Cervantes grants only a few instants of peace. Nocturnal peace, among the goat herds.

Those lines conclude chapter 10 with the comment that at nightfall Don Quixote was happy "to spend the night sleeping under the open sky, because to him every time that happened he performed an act of possession and thus had a chance to prove his chivalry." And then, the next morning (chapter 11), employing his characteristic way of linking ideas, Cervantes has Don Quixote hold a handful of acorns and speak of "the happy age," as if he were evoking his native country, of the "happy age," his words giving us, more than his genealogical tree, the proof of his blood—what might be called its chemical formula. Don Quixote is the son of the night and of fundamental distance. Of the night, that is, of thought. Of distance, that is, from an ideal time, in which we can assume that the words *yours* and *mine* were unknown. In that atmosphere of evocation and open, nocturnal sky, Don Quixote can rest in his being. Cervantes denudes him to show us exactly as he is, in his delicate nobility and then, immediately following, ties him to the post and flogs him. Because Cervantes cannot forgive Don Quixote for *having been*, he cannot placate his rancor or his anger for his having believed in him or, rather, for having felt Don Quixote's existence in himself for even an instant, as a deep *believing and loving*.

With all of the above I want to explain my affirmation that Cervantes was a precursor, not only, as the entire world has said, in literary technique. His lineage, like all lineages, branches out with many subtly different characteristics. The most medullary of those branches is the one that carries throughout Spain the *cracked* tang of skepticism, like an unsolderable break that the clamper cannot conceal but whose fissure will always be betrayed by the sound of the blasphemous curse. Just as Kierkegaard was wounded for life by his father's malediction against God, so was the man coming along the path, wounded by nonbelief, not only in God but in man, in the hero and, above all, in himself. Irony, grievous and repellent in Galdós, irritating in Unamuno, who uses it to break what he most esteems, the poetic atmosphere of his work. (Outside the genre of the novel, what can one say about Mairena's irony? It's something like pouring a hundred tons of inanity on a patch of intelligence.) And the malady reaches, without exception, each and every lesser writer.

I refer to that branch as the most medullary because it's the most genuine, the most radical among Spaniards: the other branches are common to all of Europe and to all America; I don't know if it might be different in other regions of the world. (I believe that today lack of knowledge is not a question of place—today, a person capable of knowing knows everything.) Those immeasurable bifurcations are what have produced the antihero in his two principal aspects: the hero who can be *l'uomo cualunque* and the hero *malgré lui*. No one has linked Don Quixote to the first, but a whole breed bearing equivocal resemblance has swarmed around the second. The hero *malgré lui* is the one developing on the branch that's clearly Chaplinesque, the one who tries hardest to simulate—the figure—the posture—of Don Quixote (when in fact he's the most opposite!). What does Don Quixote have to do with the hero who manages, in spite of his awkwardness, weakness, and bewilderment, to carry out some undertaking that the strong and capable fail to accomplish? Don Quixote can never triumph in the end, he can never come out ahead in any undertaking, not even by chance, he can never experience even a minimal pat from success—not even in jest, like Sancho, because Sancho, on his island, is strong against the mockery of others more uncouth than he is, whereas Don Quixote is a defenseless victim who never even notices how base the dukes are. Why? Because Cervantes said—said to himself—that's how it has to be, that's what he deserves.

Did Cervantes do or not do the right thing by returning Don Quixote's sanity at the hour of his death, leading him to disown his past chimeras? It's very difficult, in a great work, to mark the limits of what is pure, strict creation and what is the effect or product of the medium, the age, the custom, and even convenience. Perhaps there is only one sure path to follow: *the specific literary weight* of the passage in question. The death of Don Quixote is not one of the best passages in the book, but on the other hand, right before it, there is a very precise and valuable section, one so delicately poetic that it's inadequate to say it's poetically pure—it's virginal. The pristine modesty of this part has kept it from figuring among the ones discussed most frequently, and I've never heard it referred to. Perhaps some prolific Cervantes scholar has written a study, but it has never reached the general public domain. In it Don Quixote confronts the downward path, he falls from the clouds and lands: the moment when he has a presentiment, with heartbreaking certainty, that he will never recover Dulcinea. "Don't you realize, my friend, what that boy said: *'That's something you will never see in all the days of your life?'*" And then, "*Malum signum! Malum signum!* Hare flees, and greyhounds go after: Dulcinea does not appear!" One might say that Cervantes takes pity on Don Quixote at that moment, granting him a human weakness, but such is not the case: Cervantes launches pitilessly into the most challenging adventure, that of Don Quixote's leaving his chimerical universe and entering the world in which things can be.

It is very obvious that here Don Quixote confronts reality, that Sancho welcomes him to his domain as a great lord. He does not assist him like a servant but receives him like a host, or protector—strong, as the one in control of the situation to which Don Quixote arrives badly wounded by his hard contact with the real, and he tries to soothe the pain with the balm of his tenderness. "She flees," Sancho says, "I catch her and place her in your worship's power, you hold her in your arms and caress her: what bad sign is that, or what bad omen can you find there?" But this does not put Don Quixote's mind at ease, and Sancho reprimands him, criticizing him for being superstitious: "And if my memory doesn't fail me, I've heard the priest of our village say that it's not right for Christians or sensible people to pay attention to such trifles; even your worship himself told me the same thing a few days ago, leading me to believe that all Christians who pay attention to omens are fools." The adventure ends with the arrival of the hunters, they carry off the hare and the subject isn't mentioned again. But Don Quixote has died. He has died *his* death, in other words, the Christian knight has lost hope and must *enter into reason.*

My interpretation of that passage depends solely on my unmediated impression of the *life of Don Quixote and Sancho*. Unamuno, who had more information than he needed, surely worked in the same way; one deduces that from his book. And he did so because the life of Don Quixote and Sancho continues, and suddenly we see them make an unexpected gesture or utter a word never heard before; we stop then, I'm about to say that we make them stop and repeat the phrase so we can study it, return to the place, the point where the drama in which they surprised us began. We recompose the entire scene, analyze the smallest detail, confirming the rigorous construction of what we intuited in a flash. Because what's the meaning of that tiny episode with the hare? What role does Don Quixote play in it? How does this adventure rank among his many others? Don Quixote is absolutely passive here. The voice of the boy is heard—he is not speaking to Don Quixote—the hare runs by and Don Quixote does not chase it, does not make the slightest movement toward it. It's Sancho, owner and lord of reality, who captures it and places it in Don Quixote's arms. Sancho says nothing less than this: "Let's suppose that the hare is Dulcinea del Toboso.... I catch her, place her in your worship's *power* and you *hold her in your arms* and caress her." At that moment, Don Quixote hypostatically links his lofty ideal with the fragile, earth-colored creature, at that moment he knows what it is to *possess* Dulcinea. But, here, *possessing her* simply means *having her in his power*, none of the senile kisses for which the master Unamuno imagines him yearning and that in his chaste, strict lineage are repellent. Possessing her, having her in his power means understanding—*knowing*—what a life is, what a heart is as it beats between his hands, next to his heart—he can't just caress a hare like a little dog in his lap, stroking its back. He has to overcome his shyness, hugging the hare tight—as it grows larger and larger in its animality, abolishing any thought of the ideal.

What comes next, still perfectly congruent with that scene, and more than congruent, inevitable in its deference, a surrender to the evidence, is somewhat blurred, literally and poetically, because it comes trailing a certain muck: concessions to the medium and even precautions against the falsifiers, against the exploiters who could diminish the financial return from the book. Cervantes was a precursor and he knew from experience—prophecy is the nth dimension of experience—that his spirit, that is to say, his work, needed and every day would need even more to rely on material security. It seems that his battles—the battles of Cervantes the Man—on that terrain, were laborious; his inner tranquility, however, was great. So great that the accuracy of his prophecies seems unbelievable. What allowed Cervantes to rest content was not a vague confidence in the value of his work, but in an infallible feeling—a presentiment—of the *place* it would occupy in the future, since this is what he pointed to, a *position*, to which posterity has responded with textual fidelity.

Images of the abduction of Helen and the story of Dido and Aeneas decorate the inn, and Don Quixote laments not having been able to defend such beautiful damsels. Sancho affirms—since Sancho pontificates here like a schoolmaster, not a peasant—"I bet . . . that before too long there won't be a tavern, roadside inn, hostelry, or barbershop without a painting that chronicles our deeds."

Using the term rather flexibly—not vaguely: never once, in no instance *a bit more or less*—but amply, extendedly; keeping in mind its true, infinite dimension, you could say that Cervantes formulated his *judgment a priori* about things that do not yet exist but already have an area in time prepared for their reality. This is not as fantastic as it seems, nor is it metaphorical; it might be the difficult crux of an enigma that bears an axiom within. Cervantes pursues it to the end. With every conceivable sublimity Don Quixote intuits that the ideal was being hypostasized, I repeat, in reality. Humbly, at the moment of truth, Don Quixote prostrates himself before the real, absolute, mysterious truth because he has touched it. *Touching it, possessing it, knowing it* leads him fatally—sanely—to *love it*, and then the only thing left for him is to die.

The *Quixote* left all of its siblings behind, like an exceptional child, enfant terrible or, perhaps, "healer," one of those figures in whom common people—the people—see supernatural powers because they wept in their mother's wombs. Cervantes's exemplary novels have continually remained in the hands of educated readers, of scholars, while Don Quixote continues to live in the people, who recognize him for his primitive cry and venerate his image—ay! how it's represented—and with that image decorate their dwellings. Not only the Spanish people, though, but others as well, because only in Don Quixote did Spain give the ultimacy of its very core, its *confession*.

The inner satisfaction with respect to oneself, which is called pride and which has come to have such a bad reputation, is not entirely without legitimate meaning, for example, when it relates to the fact that the *figure* of Don Quixote found its *place* throughout the entire world and that, among Spaniards, it has continued to hold that place throughout time. But the burden of responsibility that can be laid on any *figure* must be measured carefully. I undertake such an analysis with trepidation because personally I'm passionately devoted to all *figures*. The *figure* is the ineffable word, the secret manifesto but, curbing my predilection, I will try to point out the traps its reverberations can set for us. The figure, in all its potentiality is a *sign*, in other words, something that offers itself to us in its integrality: we see it and there is nothing more to say. But it can also be a *type, a most equivocal term. A type* is what represents or typifies a species, and type is also what presents itself as *aspect*, the gesture, movement, and clothing that compose a figure seen from without, observed in passing, in an observation that is not *vision-possession*.

Spanish literature of the last centuries abounded with typism. Of course the great writers stand apart from the sort of typism that can be considered a trademark, but a tendency toward the *type* persists in all of them. Unamuno took this to its greatest degree as *sign;* encapsulating his *persons* in their names, he gave us, once and for all, typism's symbolic formula (Baroja and Valle-Inclán are not included here, but I must allude to them, albeit briefly. Baroja's characters have a *type*: there is a *Barojan* type. Those of Valle-Inclán are invested with a *type* in a superlative way: trace, gesture, *esperpento*). Galdós sketched his types accurately and meticulously, not missing a detail: he sets us before them from the most advantageous point of view for us to watch them live, since what we see is definitely their *living*, but their life does not interest us, we don't penetrate it, we don't possess it.

What is it that's lacking in Galdós's work? Let me make myself clear: what is it that's lacking in his colossal body of fiction, in a historical-critical oeuvre exceptional not only for Spanish fiction but for that of other countries as well? To deny that there's something lacking leads nowhere: the work's positive value stands and will not diminish because we try to discover the blind spot in such a powerful retina. There is no confession in Galdós, as various critics have already pointed out, but why is there no confession? Modesty? Discretion? Yes, I would agree, but when *there is conflict* in a writer, neither modesty nor discretion can conceal it. Does that mean there is no conflict in Galdós? The issue is more serious and, above all, inexpressibly complex because

Galdós's work is like a stream that from its start separates into various streams snaking off in highly complicated meanders, some extending far, others not, but always clearly delimited. Conflicts abound in their currents, but in those currents Galdós sails full steam ahead.

We can say almost with certainty that in Galdós there is no conflict—let's leave that "almost" for what could occur. As I said above with respect to Cervantes, to look for the most deeply inspired, purest core of his work—I mean the climes in which we see him inhale most deeply—the most reliable way is to assess its literary quality. The formal perfection, accuracy, precision, and even the beauty found in numerous pages of the *Episodios*—in all of the *Episodios* in which Galdós examines Spain's conflict with the rigor of a telephoto lens—are qualities scarce in his fiction, and they desert openly in the passages where the conflict narrated becomes tangled in affairs of the heart—sexual or filial—religion, or charity. I believe it's unnecessary to add—but just in case—that *formal perfection* does not allude to the perfection of his prose nor to anything of the sort: Galdós's lively Castilian flows carefree, assured of its correctness. Perfection, accuracy, justice, seriousness, and literary beauty are qualities or, rather, categories that merge in a quality whose excellence and exquisiteness, whose delicious flavor, aroma, and range of colors consist in being *imperceptible*. The *formal perfection* I allude to is the farthest thing from preciousness, it is, simply, the penetration of mystery. What I mean is that the phenomenon that consists in finding ourselves with the idea, as if we had swallowed it without realizing, as if the idea were already in us while the word that has given it to us subtly, humbly, remains silent or rests on its *having-fulfilled*. That incorporeal condition might not seem compatible with the concept of beauty, but it definitely is: beauty can be both sensed and imperceptible, it can penetrate in silence, without leaving a trace and prompting contemplation. I will cite some examples (positive and negative) from Galdós's prose below; for the moment I'll stick to pursuing the conflict on which Galdós stumbles.

I've said above that Galdós, *in the "Episodios nacionales," confronts the conflict of Spain*, but it would be more accurate to say that Galdós confronts the *conflict of Spain in the "Episodios,"* because there is another conflict of Spain outside the *Episodios* that Galdós does not confront. His novels are filled with personal, human conflicts, but a genuine conflict of Spanish humanity hovers above them all. In the

Episodios as a whole, everything genuine is captured with brilliant rigor and precision, but in the individual novels the specific conflict is incomprehensibly avoided. Galdós's attitude here is difficult to explain, but its effects are evident. It would never occur to me that he lacked the skill necessary to analyze, much less to describe the subtleties of that conflict; what astounds me is the fact that his attitude toward it is *conformist*—his attitude, not his theories. Obviously, as we look through his entire oeuvre, we find examples of wise criticism that highlight his free thinking, his tendency to surpass and innovate. But no matter; the fact is that *literally* in his aesthetic, in his *creation* or, perhaps it would be more accurate to say in his *words*, he neither surpasses nor innovates in a single way.

If Galdós's attitude—expression—with respect to certain topics is conformist, it is necessary to think about possible contingent causes, as I noted above. Attacking the higher powers is always highly dangerous; even so, Galdós fiercely and precisely attacks the State, the army, the monarchy, and the country itself in its very being, in its deep and genuine guilt. The prevailing norms of morality concerning the emotions are at times shown in such a way that we can judge their error, their cruelty, their contradiction, in the sphere where eros imposes its drama—adulteries, betrayals, impossible and sacrilegious desires, women's virginity, reputation, chastity, or libidinousness. Since there is never a theoretical exposition, though, since every *position* is represented by one man or one woman vis-à-vis another, whatever criticism there could have been in the *case exposed* totally lacks force because the one contradicting the norms never proves to have some incontestably positive trait. But this is not an effort on Galdós's part to show us that the soul of man is complex, that within it there is both one thing and another thing. No, such is not the case because, unlike Dostoyevsky, champion of complexity, Galdós is not *tendentious*—I'm not alluding to a political, social, or religious tendency but to a human tendency, which does not consist of saying, or even showing, that one person or another is good and another is bad. If the writer—principally the novelist—does not *incline* strongly toward something, no one follows him. Even if he successfully creates a very noble, highly principled protagonist of strong character, etc., his expression, his way of speaking are commonplaces—common to even the last poor devil—they don't bind us to him, don't sweep us up, which is what every literary hero must do, unless, on the other hand, he repels us or leaves us pursued by his repulsiveness. When the reader does not *follow* the protagonist, he feels that he breathes an air as becalmed and insipid in the hero's clime as the rival's.

The task of carrying out a detailed analysis of the great characters in Galdós's oeuvre is very tempting, but it's also so gigantic that I would never be able to undertake it. In order to adhere to the topic proposed here, it's more appropriate to select a few characters that share certain basic traits and with them compose a single *type* in which Galdós's human formula is either perceptible or implicit. Galdós's oeuvre is of a dimension that could only have been conceived in his prime; consequently, the *type* to be formed must include characters that represent a man between twenty and forty years of age. I will take three as examples: Salvador Monsalud, Juanito Santa Cruz, and José María Bueno de Guzmán. These three examples, each of them highly prominent, are the protagonists, respectively, of several *Episodios*, *Fortunata y Jacinta*, and *Lo prohibido*. They also appear in several additional novels, if not more pallidly, in a secondary, collateral sort of way with respect to the other characters. But that's not to say that the protagonists resemble each other; in fact, they don't resemble each other, they're manifestations of *the same thing*. They are possibilities that in some characters appear more clearly and prominently, and in others more diffusely and equivocally. I choose those three, not only because they're contemporaries, but because they share certain things: physical attractiveness, something of an intellectual bent, experience abroad or an education that fostered familiarity with foreign countries, and a particular attitude about national, Spanish conflicts. We can imagine Galdós in the prime of life, not confessing through these types, but through them being revealed; not giving himself, but through them, giving himself away.

I know Galdós's work well, but I am less familiar with the work of those who have tried to write his biography—the one at the beginning of his *Obras completas* [Complete Works] sheds no light at all. In Ricardo Gullón's book, though, I see that Galdós suffered a severe trauma in adolescence (information that must have been discovered recently, since it's not mentioned in Joaquín Casalduero's *Vida y obra de Galdós* [Life and Work of Galdós]). The three types that I've pointed out in his work have an unhealthy childhood: Monsalud's—and that of his mirror image Araceli—were clearly painful; José María Bueno de Guzmán—and his mirror image Manolo Moreno—were affected from youth by a sickly nature and frequent exiles; Juanito Santa Cruz—and his mirror image Federico Viera—were destroyed from the beginning by an inept education, swimming in luxuries and flattery and inhaling stupidity and sordidness. So that in the Galdosian world teeming with innumerable characters of the most diverse aspect, we find the frequent appearance of that figure the *young Spaniard*, son of his century. Galdós's sure critical vision, marked by a sharpness and minute detail it would be difficult to surpass, is almost always formulated on the basis of one of these three *types*. That is especially true in the case of Monsalud and Bueno de Guzmán, because in Juanito Santa Cruz Galdós shrewdly inserted only cunning and subtle hypocrisy.

When it is not the character that speaks, however, when a judgment and harsh sentence fall on the actions and traits of the nation—social classes, politics, customs—we sense then that the speaker is the *persona*, from which all of those types originate. The voice responds coming from all of them, rather, it demonstrates that all of them are moments of that voice. In my opinion, Salvador Monsalud is the most important—the most serious—of the three types. First, because his world is that of the *Episodios*, much more valuable and exceptional that that of the novels; second, because in him, measured out with admirable deliberation, there are shades of heroism, daring, agility and resistance, disbelief, skepticism, disorientation. Both of those reasons concern not only the actions and undertakings in which he risks his life, but also his equally daring adventures with human affections, passion, gradually increasing rage throughout a long career, followed by fatigue, accommodation, and attachment to sedentary home life.

I've stressed the importance of Salvador Monsalud, believing the figure of his mirror image Araceli to be less prominent—more shrewd— one could say more admirable, grandiose, although Araceli is the hero of the entire first series of the *Episodios*—and although his comportment and deeds are in no way inferior. The difference lies in the fact that Araceli is a novelistic *type*, he belongs to what there is of the novel as genre in the *Episodios*—areas, alas!, full of potholes and marshes—where he's been placed in order to maintain cohesion or sustain within a logical structure the large coefficient of pleasantries the reader demands. There is a detail important to note here:

in the first series of the *Episodios*, it's the protagonist who speaks, the *Episodios*, in this series, having been written in the form of memoirs, so that most things of real substance that happen in them are spoken and, consequently, thought by Araceli. Araceli, however, *is not made* of the conflicts lived in those novels. Araceli confronts them and gives himself to them. Monsalud does not have to give himself, rather, sometimes he dodges those conflicts, but no matter how much he runs from them, he never manages to place a single barrier thicker than a hair between them and himself, because he *is* the polyhedric conflict, rather, the inextricable *knot* (if we separate a polyhedron, its diverse knots remain, broken or intact, but remaining; if we untangle a knot, of that knot nothing remains). And finding a character who *is* conflict in Galdós's work leads us to suspect the conflict that might echo in Galdós himself, like a voice from beyond the grave—with that word I evoke the memory of Chateaubriand and his somber, vital, fundamental concomitances with the *Episodios*. Galdós's confession I will leave for later—like a voice smothered by enormous repressions.

In the confession I'm looking for, facts, as I mentioned earlier, are of no importance. It means nothing if Monsalud's story differs from that of Galdós, because what a man has to confess is not what he did or failed to do, but what he carries throughout his life between breast and back. So that to have confession through the character of Monsalud is not even the most veiled *indirect* confession, but *irrepressible, involuntary* confession. There is another piece of information that lends credence to this assumption: the six characters that I've singled out have sick wills—Araceli, the most superficial, to a lesser degree. The entire vision of Spain that Galdós offers is one of a people with a dislocated soul. I know that this assertion will irritate many and that it could be interpreted as an attack on, or devaluation of, Galdós; the contrary is true. I do try—and openly—to devalue his accommodating commonplaces that are nothing but a smoke screen in order to defend his comfortable prestige, but that represent the Spain he tolerated—perhaps endured—so he could circulate with peace of mind. I also take pains to devalue those commonplaces to highlight his *unconfessable* Spain, the one screaming its conflict, though the screams are muffled, between the lines in which Galdós skillfully painted its episodic appearance.

The character of Salvador Monsalud has a *decisive* importance in

Galdós's oeuvre. Whether we approach him critically from a psychoanalytic point of view or as only a literary creation, his importance is *fundamental*—profound and basic, but if we consider the figure itself, with everything that frames him as an episode, as an historic event that weighs on the destiny of Galdós's work and that of *all Spanish literature that follows it*, his importance must be defined as *decisive*. A rigorous explanation of that decisiveness would require a book, which someday I might be able to write; here, to outline in a way that won't be entirely enigmatic, I will have to rely on brief, summary, and allusive comparisons.

The *Episodio* in which Monsalud figures as the protagonist is *El equipaje del rey José* [King Joseph's Luggage]. In the other novels of the second series, his figure appears and disappears, but he is always present for the reader. (I realize that these allusions are meaningful only to those who know the *Episodios* well; for those who don't, I hope they will serve as an invitation.) These *Episodios*, which refer to the Napoleonic Wars, bear a surprising resemblance to current literature and film; principally concerning everything that has to do with the French *Resistance* during the *Occupation*. The resemblance consists of two elements. One is the obvious, narrated drama. The other, much more complex, consists of the essential *equivalent differences* underlying the similarity of the situation. And the situation, in both cases, is this: a people invaded by an irresistible army that, in addition to the material imposition of its force, tries to inculcate that people with a spirit or way of life diametrically opposed to its tradition. In the case of Spain, the innovation brought by the invader was the fatal evolution of European thought, with all its crises and agonizing struggles. In the case of France—in our day—the imposed change that was attempted represented a novelty—regression. Regression, because it cut off the progress of all speculative endeavor and erased the paths recently laid out; novelty, because what it supported was not the old Europe still standing, but the establishment of a new authority, a new dominion, with which twenty centuries of Christianity were eliminated.

Those are the obvious differences and what's curious is that phenomena so opposite at heart are manifested in absolutely identical actions and patterns of conduct. The story of the Napoleonic Wars breaks free from the *Episodios*: as in a 3-D film, the image moves off the screen and hurls itself at the viewer. In other words, the historical greatly increases in depth, becomes current until it blends with the experiences that we've just lived, so much so that, when we recall it, narrate it to ourselves in the mental colloquium that prevails after any wounding reading, we use the terms of the bellicose world we frequent daily, more than in books, in films—our daily bread—*guerrillas, maquis, partisans, police, denunciation, betrayal, rape, plundering, crimes*. Galdós might seem to be the precursor of the war story that accounts for eighty percent of what we see in films today, but in reality its first practitioner was Chateaubriand, right before him. (Galdós was undoubtedly influenced by his *Memoirs*. The figure of Chateaubriand appears in *Los cien mil hijos de San Luis* [The One Hundred Thousand Sons of Saint Louis], but not in Spain; Galdós takes the noblest of his heroines, the woman whom Monsalud truly loved, to Paris and sets her before Chateaubriand, in a brief diplomatic exchange. Nevertheless, Galdós must have read in the *Memoirs* how Chateaubriand, dramatizing to the hilt as he describes the Emperor's campaigns or the fury of the revolutionary mobs, spreads a discreet veil over the events in Spain, which he experienced firsthand. Chateaubriand stresses insistently the importance of his role in those events, but with respect to what those events were, silence.)

In my opinion, Galdós undoubtedly launched the *Episodios* as a reply to that exculpatory silence. Between those two great works there is a tacit battle and it's evident that Galdós could not win. Why not? Ah, the reasons are revealed in the *Episodios*, they abound in them, pertaining to all the literature that follows and the entire life of Spain. For those who have ears, I believe that's enough. Galdós does not prophesize: he confirms what is present for him, what he has in front of him—within him? It would take a lot of digging to find out—besides, that present of his is persistent. Salvador Monsalud is not the man coming along the road but the one who springs from a specific moment—thanks to an unforeseeable constellation—and there he stays, stunned in its enigma. But there is another, more complex aspect, in which the similarity between Salvador Monsalud and many other figures in current literature is even greater, and the difference between their meaning and their fate more opposed. Monsalud is *Frenchified*, that is to say, a *collaborationist*. For this behavior, in whichever case—in both peoples and both moments—there is a more explicit definition: *traitor*. And it happens that, with respect to the current moment and the drama that has not yet receded one bit in our memory, the definition has not been contested by either facts or ideas. The invading army was repelled and the world resumed its spiritual task with the same tendency that prevailed when it was interrupted. Characters that staked their lives on the side of the invaders achieved at best tolerant oblivion—never true rehabilitation.

Is that the case of Salvador Monsalud? No, his case is very different. The constraint of poverty, the lack of premeditation during his early years, circumstances in which the *collaborationists* have also found themselves in the recent past, all count for little here; what counts is the meaning of the invading spirit to which Monsalud acquiesces and the tradition that opposes it. The people who oppose it by brandishing that tradition also count—a great deal. Those people are the point of departure: his mother and his fiancée, howling like dogs in the face of death, faced with the death of their honor, represent the rending of matter, the cry of blood faced with the corruption of the spirit that inhabited it; and his brother, the person who is like his *I myself*, who, in essence, is the *other* and the *self*. At the beginning of the novel, Monsalud does not know that Carlos Navarro is his brother, but the reader knows so that the origin, cause, and roots of his *being* is an obvious detail—an unavoidable detail in Spanish history that, much later, Unamuno will untangle until he reaches its climax. This passional, irrational base shakes seismically, belching out its inner fire, its spirit. But at that specific moment it happens that the distant and burning veins of Spanish tradition were blazing, laying waste to lives and riches in a sacrifice to Ferdinand VII. Napoleon's army was repelled, but the European spirit that, through him, partially entered Spain, followed its course and Spain incorporated it, slowly, by fits and starts. So that Monsalud's betrayal—evident when the time came to take up arms—looks very different as the opponents' corrupt ideals are unmasked.

The conversation in jail between Monsalud and Fernando Navarro— with Monsalud unaware that Navarro is his father—proves not to be very substantive: it has value only in terms of the novel and so they talk, skirting that lack of awareness, thanks to the fact that Navarro's stupidity is great and Monsalud's intelligence at that point is dulled by alcohol. Shortly before, however, Navarro has revealed himself in all his splendor: he has spoken at great length as he set out with the guerrillas, offering an incisive explanation of why he wants to fight: "We must fight," he says, against "a serious evil. . . . the French have come here with the idea of altering our customs, of smashing our entire system of governing these kingdoms to the ground, of changing our life, of making all of us French, nonbelieving, effeminate, moronic, blockheaded, and eunuchoid." And he goes on and on, without stopping to take a breath. "But there is still a canaille worse than the Frenchified kind, since at least they're out in the open, and the others are infamous hypocrites. Do you know who I'm referring to? Well, I'll tell you. I'm talking about the ones in Cádiz who have made what they call the Constitution, and the ones concerned with nothing but new laws and new principles and other ridiculous things that would have me in stitches if I didn't see that the constitutional torrent brings a lot of muddy water and makes a horrific racket because it sweeps along filled with rocks, corpses, and muck." When Navarro launches his harangue, Monsalud has not yet entered the fray; he is twenty-one years old, but with the perspective of his father's ideas Galdós already outlines a future path in which Monsalud's betrayal will vanish—in anguished swerves of indecision, to be sure.

I will say again that I'm familiar with very little of what has been written about Galdós, but I've *heard a lot of talk* about Fortunata, Benina, and Nazarín, and I admit that they interest me less than Monsalud. They are all great characters and, of course, very much ours, very Spanish, but they are all individuals who fulfill their mission through one action—a single movement of their passion—and in that action they are realized. Monsalud represents the unrealizable, the passion gradually squandered in unsatisfactory actions, and who succumbs, without dying, sliding toward the risk-free zone in which his core, wounded with fatigue and despair, finds a balance in which he can *be present* and minimally *be*.

I'm particularly interested in this character not because I like him more than the others, but because I think that in him I discover the enigma of Galdós's oeuvre. I think that deep within him I see Galdós as a child of his century. In other words, Galdós does not herald the man coming along the path but draws from his memory—a memory that extends beyond his life—the image of his precursor. He, Galdós himself, is the one who comes after Monsalud. But an after in which there is no overcoming, because Monsalud has nothing to *realize*. Monsalud is wounded at the vital core and Galdós, son of Monsalud—not Monsalud son of Galdós, an apparent absurdity that I don't believe Unamuno would deny—justifies him, verifying his formula precisely. Monsalud's wound occurs at the moment he loses faith and *remains* bound to reason. Faith, in the religious sense of the word, he never had much of when he was young, but *faith* is a word that cannot have a meaning other than a religious one. Which means that Monsalud loses faith in love, in man, in all earthly hope and, irately, in God. Around him Galdós constructs a densely nuanced social milieu: common people, nobility, clergy, ministerial offices, etc.

It is important not to forget Pipaón, another of Monsalud's contemporaries and compatriots. Galdós also takes him from his beginnings and lets us see how he develops. Naturally, Pipaón is quite a character, a cunning, intelligent, and malleable office worker. In addition, Pipaón is ugly, just as Monsalud is extremely handsome. Galdós makes it very clear that these details about the two types are significant. Monsalud's handsomeness protects him, is placed on him as an essential sign that makes him superior to his actions. Pipaón's ugliness betrays him and at the same time excuses him, without managing to exonerate him totally: his actions are explained by his ugliness and tinged by it. By being what he is, Pipaón climbs until he represents more than he is. But with this social octopus, who plants his scheming suckers on every covetable thing imaginable, Galdós does more than define a type: with an inexhaustible wealth of detail, he shows his technique, makes him speak with his heart on his sleeve. In other words, he makes Pipaón expose the workings of an hypocrisy radiating indiscriminately toward all the crevices of human nature. He makes him show how the reasoning behind his flattery is like a surgeon's instrument with which he can operate on vanity's deepest and most delicate viscera, touching the most sensitive points of belief and making them grow calloused. By showing us Pipaón's behavior and the success that follows it, Galdós outlines technique itself as a phenomenon, freed here from the type that employs it—simply as a social fact that *can be*. Pipaón's victims never manage to catch him in the act because his devious mind knows how to flatter while passing from left to right with infinite disdain for one person as much as another, knowing that in everyone there is a point receptive to adulation, corruption, confusion.

Although I'm not familiar with many of the opinions held about Galdós, I have been able to confirm that such praise includes the opinions of many different tendencies. That doesn't surprise me because in truth it's difficult to know with certainty which way Galdós himself leaned. In his work one definitely finds very harsh criticism of reactionary norms and a decided sympathy for the oppressed and the humble; but at the same time the work is filled with commonplaces that bestow tacit validity on the tritest forms of morality and religion. The religious facet is undoubtedly the most inconsistent, despite the prestige of his most pious characters, who would not hold up well under any scrutiny. I can't even approach such an analysis, though, because it would lead to an exhaustive investigation inappropriate for this study. Besides, that's not what I'm after. What I've proposed to do is find traces of the confession that Galdós does not want to let escape: consequently I must continue confining myself to my three masculine types, which are like the possibilities of *one and the same man*. Galdós can present them to us like figures who pass before his lens: if we believe what he says about them or what he makes them say, they will no doubt seem very well delineated, but if we merge them all into one, we obtain a third, reinforced dimension and, consequently, we will find that the mystery of their essence is much richer. Taking *this man*, then—a young Spanish male, twenty-four years old, kept in that bloom of youth for about a century—we can systematically squeeze him, until expressing from him at least a drop of that essence.

Where is the conflict of *this man*? When *this man* is Araceli, the conflict of Spain *is facing him*, and if he throws himself into its vortex—the admirable focus in the first series of the *Episodios*—all of Spain's maladies undergo a bloody scrutiny. And that is not a metaphor, because no one remedies, or channels, or contains those maladies: instead, many, massive numbers die for them. When *this man* is Monsalud, the conflict *is he himself.* Since Carlos Navarro is Monsalud's brother, Navarro also fits within *this man* being discussed here, and it's clear that the cainite drama develops between the two of them. The conflict, though, *is* Monsalud and Navarro is unaware of that conflict. Perhaps Navarro's conflict is sensing the conflict that *is* the *other*, and knowing that he is incapable of achieving it. The fact is that Monsalud *is* conflict and Pipaón *is* its shadow. I mean that Pipaón is the photographic negative in which conflict does not suffer, being in its element. This is demonstrated quite clearly in the dialogue between Monsalud and Pipaón found in *La segunda casaca* [The Second Turncoat]. Monsalud throws himself—with fine accuracy and subtlety—into an enraged exegesis about Spain's maladies: it is into this that Monsalud plunges. We're aware that he fought and took great risks, but we don't see him fight. Monsalud escapes us, he continually slips away like a ghost, throwing himself—before the reader; let this be clear—only into that passionate speculation. Beside him, Pipaón develops the theory of his skepticism, his treachery, and ambiguity. But we've abandoned some while back the other characters who also make up the composition of *this man*: Juanito Santa Cruz, José María Bueno de Guzmán, and their mirror images.

I say that Monsalud *is* the conflict of Spain because in him this is an intimate issue, the vital core: it's not easy to find anything similar in the other characters I've just mentioned. They will have to be judged according to the results of their actions in order to see what they give of themselves. The two that are most important act exclusively in the sphere of the erotic. Their eros, however, is miserable. Juanito Santa Cruz is the quintessential representative of *wretchedness not* exactly because he's *a wretch*, in the sense of wickedness usually associated with that word, but because he's wretched *in his being*, he's rather like a hypertrophic return on wealth. Comparing Galdós's commercial and financial world very briefly with that of Balzac shows us that in Balzac the financial is something intimate, located in its own right in the area of affect, and it receives the same treatment as affect does, is cherished with the same warmth and tenderness. In Galdós, the commercial world, finances, occupy a place among one's obligations, they're treated like laws or strict norms that must be observed and borne in all their cruel sordidness, placing in them the same confidence that one does in the effectiveness of bitter-tasting medications. The parents of Juanito Santa Cruz observed or, rather, respected, those laws; perhaps they even venerated them because they managed to get free of them without ill-effects, as if they had achieved the comforts of wealth thanks to the natural magnanimity of the laws themselves. Settled into *well-being*, they cultivate the childhood of the son who seems so handsome.

That son's handsomeness, however, is like an advantageous appendage to his *nothingness*, which is what he *is*. He is also said to be highly intelligent, but he does not demonstrate that until he needs his cunning to defend his utter license. Intelligence figures among the traits of his character as simply one more detail of his well-being: his mother surrounds him with books. Later, women adore him: Jacinta, while she believes in him; Fortunata, until death (I can't pause to analyze Fortunata's love, but suffice it to say that I don't agree with any of what *I've heard said*). The fact is that if we're determined to discover something truly because it belongs to him or defines him, we will have to point to his habitual instability: he moves from one love affair to another, rather, from one woman to another, simply, like someone who moves from the armchair to the chair and from there to the couch every time his position bores or numbs him. But who is it who moves from one woman to another? It's the spectacular mask of Juanito Santa Cruz. In this character, whose sole obligation in the entire novel is to love, Galdós places nothing but vacuity, negation, nullity. Santa Cruz's parallel, Federico Viera in *Realidad* [Reality], embodies that adjective only because his activity is limited to the erotic. Like Santa Cruz, Viera is lazy, but his situation is very different. Of noble lineage, penniless, and totally ruined with respect to both material and moral assets, Viera is an exemplary specimen of *nobility in ruins* because all that remains of his nobility is an irritated pride powerless to prompt the smallest positive action. He prevents himself from sliding into dishonor by shooting himself because suicide is the only exit that occurs to him. The meagerness of his intelligence becomes obvious when he ventures into psychological analysis of his intimate problems with a clumsiness comparable only to that of his *partenaire*, Augusta.

José María Bueno de Guzmán in *Lo prohibido* [The Forbidden] inhabits a sphere of action similar to that of Santa Cruz: he is a wealthy man who devotes all his energies to amorous adventures, but in Bueno de Guzmán there subsists the hint of a soul that makes him a relative of Monsalud. Bueno de Guzmán is not Frenchified but Anglophile. In truth, he's a man who lacks sufficient entirety for any philia, whatever it might be. But he's an Anglophile because his mother is English and his father Andalusian. Galdós wanted to inject ambiguity in his being but without giving him Monsalud's courage for assuming conflict: he gave him an ambiguous being in the form of an inherent fatality, which Bueno de Guzmán can bear calmly, rather, without struggle, taking the fullest possible advantage of it. The two elements of his nature are equally lax, giving him an elegant flexibility, although they never move beyond a mere feeling of ease with social conventions. His last redoubt is a dead end that can only be described appropriately with the adjective that describes all of Galdós's wealthy characters: *wretched*. Bearing in mind that one of Bueno de Guzmán's characteristics is generosity—he bombards his relatives and friends with gifts, favors, loans—his lack of grandeur when it comes to love suggests that his weak or small point is found in the deepest part of his being. But I won't get tangled up here in a narration of each and every one of his actions without exception, which would be excessively lengthy, or his reflections, or the outlets for his desires, or the adjectives—whether tender or cruel—that define the women he loves, while he loves them and when he no longer does.

I believe that this test of *literary level* is decisive for discovering the relation that exists between the intimate values of the mind—the vital values of thought that admit only authenticity, the modulus of truth—and those of the work. Galdós *stumbles* literarily in all amorous dialogue. It's clear that he reaches an unsurpassable perfection in the description of milieu with which he feels an affinity. In those descriptions, both the human and urban backgrounds that frame them and the (social, political, economic) drama driving them, *he moves beyond the frame*, in other words, they seem not to have frames, not to belong to an intellectual—therefore, limited—concept, but to spring from the world we inhabit and to circulate in it. The heights of Galdosian perfection are undoubtedly found in the passages of social analysis. Analysis that includes not only such episodes as the French occupation of Spain, civil wars, intervention, hidden wars of ambition, envy, and lies revolving around high—and low—positions; but also the major figures, from the king to the most uncultivated cacique, and in the commercial or financial worlds—climates or environments—an analysis that encompasses the characters through a reading of their money-magnetized souls and through long authorial digressions about the plotting and intrigue of the stock market, about the *mysteries* of banking—reasons one can see only from within. In all these spheres—spheres that fill many pages—accuracy of meaning and perfection of form excel at the same high level. At that level, meaning achieves its full moral value and form its full beauty—its efficient purity. Galdós's form also reaches its maximum in passages that seem not to rest on their meaning but irresistibly *make themselves felt*, since they evoke, never describe, places, tenement buildings, slums outside Madrid, narrow Madrilean streets. I cannot, however, take the space I would need to prove this by citing the additional examples required for a conscientious study of Galdós's prose, in order to make it perfectly clear that his prose can be splendid and that, if, in some passages, it is not—as *indisputably* it is not—there is *inevitably* a profound reason.

To put it as simply as possible, we could say that Galdós writes poorly whenever *he does not want to confess*. And it might seem that not wanting to confess when it comes to affairs of the heart, so as not to reveal incidents from one's own history, is perfectly legitimate and reasonable, since those details inevitably become entangled in the stories of others, but in fact the most important things in a good writer's own history always seep into his work. Consequently, we might remain uninformed about Galdós's adventures or love affairs, but he will never be able to hide from us the *tone, kind and quality* that love attained in him. I have italicized those words to stress that I'm not talking about *intensity*. In Galdós's work there are great loves, that's well known, but, my God, what loves! Their quality does not consist only in the type of woman who embodies them, although this is undoubtedly important. We could say that to analyze love in Galdós it's necessary to divide the topic into two categories: *what she loves and how she loves*. The two women who have usufruct of the greatest reserve of love are Fortunata and, in *Lo prohibido*, Camila: two women who, although very different, have in common an invincible temperament, which gives them a sort of eternal virginity. To Jacinta's lot falls the fate of a very meager share of love: Jacinta is solitude, sterility. Eloísa and Andrea, the young Creole, coincide only in the framework of wealth that envelops them—luxury, voluptuousness—so that in them the *how* is more important than the *what*. Eloísa, however, coincides profoundly with Augusta. These two women could also be considered one single woman, particularly because the husbands they betray are *one and the same man*. Jenara is quite singular and to her corresponds the greater—although brief—portion of clearly expressed love: Monsalud's youth, love pure and violent, which becomes frustrated without being tarnished by deplorable scenes and accusatory conversations. There are also the good girls, Inés and Solita. The latter is ugly on top of everything else. I will comment briefly about how these women *are* as I discuss *how* they are loved. Fortunata is undoubtedly the most prominent and the best known. Camila is her counterpoint. To concentrate on Fortunata, though, Galdós's *great* love, the important thing to note is that he assigns her a lover who is the scum of Galdosian characters and, more precisely, the scum of the Spanish man. But over Fortunata Galdós pours *his* love, even though it might be said that he poured into her the (inexhaustible) love he had left after he had loved Camila—by creating her.

In Fortunata there is a magnetic force strong enough to activate the pseudo-man fate sent her way. We witness the scenes of that man's conjugal love with his unfortunate Jacinta, blushing as if the situations described were the most obscene imaginable. But the important thing is this: the scenes are very chaste. Clearly, the author has not wanted to describe, or even to suggest anything that would have concerned physical contact, instead showing us—unadorned and fully displayed—the foolishness of two bourgeois young people in love, in the intimacy of their bedroom. Of course Juanito does many silly things because of Fortunata; but to show that he is a *type* absolutely incapable of love, without resorting to insults, I will note a single detail, which will suffice, from the depths—from the sediment stuck to the very bottom—of his soul. When Juanito Santa Cruz spends a few days closed up in his room with a cold and Ido del Sagrario comes to visit him, the spoiled child is in a bad mood because he's bored being shut in and tells his wife to admit Ido immediately: "He's the most amusing lunatic you can imagine. You'll see how we laugh. . . . When we get tired listening to him we'll throw him out. A really eccentric type of guy . . . I saw him a few days ago at Pez's house and he made us die laughing." Since it's clear to look at Ido that he is truly wretched, they suggest that he have a chop right there and then: "'Bring him two,' the señorito said, delighted by the idea of watching a starving man eat." And the rapid gorging—Ido swallows the meat whole because he has no teeth—has him so congested that he comes out with his usual delirious nonsense about offended honor. "But the other man, wanting a little amusement, piqued that poor man's madness to get it going." Compassionate Jacinta can think of nothing to say but: "'Calm down, poor man. It doesn't matter a bit to us what your wife is like.'" Juanito knows that soothing words excite him, and wanting a bit more amusement, tries to calm him: "'Sit down, don José, and don't get so excited. You have to take things easy.'" The scene fills four pages, in which the domestic chorus is not lacking: "The servant was in the doorway laughing, waiting for his masters to ask him to put that clown in the street."

I've quoted the lines above because they demonstrate more unquestionably than my own opinion a resemblance to the abominable passage about Don Quixote in the house of the dukes. The fact that this vile sarcasm abides in Spain's *Christian people* calls for serious thought, seeing that Spain's people, so little given to pleasure, delight in offending the weak—to use "people" here in the widest possible sense, not limited to class or period. We could consider it a donjuanesque feat that such *unloving* has traversed the entire social scale, from the Cervantine dukes to the nouveau-riche Madrilenian philistines in Galdosian—and post-Galdosian—novels. Well, that detritus of humanity is what Galdós bestows on the greatest lover of all his heroines. I said that I could not write an extensive analysis of Fortunata, but it's impossible for me to omit the phenomenon of *identification*—in the Freudian sense—that occurs in her. This is expressed so subtly in Galdós that I cannot tell for sure if he only hints at it because of his proverbial discretion or if it was the result of an intuition so blind that he did not try to develop it fully. Fortunata identifies with Juanito Santa Cruz's *absent masculinity*. But this does not seem clear if we focus on the fact that Fortunata's love is essentially sexual. She loves Santa Cruz simply, like a bitch in heat, and she loves him and no one else, because he *responds* to her personal yearning. But despite this *response*—a question of condition and not correspondence—a large area of her person remains idle, as if unrealized. Santa Cruz lacks something he would need to fill—or possess—that area: he lacks *manliness*, and it's precisely with that *absent manliness* on the part of Santa Cruz that Fortunata identifies.

Earlier, I used the term *masculinity* and I've corrected it with "manliness," because what Fortunata desires is the whole man—material and moral—and that *wholeness* of being is what she can nurture in herself. Her bravery and lack of feminine vanity would be enough to demonstrate this, but there is much more. Fortunata feels a mysterious attraction to Guillermina, a benefactor and spiritual activist; and, with the particular sense of fraternity shared by combatants, she feels deep friendship with Mauricia, the tough streetwalker. In other words, Fortunata yearns with *all her being* for the *absolute* masculinity she sees hovering above these women—one a virgin, the other a prostitute—like a tongue of fire, infusing them with its spirit. They hold a mysterious attraction for Fortunata because she sees in them precisely what she herself yearns for, and seeing it in those fellow women makes it seem more real and more possible. So possible, close to and consubstantial with her does it become, she ends her life with her effort to *give a child* to Jacinta. The rival at first hated and disdained ends up *seducing her* into pity or, better, into masculine generosity, magnificence, magnanimity. Jacinta's femininity, so weak, so barren in body and soul, arouses in Fortunata the desire to give Jacinta the thing for which her whole being hungers and, in that way, to *possess her*.

Fortunata is undoubtedly the great lover among Galdós's heroines, but I said that she was created with the love that was left over after he had created Camila, which is true; Camila is not the one who most loves but she is the one most loved. To return to a literary perspective, which I seem to have abandoned, but to which I'll return soon, it's necessary to note that *Lo prohibido*, written from 1884 to 1885, is a novel much more modern—in terms of novelistic technique—than the later ones. Not in terms of style—I'll have to return to this—but with respect to its conception and structure. In this novel, Galdós confronts psychoanalysis from the point of view of the first person, which makes the work read like a confession. Of course Galdós assumes that it does not have to be taken that way: the facts of his life probably showed him that he was quite mistaken. But in a confession, what can demonstrate the events of a life? Galdós *places* José María Bueno de Guzmán in the presence of three women, making him, as narrator, conscientiously and systematically beam his amorous powers in their direction. The book's chief modernity lies in Galdós's restricting of the drama to four characters (just two steps removed from that "personal novel," whose beginnings Marías situates in Unamuno), without diluting it in contingencies or highlighting marginal characters. Of the three women, two are loved intensely by José María, the third he loves only out of *kindness*. Within the Galdosian norm, there is nothing exceptional in Eloísa's love. One could say that he presents Eloísa as a classic example of love that is passionate and elevated at first and ends with boredom and contempt for the object that inspired it. I cannot dwell here on the husband Eloísa betrays, but he must be mentioned briefly. This man, Pepe Carrillo, from the same generation as the three characters I merged into one, could never be merged with them. Pepe Carrillo belongs to another breed, about which Galdós has nothing to confess: he is *one and the same man*, along with others of his kind—Orozco, Nazarín. A man whom Galdós sees from without. In both

Lo prohibido and *Realidad*, the very existence of such a man prompts in women—Eloísa in the first and Augusta in the second—the arousal of the passion their senses crave, since they live adrift between luxury and a moribund virtue, the spirit of these two such saintly men being heavy as lead. Eloísa's love ends, then, as a love usually ends, and Camila's begins, one of those loves that cannot end.

For the protagonist of *Fortunata y Jacinta*, that tempestuous drama of passions, Galdós created Juanito Santa Cruz, an inept character with an impotent soul, a dazzling mask of a man; and for *Lo prohibido* José María Bueno de Guzmán who, like an invalid, like a man bearing a serious defect who is *going* to die—*he goes* toward his death and reaches it. This character has the mettle to tell us about his death—having admirably experienced his death after his hemiplegia—and about the persistence of his love. Consequently, we see *how* José María Bueno de Guzmán loves, but *what* is it that he loves?

The title of *Lo prohibido* suggests Bueno de Guzmán's inclination: no licit love can attract him, the only thing that stimulates him is the risk of something difficult. Under that premise as an accepted fate, he undertakes the conquest of his three cousins, women married to respectable husbands, and with the first two the cycle of conquest, possession, and abandonment runs its course in the normal way. But in Camila the seduction of *the forbidden* culminates, acquiring the supreme category of *impossible*. There is a fierceness in Camila, the youngest of the Bueno de Guzmáns, that does not seem to fit with the style of her parents and sisters, moderately educated, well-bred bourgeois educated with pretensions to refinement. She's married to a poor and supremely uncultured minor military man, whom she adores.

When Bueno de Guzmán first sees her, José María finds Camila detestable. She's pretty—all three sisters are extremely pretty—and she exhibits her charms in provocatively chaste ways, playing the piano in her nightdress, making continual allusions to her budding pregnancy and extolling the bounteous parts of her body reserved for her little son. José María's relationship with his cousin's household—he never manages to have a relationship with her apart from that household— is exactly right as a psychological process. Gradually he infiltrates the home with gifts—becoming the child's godfather with that in mind— loans, trips paid for. None of that allows him to advance one step in Camila's esteem—much less her love. From the beginning, when their relationship has not yet become violent because José María has not yet undertaken anything openly, she treats him as shown in the following examples. One day he runs into her on the street, when she's out shopping and he tries to invite her to a restaurant for a bite to eat. "'Get away, *tísico*'"—her nickname for him is "consumptive." "'Are you crazy? Me in a restaurant? It wouldn't matter to me, but Constantino would have a fit . . . Wouldn't that be a fine thing if after making him give up the vice of going to the café, I adopted it.'" Constantino's physical strength is highlighted on numerous occasions and is best defined by a portrait placed in Camila's study—he's wearing an undershirt and displaying his large biceps. There is also a dramatic moment on the beach when José María, confident that he's the better swimmer, violently knocks Constantino over, forcing him to swallow a large quantity of water, but the athlete rallies quickly, knocking José María down even more brutally. His head under water and unable to defend himself, he hears Camila shouting from the shore: "'Drown him, drown him.'" His long fruitless struggle with Camila's virtue is perfect; she yields to neither his protests of love nor his temptations of luxury. And José María's passion, daily more ardent, finally reaches the point of explosion when they meet by chance in the kitchen. I prefer not to summarize such a masterly scene—Galdós's best, if not his only good love scene—but I will try to excerpt from it because Galdós's *style* in that scene makes clear Heidegger's assertion that "If a manifestation of being is produced in a work—in what it is and how it is—this sets in motion an occurrence of truth."

José María goes to Camila's apartment to show her a small picture someone has given to him. "Camila herself opened the door. She was alone. Having dismissed the maid, she had to make dinner herself. . . . She was wearing an old skirt and her blue and white apron. Kerchief tied around her head Basque style; sleeves rolled up; a rather loose blouse; no corset, since the heat and the effort of the work wouldn't permit it; her bosom well covered, but very pronounced in all the elegant roundness of its solid architecture. On her feet, a pair of Constantine's old boots completed the outfit."

"I went to the kitchen with her and sat in a chair she had way in the back." Here, a short, perfect description, like a landscape, of the kitchen. "She started to wash the dishes, saying: 'That giraffe left everything for me exactly how you see it, unwashed . . . What whores.'

And I watched her, enraptured, looking at her hands red and fresh in the water . . . and, especially, contemplating her face smiling with a youthful vigor and peacefulness that cannot be expressed in words. I was seized by fever, delirium; the chord of my spirit vibrated as if it would break. I could not control myself, nor did it occur to me to use indirect, hypocritical language, as I had other times. I went over to her, holding my chair in my left hand; I sat down beside the sink, all of this very quickly . . . Grabbing one of her arms, I pressed it against my forehead, which was burning. The freshness of that hand and the hardness of her elbow, which ended up falling on my forehead, produced a delightful sensation. Everything happened in less time than it's taking me to tell it, and these were my words: 'Love me, Camila, love me or I'll die. Can't you see that I'm dying?' She backed away from me, and with a great hullabaloo of arms and words, forced me to retreat. 'Look at this *tísico*. If you die, what fault will it be of mine? Get away and let me work. If you continue to be so annoying, I'll have to give you a good whopping.'" Following this, Camila bursts into laughter and she herself makes fun of her garments. Using coarse, comical language, she scolds José María for his ridiculous infatuation: "'Get out of here, you're an adulterer, and you want to make an adulteress out of me.'" Then she threatens him with her tongs and José María throws himself to the floor, hugs her knees, and makes her fall on top of him. They roll for a moment in a heap, but they get up and she threatens him more seriously.

When Camila thinks that he's calmed down, she tries to change the subject and begins to tell him details from her married life: the little gifts she gives to Cacaseno—her name for him—and the surprises she prepares for him, making him get up in the middle of the night because of a suspicious noise and finding the thing he was looking for hanging from the door. "I didn't let her finish. The desire to press her against myself, to cover her with caresses, was too strong for my weak will to restrain. . . . 'Love me or I'll kill you,' I said, with epileptic anxiety, beside myself, clutching her in my arms and nuzzling any part of her that wound up in front of my face. 'Love me or I'll kill you. Not all of you for him, something for me. I'm in love with you like a child, and you, nothing.'" He throws himself on her again, they again roll on the floor, and again she gets the upper hand. The beauty tells him: "'See how I hold you in one fist, *tísico*? You're a little puppet; there's not a drop of blood in your veins; your vices make you revolting. You're not enough for a real woman, just for those consumptive whores, worthless as you . . . a loser.' Seeming more beautiful the angrier she got, she raised her right leg, kicked off one of those enormous boots with a quick movement, brandished it in her right hand and planted the sole on my face one, two, three times. . . . She looked at me so hard that I put my hands over my face. 'How's that, does it sting?' she asked me. 'You're the one who's guilty, for being such a pest. That's how I wear them out. What's that, blood? I'm glad: come back for more. Take this, and this. I want you to have the soles of my husband's boots stamped on your snout.'"

The scene is reduced here to a minimum; with the paragraphs I selected I can give only a hint of Camila's nature and of the words bombarded between the two of them. Those words are crude, on Camila's part; José María's are correct and intense; you could say pure, the real truth, or true reality. I mean that his words speak about something that one has lived, wanting to live it: something that truly *happened* and, because it's true, *it cannot happen*. Concerning the language of José María Bueno de Guzmán, I need to take a small inventory of the amorous conversations between *this* (synthetic) *man* I've composed and his various women. Monsalud is the one who remains most free of guilt, because he barely speaks in his sad love affairs. Not even in the bedroom of the beautiful Indian woman coiling herself in snakelike undulations on a tiger skin among flowers, jewels, and the like, to the point that even the most patient reader gets gooseflesh, does he say much of anything in particular. Nor does Araceli utter sentences worth singling out, although there is one very long passage, a comic-moral-sentimental discourse, underpinned with solid chauvinism that merited a separate chapter; I will comment on it later.

Where one finds the best examples of Galdós's *amorous* style is in *Fortunata y Jacinta*, *Realidad*, and *Lo prohibido*. In those novels, we can gather the expressions of love such as "Dark, darling" that Juanito Santa Cruz uses with Fortunata and the endearments common between married couples that he and Jacinta exchange. "'How much do you love me?' 'This much.' 'That's not very much.' 'Well, from here to Cibeles, no to the sky. Is that enough?' '*Chi*.'" In a very dramatic moment when Jacinta presses him to calm her feelings of jealousy, he tells her—jokingly, Galdós assumes—"'Shut up, *you whore!*' . . . Saying this, he turned toward her, sitting down on the bed and uttering all sorts of endearments." In *Realidad*, the complaints of love are in this same style, here in the case of the licit and passionate relationship between Federico Viera—noble, devoted to the gentleman's traditions—and Augusta, an educated woman surrounded by a highly spiritual environment. Defending himself from Augusta's accusations, Federico says: "'Be careful with your suspicions. No, clever kitty, there's no reason for you to be angry with your *good-for-nothing*.'" I've italicized that expression because it's the term of affection Augusta uses with him. And with Leonor, a friendly, magnanimous prostitute, things go like this: "'What are you thinking about, sweetie?' 'About things happening to me.' 'Love affairs? Ah, little vixen, don't deny it.'"

I'm not at all sure if in the time between Galdós's generation and mine such terms have fallen in disuse, to the point of becoming intolerable, grotesque, but I remember very well how people in my family talked; I never heard anything similar in the stories my aunts and grandmothers told. It might seem that Galdós transfers the language used in situations of a coarse nature to the elevated sphere of refined society—an ambition never realized—but I don't think that's where the dissonance lies, because even in the case of one of his most uncultured characters, a grotesque comment reveals the artful state of a mind, when Manolita takes Fortunata, now in the reformatory, to church and shows her the treasures on the altar. "'Don't go believing it's gold,' she says as she points out a monstrance: 'it's gold-plated silver; but it's really sweet, isn't it?' Fortunata was so deep in thought that she didn't notice the foolish reference to the monstrance as sweet." Ten pages later, though, after Galdós has noted the foolishness of that expression, in a passage that aims to be dramatic and very profound, Mauricia, in a fit of mystic intoxication, believes that she has seen the Virgin dispossessed of the baby Jesus; she goes to the church to steal the monstrance so she can take her the child enclosed in the Host, but she finds the door locked and stumbles in the doorway, where she falls asleep. In her delirium, she carries out the planned robbery and, when she has her hands on the monstrance, she starts to talk to it: "'I won't hurt You a bit, my little God; I'm going to take You to Mama, who's outside crying for You and waiting for me to get You. . . But what's the matter? . . . Don't you want to be with your Mommy? . . . See how she's waiting for you . . . So beautiful, so fancy, with that shawl all covered with little stars and her feet on the moon's two-cornered hat . . . You'll see, You'll see, sweetie, how carefully I take you out.'" Who can believe that a woman from the Spanish people—and here, "people" means, literally, people—calls the transubstantiated Christ *"sweetie"*? Galdós continues fabricating Mauricia's delirium, which in fact he does very skillfully, since he undoubtedly knew the oneiric world, as Joseph Schraibman has explained in his excellent article, "Onirología galdosiana" [The Galdosian Dreamworld].

Yes, Galdós did know that world, but as soon as he tried to perfect it, he destroyed it. He comments: "She continued to walk straight ahead through the church. The sanctified Host, not having a face, watched her as if it had eyes." Mauricia begins to feel afraid, but she does not let go of the monstrance, and it speaks to her: "'Girl, don't take me out of here, put me back again where I was. Don't do foolish things . . . If you put me down, I will forgive your sins, which are too numerous to count; but if you persist in carrying me, I will condemn you. Put me down and don't be afraid, because I won't say anything to either don León or the nuns, so they won't scold you . . . Mauricia, girl, what are you doing . . . ? Are you eating me, you're eating me . . . ?'" Fabrication, obvious artifice. This is neither a dream nor the soul of a woman from the *people* in *true* religious ecstasy. The entire situation is intellectualized; Galdós tries for the grotesque, but never reaches beyond the picturesque, with thick brush strokes of ineffective *tremendismo*.

I repeat, for the umpteenth time, that what I'm doing here is not literary criticism. Is there an exhaustive, systematic study of Galdós's work, one that identifies each and every one of his topics and investigates all of its ramifications, even the least important? I don't know of one, and I wish I could count on the time it would require, because the fates of Spanish literature are knotted within it, and the knot can't be cut at one go. Only the patience of a Chinese carver able to release one ivory sphere within another, within another, and so on successively, would be able to take a step in this direction. In truth, though, what I'm looking for here is the confession that Galdós holds back. It's not easily found, despite *Lo prohibido*, and despite the moment of Jenara's contrition in *Los cien mil hijos de San Luis*: "And one continues to live after doing such things. And it seems as though nothing has happened and happiness returns, and sometimes it's even possible to forget completely the perverse, villainous act. I don't hesitate to write about it here because I intend this paper to be my confessional." In this paragraph, Galdós demonstrates his belief in the need to confess deeds, but if I'm not interested in deeds here, it's because I'm looking for the deeper cause, which rational analysis can barely reach but is perceptible, nevertheless, like the unarticulated stammering sensed in the inability to speak.

Earlier I said that in Cervantes there is a *fêlure*, fissure, or crack in his unity, of which he was aware to the point that he enveloped it in an incomparable poetic form. In Galdós there is a fracture or, rather, a dislocation, which he does not face with the poet's supreme courage. In all fairness, however, neither does he dissimulate nor mask it with a stiff upper lip like most—if not all—of his contemporaries. But the fracture is at the core, which means that affects the most basic and central things. *Skepticism* is an accurate definition, as long as we consider both of its phases. The positive aspect of Galdós's skepticism is the extraordinary lucidity it gives him with respect to social conflicts, historical facts, Spanish idiosyncrasy, the two sexes, and diverse social classes. But even though that lucidity leads him to formulate very harsh accusations, he formulates them with little despair. In his conclusions he places irreducible contradictions head to head, human natures in agonic opposition; he recounts battles in which men die like bedbugs, but there's a composure—when not an irony—in the story that cools down the drama. If we follow the rational aspect of his skepticism, we see how the fact that he has traveled, is knowledgeable about other countries, languages, and customs, helps him to see the faults of his own nation, to recognize that Spaniards are dragging baggage that has them trailing behind European thought. Nevertheless, the judgments he hurls at foreigners, his coarse censure of French women's morality, the extravagances he attributes to the British, differs not a bit from the most simple-minded opinion. This becomes evident when we turn to the aspect of his skepticism that we might call vital—the amorous and religious spheres—which allows us to suggest that Galdós's unconfessable fracture is in his *faith*. I said above that it was at the *core*; it's the same thing.

There is still one more sign of a vital lack in *this man* I have forged from several Spanish, Galdosian types: there is not the least symptom of paternity. Santa Cruz, the most morally sterile, is the only one who fathers a couple of children—by chance, and he regards the events with complete indifference. Carrillo fathers one and never finds out; the rest don't even think about the subject. Maternity is anguished yearning in Jacinta, enterprise and triumph in Fortunata, and ostentation in Camila. Of course, sentiment figures in the relationships between other characters who are fathers or mothers and their children in Galdós's numerous novels, but the issue of *paternity* is not a question of sentiment—it's a *generative impulse for eternity*.

That concept, a *generative impulse for eternity*, I want to take now as a touchstone and place it in the context of Unamuno's work, to determine the degree to which the phenomenon it signals might be important there. The first thing one notices is that the *degree* is difficult to calculate because of the ambiguous *way* it underlies its context. With *way*, though, I'm not referring to form—form concerns things manifest—but to the *ambiguous way of being* associated with that urge in Unamuno, perhaps even to the point of involving more *yearning* than *impulse*. In truth, analyzing everything ambiguous in Unamuno—which is almost everything—is a difficult task, because everything, on both of its sides—two, so as to simplify, although, in truth they're infinite—arises overwhelmingly and imponderably, so that we need to give credence to each, as if at every moment it were not threatened with annihilation or substitution by its opposite.

Fortunately, the difficulty of that task is mitigated by the possibility of drawing on the numerous, extensive, and very good studies of Unamuno's work. Consequently, there's no need to venture a simple explanation of my own, because the ones I know are too sound to ignore. I will limit myself to citing first the three I most admire; each of them addresses one of the points that must be considered if I'm to find what I'm seeking: Marías's "personal novel," that is, Unamuno's *persona* and his "sole question," the *meditatio mortis*; Gullón's *Autobiografías de Unamuno*, in other words, his indirect confession, which Gullón describes as a "confidence," and therefore a relationship with *his* (Gullón's) fellow human beings; Antonio Sánchez Barbudo's *faith* and, consequently, *truth*. Equipped with such sound instruments, I will use as my testing ground a novel these authors consider transitional, but independent of what it represents as a *work*, one whose drama has a particular *accent*—a particularity that, perhaps, consists in totality. Does the fact that Unamuno chose "A Real Man" as the first—embryonic—title of *Amor y pedagogía* [Love and Pedagogy], which Gullón notes referring to a letter from Unamuno to Pedro

Jiménez Ilundain, not signify totality? In the definitive title, there's a freedom vis-à-vis its author, who seems to be laughing at his own joke. The irony placed like paprika on that binomial is destroyed by the gentle power of those two words, those two *voices*, which are perhaps one and the same.

Marías shows what there is in this novel of a "transition to individual life," and he cites sections from the prologue to the second edition, in which Unamuno points out the differences between this novel and the preceding one, *Paz en la guerra* [Peace in War], observing that in it "there is the seed—and more than the seed—of the great and the best part of what I revealed later in my other novels." Marías adds, "To what extent and in what sense are those two claims true?" My understanding is that they are both perfectly true. Marías argues that in this story with "a vital, individualized, but rigorously *inauthentic* atmosphere, there is not the radical situation, the *scream* that allows one to strip bare a character's soul, as Unamuno would require some time later."

Gullón thinks that he does sense that *scream* in *Paz en la guerra* and points to sections from the prologue to the second edition of 1932, by which date Unamuno's own work has been fully realized, and in those sections he seems to allude to the *ultimate scream* or accent. "To the reader [to whom the prologue was dedicated] and not to the readers, to each one of them and not to the—mass—the public they form. And with them I will demonstrate my intention to speak to the ultimate in individuality, the individual and personal intimacy of the reader within that mass, to his reality, not his reality as it appears to others. That explains why I speak to him all by ourselves, hearing each other's breathing, sometimes the beating of our hearts, as in a confessional. Because this is not a work from the pulpit. Nor the political platform. Which frees it, insofar as possible, from a particular rhetoric inevitable in those activities. A work of the confessor, not the publicist. Of confessor and confessed." Gullón comments, "Of confessor and confessed, Don Miguel says, where I write 'confidence.' But the context of the work proves me right, as do the text and even the pages where Unamuno sets the demagogic task, characteristic of an Unamuno sure of himself (or who believed or said he was), against the longing for intimate expression revealed in the novel, where he will speak of personal conflicts beneath transparent masks. And confidential novel means lyric novel (something we saw at the end of *Paz en la guerra*)—not 'poematic' novel with purple twilights and old parks, but a novel in which the author speaks revealing words about himself."

Gullón studies *Amor y pedagogía* under the title "El filósofo en chancletas" [The Philosopher in Slippers], and argues that "the character Don Fulgencio should be called the novel's protagonist," agreeing with Geoffrey Ribbans, who, according to Gullón, "read accurately: for him Unamuno reserved the principal role beneath the mask of the intellectual saturated with intellectualism who rebels against his author, knowing full well that he will not be able to free himself from that yoke." "When he [Don Fulgencio] goes out to receive Avito for the first time, he'll be 'wearing slippers.' Both his attire and the setting tend to make the character look ridiculous, to prompt laughter at his mere appearance. His philosophy is presented as equally comic—'combinatorics carried to the ultimate extreme . . . four principal ideas, two related to the ideal, two to the real,' which, coordinated 'in every way possible,' in binary coordinates first, then tertiary, later quaternary, and so forth, successively, 'will allow us to decipher' the mystery of the great hieroglyph of the Universe and to grab 'the thread, thus untangling the eternal drama of the infinite.'" There is a burlesque tone to the narrative itself; every time the author describes something, the very description is deformed, so that it seems more a caricature than a portrayal. The scenes between Don Fulgencio and his wife Doña Edelmira draw on the *sainete*, including even the use of diminutives associated with the style of writing credited to Arniches and García Álvarez; inserted among the scenes in which Don Fulgencio plays the role of mentor, they break the solemnity of the pedagogical comedy with an abrupt change of attitude and vocabulary. Consider the following dialogue:

> The philosopher cups the chin of his solemn wife in his hand and says to her:
> "Come, *Mira*, don't be naughty."
> "You're the naughty one, Fulgencio."
> "We're both the naughty ones."
> "As you like, but I believe we're both very good."
> "Maybe you're right," he adds pensively and then: "Dammit, how could I find you just as gorgeous, even after all . . ."
> "Ssh, ssh, Fulgencio, the walls have ears . . . come here . . ."

Later, Gullón continues, "the elements used to highlight the comic serve various purposes: the skeletons and inscriptions are a mockery of nineteenth-century scientism watered down for the public; Darwin's theories are simplified to such an extreme they seem silly; the philosopher's pieced-together outfit suggests indigence and, indirectly, failure and is a sign of how, having nothing better, the person who wears it feels different. Those 'my' hips, 'my' knee patches testify to 'originality' and suggest that most likely the philosopher's claim to being original merely shows how, of necessity, he turns the limitations posed by poverty to the best advantage possible. Because the allusion is so transparent we can see Unamuno's silhouette in the background, becoming agitated by the obsessive I, I, I."

I said above that confession is the spectral analysis of the will, and the will hurled by Unamuno with an indifference that makes it seem *involuntary* is, in reality, *subvoluntary*; it has the oneiric obstinacy of things that surface in our sleep when our ultimate will wants something that we don't want to want. In that subvoluntary will Unamuno is not daydreaming, dreamily planning a work, as when he autobiographies—confidentially—his yearning, but it is a truth—the only, the *ultimate* truth—that truth that asserts itself over him, with the accent of one disdained, and it does not succumb to the disdainful author, no matter how much the author persists in stoning it with trivial sarcasm.

Gullón points to the origins of Unamuno's novel: "In letters from 1900 and 1901 there are frequent references to *Amor y pedagogía*, when he speaks of fusing grotesque and tragic elements, emphasizing in particular the humoristic form he planned to give them. There might not have been enough attention paid to that fusion and form, which, together, give the novel an esperpento-like character. The attack against the ideologues is probably directed toward Unamuno's possible Unamuno: a warning whose vibrations will remain in the air, summoned to resonate each time the theorizer tries to raise his head: a connoisseur of intellectualism, as the chronic sufferer of his affliction, he intended to confess in the novel, by declaring his malady the same way he did in a letter to Clarín dated May 9, 1900, several months before writing the book: 'intellectual, intellectual with respect to and above everything else, feeling himself a victim of intellectualism,' he says, referring to himself in the third person, 'he waged campaigns against that intellectualism and it turned out to be the most intellectual possible. And he suffered, he suffered a great deal.'

"These words are followed by an allusion to the crisis of '97, Unamuno's passing rapprochement with religion and religious practices and the 'most routine devotions,' when he made a great effort to believe, until the false nature of his attitude became unbearable and he 'again found himself disoriented, once again a prisoner of his thirst for glory, the longing to survive in history.' He suffered because he found it impossible to believe, and since the cause was reason, the destroyer of faith, in order to take revenge he attacked that corrosive reason, embodying it in science." Gullón adds a footnote in which he cites a letter from Unamuno to Federico de Onís as evidence of Unamuno's assertion: "'Science frightens and saddens me. That is to say, I'm afraid of and saddened by truth.'"

Cervantes's rancor against a moment of his own being, against a spark of his past faith, ignites in Unamuno against the aspect of *his* own person that looks at reason and, by setting that aspect free among his personal fictions, he sends it—to the reader—loaded with a ridicule not found in Don Quixote's cruel purity but a ridicule that envelops more than denudes. Which is to say that he shows that aspect of himself in all its incontestable absurdity, but in that absurdity it's armor-plated: it does not bleed like a living soul; comically invulnerable—no doubt unbeheadable—it takes the blows, never threatened by death, never on the way to dying in truth, in reason.

Marías points to the "inauthenticity" of the *persons* who make up *Amor y pedagogía* as a distinctive feature of a transition phase of what we might call evolutionary process of Unamuno's creative technique, which it undoubtedly was. Studying the successive steps of that process, we see that it did happen that way, although something more determined the existence of that "inauthenticity"; its meaning is attached not only to a question of surmountable difficulty or, rather, of the atmosphere or world in which one does not want to employ an emphasis appropriate to a pulpit or a political platform, but in which "a certain rhetoric inevitable in these activities" gets inserted just the same, because there is something that precedes confidence. Before the reader of the novel, closer to Unamuno, so much closer that neither their breathing nor their heartbeats register in their perceptible proximity, there is the polemical interlocutor.

It seems indisputable that Don Fulgencio is the true—truly inauthentic—protagonist of *Amor y pedagogía*, but if we think about Avito Carrascal, does this character prove to be less inauthentic or more so? He proves to be *other*. Unamuno sows him like a seed in a clearly fatal theoretical space; offering him no support concerning that fate, he throws him into a mephitic atmosphere where he's bound to perish, as if one of those two terms—*love* and *pedagogy*—signified a deleterious antithesis. The indifference that Unamuno shows toward this unfortunate *person* is obvious in the lengthy prologue and epilogue that frame the novel. In them, Unamuno does not use the possessive pronoun even once before the name of Avito Carrascal. He repeatedly says "my Don Fulgencio" and also "my poor Apolodoro," his very characteristic way of acknowledging paternity. About Avito, however, he says only "Don Avito, poor Don Avito." One of Unamuno's characters—or *persons*—who does not bear that *my* before his name has been disinherited. We can't help considering him as such, as one dispossessed, because we know that Unamuno is his progenitor, but Unamuno himself knew deep down that he was an adopted son. I would dare say *abducted*, snatched from his true clan and mistreated, held in clownish servitude. In Avito Carrascal, the grotesque is not an ontological drama but a polemical caricature. Unamuno does not delve deeply into the true intimacy of his being; he *takes* him in his supposed existence, as if such an existence were an inevitable effect of time, a foreseeable meteor.

What is it that Unamuno argues and with whom does he debate when he places Avito Carrascal in the world? I think it's quite clear that he's arguing with Rousseau about his *Émile*. The argument is a cordial one because, in an article written years before, Unamuno said, "I have always loved Rousseau . . . I've always loved that poor tormented soul who, despite professing optimism, in his own defense, is the father of pessimism." So the argument is cast more as an exchange of ideas than a polemic. Of course, Unamuno was aware of the infinite absurdity of *Émile*, a prefabricated youth, an absurdity that consists primarily in its being the fabrication of a natural youth. On the basis of nature and naturalness, Rousseau fabricated a deaf, mute, asexual, and discreetly avaricious adolescent. Unamuno sees his essential absurdity but nevertheless feels stirred, seduced by his *puritan* aroma. Acknowledging the rigidity, abstention—one must say negation—of Protestant *puritanism* (its decorous—although impure—adultery), he experiences the power of supreme temptation irradiated by *purity*, its magnetism, which tugs at his generative energy until it manages to trip him. Without loving him, he adopts that poor *person* borne by the wind. Avito Carrascal is made from the winds of his time and, rather than place him face to face with Émile, he dangles him, showing him Rousseau with a friendly smile, in order for Avito to see that the science and reason he detests can also take shape in a pathetic freak.

Unamuno believes that in Rousseau there is passion and faith. He also believes that "Rousseau, the spiritual father of Obermann, was always a gloomy pessimist, a denier of life." A close look, however, shows that what Rousseau openly denied was not life—he would not have dared—but man's power; it's that wind bearing the man of his time. Unamuno embraces Rousseau's negation and with it creates a being, trying to form him with two materials that will not blend. Emulsified or mixed together, they occupy the space whose perimeter describes the imaginary person of Avito, who sometimes *falls* in love and other times aspires to pedagogy, but neither is his pedagogy pedagogy nor his love love. The only love of Avito Carrascal that we might find moving is his love of science, which is not moving to Unamuno. Unamuno tries so hard to give Avito a rotten deal that he ends up rotten, because triviality as a weapon wounds but does not finish off.

There is much still to be said about the prologues to *Amor y pedagogía*; to focus on Avito, though, Unamuno defines him for us in the first chapter as "A man of the future, he never speaks about his past, and since he doesn't do this on his own, we'll respect his secret. He probably has his reasons when he's forgotten it like that." With this, it's made clear that Avito is a "puppet" created to represent *a* man of the future: never *the* man of the future, who can only have futurity in his being if he is filled with past. And with that burden of trivial ridicule that Unamuno places on Avito he makes him an obviously weak victim. As he says in the prologue: "Don Avito disappoints us, because when everything leads us to assume that he will impose his strict pedagogical regimen on his son, we find that Avito is a poor imbecile who stuffs his son with book learning but allows him to do what he wants and turns him over to Don Fulgencio, unaware of his deception." Unamuno makes it clear that Don Fulgencio's own (self)-deception is part of his nature, but gives him no trivial traits that would make him grotesque as a figure. For Gullón, Don Fulgencio arouses the greatest possible pathos when Unamuno refutes a paragraph from the novel's first prologue: "To many readers this novel will seem like an attack, not on the absurdities prompted by science when poorly understood and pedagogical mania carried to an extreme, but an attack on science and pedagogy themselves, and it's important to acknowledge that if such an attack was not the author's intention—we refuse to believe it was, since he's a man of science and a pedagogue—at least he's done nothing to prove that." Those are Unamuno's words, and Gullón states: "It was neither 'poorly understood science' nor abusive reason that delivered the death blow to Unamunian longing for a return to faith, but plain science and pure reason, and they're what he assailed." "His anger against his enemy—reason—that made his full return to innocence impossible dictated bitter pages: nothingness was the response, and like a barbaric caudillo meeting a soldier bearing news of defeat, it condemned Don Miguel, the messenger, to death."

Gullón's exhaustive study of the associations suggested by this novel is supported at times by quotes from other critics, some of whom have seen a reflection of Carlyle's *Sartor Resartus* in Don Fulgencio's abstruse philosophy. I'm surprised to find no echo of Jean-Jacques in the work of those critics except in Sánchez Barbudo's study; a merciless excavation with the intensity, the persistent investigation that Unamuno deserves, it's like a very strong spotlight that illuminates the shadows. Note that it illuminates them, but does not disperse them. The shadow that pursues Unamuno, nothingness is outlined like a hollow in reality, like a hole where one can trip, fall, succumb. Unamuno moves—in his life and in his work—on a profusely perforated plane, avoiding the openings by zigzagging around them, his gait sinuous. When the final moment arrives, he makes his last will and testament. Gullón refers to his confessions as "confidences" and the last one, *San Manuel Bueno, mártir* [Saint Manuel Bueno, Martyr], he calls "Don Miguel's Testament." Here sinuosity is not feeling one's way, it's no longer maneuvering right to left and left to right to clear the potholes; the search for salvation is abandoned or, rather, transformed into a spiral— movement of ecstasy—curled over itself.

Amor y pedagogía and *San Manuel Bueno, mártir* are undoubtedly Unamuno's most "authentic" confessions. That statement does not refute what Marías points out as "inauthenticity" in *Amor y pedagogía*. Not only does it not refute Marías, it uses his comment as proof:

"inauthenticity" is the primary element of his most "authentic" confession. This Sánchez Barbudo has seen with clarity and microscopic detail and has spelled out the equivalence—more than the similarity—between San Manuel Bueno and Rousseau's Savoyard Vicar: "Through their respective works, both Rousseau and Unamuno express fear of, and repugnance toward, the materialism then triumphant, whether that of the Marxists or the republicans and the masses that followed them, or that of the encyclopedists and their many admirers; antipathy toward, and fear of, that wave of atheism and revolution that, with their preaching, they themselves had been instrumental in shaping. And they both defended themselves, by attacking, against the accusation they feared would be hurled at them for being deserters of a cause."

"They were both instinctive, romantic, sentimental, although each of them, especially Rousseau, was more tied to reason than it seemed. Both were exhibitionists and egotists, destructive and confused; both were instrumental in rekindling spiritual anxiety and both regretted it. A possible parallel exists, then. But the truly surprising thing is the resemblance between the two novels to which we have referred."

Sánchez Barbudo's comparison is detailed; he discusses the basic points of the two novels and relates them—especially Unamuno's—to the fundamental conflicts of their authors. This involves studying Rousseau's influence on—it might be enough to say presence in—Unamuno's very early work, as Unamuno notes in *Recuerdos de niñez y mocedad* [Memories of My Childhood and Adolescence]. Fragmentary readings when he was fourteen were enough for him to mention Rousseau in his first lecture. As he recounts, "I had to speak about the divinity of Jesus Christ," and when "In oratorical tone . . . I reached the death of Jesus, I cited, rather, recited, the part in Rousseau in which he says that if Socrates died like a sage, Jesus Christ died like a God." That quote shows not only that Rousseau had always been present but that Unamuno's contact with him was based on the question of belief—or of disbelief.

The relationship—I repeat that when I speak about relationship I don't mean similarity because there is none between the two novels: rather, there is an identity of elements, combined like the genes in individuals of the same lineage (this will not be left unexplained) that causes a brotherhood less apparent, although more real, than resemblance—the relationship between Don Manuel Bueno and the Vicar determines their essence or structure, which is wrapped in very different coverings. There is a great difference between their tone of voice—a notable characteristic in the case of Don Manuel, nonexistent in that of the Vicar—as there is between their attire and their overall appearance. They're two brothers who don't resemble each other, but they are brothers, sons of the same cause.

Although it might be a digression, I can't fail to note that Unamuno does not refer to Rousseau as "my brother," and that he does refer that way to Kierkegaard. Like Kierkegaard, he frequented certain places—in the mind, the conscience—but in terms of their essence, makeup, chemistry, dynamics, they differed greatly.

But I was discussing the brotherhood between Unamuno and the Vicar, not between Unamuno and Jean-Jacques. The thing is, though, you can see the Vicar in San Manuel Bueno—late Unamuno—whereas the accent or genuine trace of Jean-Jacques is already visible in the prologue to *Amor y pedagogía* (1932), the beginnings of his most *personal* novelistic style. "There are some who believe, possibly with reason, that this work represents a lamentable, very lamentable error on the part of its author." "What is most detrimental to him is his aversion to the epithet of scholar and the ridiculous effort he puts into making sure that it's not applied to him. We cannot understand either why he finds such an honorable title so upsetting or why, since he writes so much and he is a professor of Greek literature, he would go to such lengths never to write about it. Maybe he does not really know Greek literature well at all and he's afraid to show how weak he is in the area in which he is officially supposed to be an expert? We couldn't say." "All these and other aberrations of his spirit, which we'll pass over in silence in order for our opinion not to seem exaggerated, led Señor Unamuno to produce a work like this one, which is, we repeat, a lamentable, very lamentable error." (The speaker here is Unamuno.) Jean-Jacques definitely never jokes about himself so excessively; very much on the contrary, he pleads, haggles, begs on behalf of his prestige. Unamuno risks his, tosses for it—really tosses for it? Throws it into the air to see if it falls heads up, or to make it shine? Whichever the case, he adopts a distance from which, speaking about himself, he can say *he*, respond when called *Señor Unamuno*. In other words, he renounces "the epithet of scholar," but he makes sure that *Señor Unamuno* gives people something to talk about.

There is another paragraph in the prologue that comments on one of the last chapters in the book—referred to in a way that indicates early on a passage in which there will be a *conclusion*. "We would be happy to stop and analyze Don Fulgencio, *who is perhaps the key to the novel* (emphasis added), but the author himself has revealed this, revealing at the same time other things that would be best hidden, when the grotesque philosopher talks about Herostratism in his last interview with Apolodoro." "Was Jean-Jacques thinking about Herostratism when he categorically defined all past, present, and future philosophers?" The Vicar instructs the young boy as follows: "When philosophers are able to discover the truth, who among them will be interested in it? Everyone knows very well that his own system is no better founded than any other, but he sticks to it because it is his own system. There is not a single person who comes to know the true and the false but does not prefer the lie he has found to the truth discovered by someone else. Is there a man who, deep within his heart, proposes anything else but to distinguish himself? Provided he elevate himself above the ordinary, provided that he outshine the brilliance of his rivals, what more does he require? The essential thing is to think in a way different from anyone else. With believers he's an atheist, with atheists, he's a believer."

In the last interview Don Fulgencio says: "'Do you know what Herostratism is, Apolodoro?'

'No, and it doesn't matter to me.'

'Yes, it does matter to you, it matters a great deal that we all know about it. Herostratism is the illness of our century, the one I suffer from, the one with which we have tried to infect you.'"

There is a marked shift in emphasis. In Don Fulgencio's case, Herostratism is an ailment suffered; for the Vicar it's a healthy attitude adopted—adopted pragmatically—that he theorizes and recommends.

Pragmatism is the decisive note in both preachers, but the very individual stamp of each, what gives them both a unique physiognomy, is not only the inevitable uniqueness that marks different versions of a theory, depending on the mind that develops it. The process of the—very different—experiences lived by the two authors is highly significant. Rousseau sowed, the ground having been previously worked, fertilized with manure and rain. In other words, he tended his ground diligently, in it he deposited substantive principles—axioms—and his pithy words moved, softened, melted hearts. But he did not live long enough to harvest. There is no doubt that he felt an unspoken certainty that his efforts were fertile, but he was not able to see that corroborated by spring's celebration. Until the day he died, he had that certainty lodged in his throat, beneath the cold shell of his pessimism. Unamuno sowed too, but he sowed on stony ground, violently, with his fists, like a man sowing seeds that germinated too quickly. Well, that's not exactly accurate. Gestation— as Kierkegaard has said before me—is always slow, but Unamuno's action provoked a rapid, you could say independent—although I won't because there was nothing independent about it—reaction, remarkable and striking like the repercussion of a blow. A repercussion that was like an immediate response, an audible *yes* or a *no* of the material, its wave traveling very deep within, the radius of its tremor limitless. Could that tremor be fertile? Evidently—it was—but Unamuno could not prove that. He did witness, however, the sparking his steely paradoxes provoked on the flint (a use and abuse of the metaphor, because, as Marías says, "It's important, above all, not to be too precise; in this particular case, it might be the only way to be exact"). In short, Unamuno saw the spark, *his* spark, but he refused to protect it with his loving, possessive pronoun.

Sánchez Barbudo has studied and copiously documented with facts and dates the battle waged simultaneously in Unamuno's soul by his religious drama—intimate and personal—and the drama of Spain, of which he witnessed what was clearly the prelude. "I was again resuming, here in the heart of the fatherland, my civil or, if you prefer, political campaigns. Immersing myself in them, I have felt my old, rather, my eternal religious anguish arise, and in the fervor of my political proclamations heard the whisper of the voice that says: 'And in the end, what's it all for? What for?' And in order to quiet that voice or the one who gives it to me, I continued holding forth to believers in progress and civility and justice—also in order to convince myself of their virtues" (Unamuno, *Ensayos* [Essays]).

To that, Sánchez Barbudo adds: "He [Unamuno] did not convince himself about their virtues and for that reason, during the same days in the fall of 1930 he wrote *San Manuel Bueno* . . . Once again, in the summer of 1930, he had sunk into the depths of himself, into the painful truth, down to the void, and when he abandoned the role of warrior against himself he also abandoned the role of instigator of civil struggle; or perhaps on the contrary, by separating himself from the revolution, fearful of the direction it was taking, abandoning his role as liberator of galley slaves, he also abandoned, even if momentarily, his legendary vestments and fell again into his real grief. In other words, he again became aware that deep down inside himself there was neither 'struggle' nor 'doubt' but a complete lack of faith.

"That ultimate unbelief on the part of an Unamuno tormented by the contrast between what he was and what he seemed, between the inner and outer Unamuno, is what he wanted to confess, and in a way did confess through his character, the priest Don Manuel." Shortly after the Republic was installed, he wrote: "I find it upsetting to see such a surge of illusions about a wealth-filled future ... we must rein in the illusions, above all we need to ask ourselves what for ... to what end that improvement" (*La enormidad de España* [The Enormity of Spain]). As Sánchez Barbudo states, "The voice—echo of Ecclesiastes—would do its part, and his [Unamuno's] fear of the revolution would do the rest."

At that same time, an outer impression internalized by Unamuno in an intuitive ecstasy was added to the two elements locked in the battle whose duration can be marked with the dates of his birth and death. It was thus something like a living, real metaphor; Unamuno clashed with it and confirmed it as a perceptible reality swollen with mystery. As Sánchez Barbudo explains: "In early June, Unamuno visited the lovely, melancholy lake Sanabria in the province of Zamora, the site that inspired the setting for his short novel [*San Manuel Bueno*]. Contemplating the surface of its water always produced a strange impression on him, since it made him think about the innermost peace hidden in him beneath the Unamuno of impassioned words." And Unamuno himself tells us in *Paz en la guerra*, that "[t]he sight of the immense, restless liquid plain" plunged Pachico, that is, the young Unamuno, into an obscure intuition of pure life. Later, however, contemplating the stagnant water must have plunged Unamuno into an obscure intuition of death.

San Manuel Bueno might be the only one of Unamuno's novels that sprang from an aesthetic intuition—not planned with an aesthetic purpose but prompted by a *vision* of the unseeable. (Marías says that "Unamuno's entire oeuvre exceeds and transcends poetry and literature in general. From the first glance you notice that the purpose is not merely aesthetic.") As Unamuno explains in the prologue, "[t]he setting in *San Manuel Bueno, mártir* was suggested by the marvelous and highly suggestive Lake San Martín de la Castañeda, in Sanabria, at the foot of the ruins of a Bernadine convent and home to the legend of Valverde de Lucerna, a city that lies at the bottom of the water." It would be impossible to find a setting more different from the one framing the conversation in which the Savoyard Vicar lays out his profession of faith: "One might say that nature spread her entire magnificence before our eyes, offering the text for us to discuss." The young listener speaks, his right hand pressing that of the Vicar and his left extended in awe toward the luminous space of the valley. He puts one foot forward, leaving the other one suspended, utters an "Ah. . . !" which the Vicar receives as recompense and encouragement, and which gives rise to the long confidence in which breaths and heartbeats communicate beside a pleasant tree at the edge of a hill (this dynamic scene arose from Moreau de Jeune's exquisitely ridiculous illustration in the illustrated Classique Garnier edition of *Émile.*).

No matter how long I might spend commenting on those two settings, I could never stress the phenomenon enough. Natures, situations, circumstances diametrically opposed are home to dramas and determinant of behaviors that, practically speaking, are similar. That issue of practice could be considered decisive here. Both the Vicar and Don Manuel try to put goodness, peace, and the happiness of their parishioners into practice, concealing the desolate solitude of their souls. The Vicar maintains a moderation that at the same time serves as a very practical resource for his own tranquility, an accommodation to his dead-end social situation. You could say that what the Vicar has lost totally is hope in society, and that in order to bear it he confesses that what he hides in his soul is doubt. Don Manuel triumphs in the world. Not only because he has enjoyed various opportunities to shine in the ecclesiastical sphere, but because in his harsh, miserable village he walks on a soft carpet of love. His proven effectiveness sustains him and justifies his pragmatic conduct. The soul of his flock belongs to him or, rather, the opposite, he belongs to his flock, he is the truth in which his flock believes, and since he knows that finding oneself without truth is a living death, he assumes for them the role of the living truth.

I believe that the radical difference between the two preachers lies in their human relations, with both the faithful in their parishes and with the favorites to whom they make their confessions. The Vicar, rather than conceal his disconsolate doubts, cloaks them in a theoretical concept he considers more sound than everything previously theorized. The security he feels in doubting everything helps him to remain silent in the presence of the faith or simple confidence of others, of those who live with their inherited faith, alive within them, a faith thoroughly fused with their lives. With respect to the beloved confidant ... (The traces of Rousseau are incalculable in Unamuno; wherever we open *Émile* we find decisive characteristics that concern both the contents of Unamuno's conscience—the things he counts on, definitively—and his approach to form, the way he resolved or tackled situations. There has certainly been mention of coincidences between Unamuno and Pirandello, but the harmony between Unamuno and Rousseau is earlier and more fundamental. Rousseau, readying himself to unfold the *Profession de foi*, prepares the reader: "Instead of telling you what I think on my own authority, I will tell you what a man more worthy than I, thought. I guarantee the truth of the facts that will be reported, they actually happened to the author of the paper that I am going to transcribe.... Thirty years ago, in an Italian city, a young expatriate found himself reduced to utter poverty. He had been born a Calvinist; but as the consequence of a careless mistake, finding himself a fugitive, in a strange land, with no resources, he changed his religion for a bit of bread." This is explained in a note: "It is about himself, naturally, that he speaks. He is retelling, in the form of a romance, his story, in Turin in 1728." This game of displacements, which Kierkegaard also employed—although in a very different way—was adopted by Unamuno in 1902. Characters at large, realities fluctuating between what is and what seems to be, will come to have Pirandellian correlations, but the sleight of hand with the "I," the acceptance of *Señor Unamuno*, when everything is Unamuno, I, I, I Unamuno ... is a vestige of *ascetic Jean-Jacques, poor Jean-Jacques*.) The Vicar takes a sincere interest in the misguided youth and tries to guide him by engaging him in rational, clear reasoning presented so skillfully that we assume his success, but the author—of the real document—does not let us know how the Vicar's young confidant reacts.

Don Manuel Bueno's endeavor occurs in a different climate. The authors I draw on here have already explained the pragmatism on Unamuno's part that lets him come to terms with the fact of consciousness. What I want to stress is that the personal novel culminates in *San Manuel Bueno*, because ideas and facts, doubts and beliefs, experiences and interests are totally subordinated to, or spellbound by, Don Manuel's very singular person. The reader is interested only in that event which represents the overall attention of an entire village in ecstasy, or a state of loving fascination.

"In *San Manuel Bueno*," Sánchez Barbudo explains, "Unamuno identifies Christ with the priest, into whose mouth he puts words analogous to those Christ uttered in his agony; which is why Angela faces the crucifix after Don Manuel has died and prays piously, recalling the 'my God, my God, why have You forsaken me?' of our *two Christs*." The identification is echoed by Gullón: "through the unequivocal allusions to Jesus Christ, one might wonder if the author wanted to establish a parallel between the character's sublimation and attitude to that of the son of God; if, by merely suggesting the possibility that the creator of our religion did not believe in it, did not believe in the truth of what he preached to console the sad and sustain happiness, imagining, as Don Manuel tells Lázaro, that 'the truth is something intolerable, something mortal: simple people could not live with it.'" Each of the critics meticulously studies the comparison, and we can assume with certainty that Unamuno intended to suggest it. In both moments of faith and hours of doubt, Christ's humanity becomes obvious to everyone who has faith and doubt at the root of his consciousness and, of course, also in the lamentation during Christ's divine agony one senses—those who sense something—a fearful breath of abandonment and, therefore, of doubt.

All of the above reasons suggest that it is not possible to establish the comparison, but then again . . . up to a certain point. I don't reject it because I consider it sacrilegious or because I'm alarmed by the pride it involves, but because in both cases the *practical* consequences of that doubt are as stark as black and white. Unamuno frequently pointed out on other occasions that Christ did not come to console the sad, much less to sustain happiness: he came not to bring peace but a sword. He came to separate the son from his father and the daughter-in-law from her mother-in-law; he came, like Don Manuel— the terms are obviously inverted here: it was Don Manuel who came like . . .—to seduce or fascinate with the power, its range universal and everlasting, of his divinehuman [sic] person, making him renounce everything in exchange for the person he gave them. And above all, with respect to practical consequences, he came to destroy, he came to uproot the old religions in which people lay slumbering, and toss them on the ground. For him, the wise men of Israel were dismissed and the Greek gods beheaded. He roused Lázaro—the entire village, the people—from the grave, not to confide to him a truth the simple would find unbearable, but to hurl the simple and the complex into a vortex of martyrdom in which earthly lives and loves burned with the happiness—only certainty, the possession of the truth can bring happiness—of knowing that they were guaranteed to be *with Him tomorrow, next to His Father.* It is Kierkegaard who confronts the hopeless truth, without trying to sweeten it for the simple, on whom he hurls his Olympian disdain—there was much of the Olympic in Kierkegaard, who adored "the divine majesty of the rule of faith"—with the sarcastic epithet of "happy Christians." So that when Unamuno Christifies *his* Don Manuel Bueno, he forgets Kierkegaard and follows William James, in company with Rousseau.

Of course, in spite of that violent attack, like Gullón, I consider *San Manuel Bueno, mártir* Unamuno's most perfect novel. I would dare say indisputably his most poetic, most *essential* because, being his most personal, events, passions, and situations are structured around a person so intimately that it's almost impossible to say *around*—with it they form a *whole* in which everything belongs to everything. The submerged city *of* Don Manuel is the city *of* the lake and Lucerna *of* the lake is the faith that parts from it as part *of* him and is returned to him in the love *of* others because, likewise, *it is of him.*

I also believe, along with Sánchez Barbudo, that what results from this novel is not doubt, but the total lack of faith. But still we might ask, what is total lack of faith? Because Unamuno was already saying in 1930, when political convulsions had shaken, had so battered his conscience that any living fruit had fallen to the ground: "What's it all for? What it's for? And in order to quiet that voice or *the one giving me voice,* I continued to hold forth." I emphasize that unmoored *one,* which might cause disquiet, because here there seems to be a glimmer of suspicion on Unamuno's part that the voice may have been *given* to him and his faith *taken.* By *whom?*

I don't know if that avatar of doubt has been properly classified in the history of faith. For me, classifications are an article of first importance—although this idea is not in vogue—but the extent of my knowledge in this area, one admirably studied by others, is very limited. On the other hand, I do know—and I say that I know it because I know it well, in other words, vitally—the vicissitudes of that phenomenon today. Some writers, still alive, have left it in their work—which doesn't mean that the phenomenon has left *them*. Graham Greene, in *The Potting Shed*, shows the terrifying mystery of a priest who asks God for a miracle—the life of a beloved person whom he believes dead—proposing to him a most risky transaction: "Grant me what I ask and take from me what I love most" (I cite here without having the text). God grants him the miracle and takes his faith. It is masterfully made evident that the priest is left without faith, but he feels that *it has been taken from him*. Terrible the adventure in which what is risked by those who try to take Heaven by assault, whether in a passionate, momentary rapture, like Greene's priest, or through persistent scrutiny, or in a groping attempt at—which is also a tempting of—Heaven, a constant palpitating, probing, manipulating that ends up turning perseverance into habit, withering the passional impulse, turning it into domestic, daily, marital commerce. Another modern author . . . *Vade retro, austère Jean-Jacques*, you cannot tempt me because forty years ago I said I, I, I, and I am not going to take it back. It was I, I, "ne vous déplaise," who said, in 1960, in the words of a masculine character who, nevertheless, "c'ést moi," a defiant "You don't have me fooled" to the God hidden behind the glacier of his dead faith.

It's not from modesty that I insist on apologies without fear of being impertinent, but I'm studying Unamuno and, according to Marías, in my work I continue the line of the personal novel. Which is true, in fact; consequently, and because continuing a line is a fundamental point, to which I will return later, I've allowed myself this digression by alluding to that ungraspable phenomenon of *suspicious doubt*.

An ancient brooch or bracelet—very well known and exploited by industry today—consists of a gold or bronze ring, split, with facing ram's heads on the two ends. A shape, for the symbolist, saves many words, or the opposite, unleashes a torrent of words to gloss, sing about it, possess, or wring it out, all the more to bring to light the obscure suggestions of which it might be a cipher. For example, Unamuno's personal style as a novelist makes a circle of his ramlike obstinacy. To quote Marías: "Neither system, then, nor aphorism, but the reiteration of scattered moments. Such is the dynamic and permanent unity of Don Miguel de Unamuno's thought." A dynamic and permanent unity that tries to enclose in its circle the agonizing theory of persons; but the ring does not achieve a homogeneous integrity without beginning or end. There is a duplicity in its dynamism that prevents the repose of the complete circle. "Unamuno," according to Sánchez Barbudo, "joins in one two problems that have little to do with each other, but that, in truth, had much in common in him. And those two problems charge at each other in the two extremes of his oeuvre, *Amor y pedagogía* and *San Manuel Bueno, mártir*. Except they charge, without colliding, they are face to face, the circle does not close in the roundness of a consequent structure. The two rams look at each other, emitting the sparks of their never-reposing power."

"The root of the problem of personality in both Don Manuel and Unamuno," according to Sánchez Barbudo, "was the feeling of Nothingness, the intuition of their own death . . . and their transformation of the certainty of discontinuity into the 'problem' of continuity was the principal source of the second problem, that of sincerity, of the ongoing identity of the outer, visible aspect of one's own person." In both novels under discussion here, those two problems are polarized; although not entirely discrete, they are definitely distinguishable, because the question of personality is so important and integral to each book. In *San Manuel Bueno* what predominates is a feeling of the end, with no hope, since here there is no problem of insincerity, despite the diametrical opposition between Don Manuel's outer, visible being and his true, inner feelings. The outer face is the purest expression possible of his love for his village. He adopts it consciously, in other words, it is the face of his consciousness, and the other—nothingness—the intuition of his own death is the nucleus, the seed of his soul. The two things are one and the same, not two distinct things, not even one ambiguous thing, but one thing that has its within and its without.

Insincerity is the predominant problem in *Amor y pedagogía*. The idea of death sustains and stalks the novel—if it were not so stalked, this would not be a novel by Unamuno—from beginning to end, although its presence is not felt at the beginning, as if the book were not going to address death, as if it were going to be only about life. And it is, in truth, about *making* a life. The supposed protagonist—the novel's entire ambiguity is distilled in the simple fact that the supposed protagonist is not the real one, the one responsible for everything that is going to happen. Poor Avito wants to direct, wants to demonstrate, to display a child and announce his presence from the moment of his conception (compare this endeavor to Rousseau's: to educate and instruct a nonexistent creature, one incapable of the least autonomous reaction, one constructed with a perfect paucity of feelings), wants to select the maternal matter beforehand and deposit in it the appropriate seed. From the very beginning, Avito, the character, strays from his author, acting more sanely than the author's instructions. Because if Unamuno shows us Avito's senseless rationalism, already anticipating—the author or, better, every author adapts or guides the reader's mind with the first words, for the sake of the proposed outcome—his inevitable disaster, Avito falls irrationally in love with a woman who receives the seed—normally and, for that reason, irrationally deposited—in her simple matter. And she harbors it until it matures, with nothing more than an abundant dose of kidney beans and a few equally harmless music lessons.

Why is that organism, which cannot be called ill-bred, annulled by his father's theories, which are as innocuous as kidney beans? Unamuno tries to show that a child needs to be raised with maternal love, tenderness, and caresses, just as a mother needs to envelop her child in that same tenderness. To demonstrate that, he sets us before Marina lavishing her kisses on Luisito (Apolodoro)—her Luisito, the name she's given him in secret—so that Apolodoro lacks neither an affectionate private name nor maternal contact. As for the rest, the dietary plan and the hygienic routine to which his father submits Apolodoro would not hurt a flea; nevertheless the poor fellow grows up having little vitality and a confused psyche, even though his growth is not stunted, so that he cannot be considered a feeble mess. Poor Apolodoro succumbs because Unamuno has to show that Avito's *passion* was deadly. Because only in Avito is a passion revealed. Passion sweeps some people off their feet, nails others, leaves them in their places, hypnotizes them to such an extent that they're left insensible to all contact—to the needle that pierces their arms, to the flame that approaches their faces. Passion can be an impetus and it can be a snare. But Unamuno does not want to admit Avito's fixation on science as a passion. He wants to show us that Avito "is a poor imbecile," and he shows this by putting him in the hands of Don Fulgencio who, in his vast wisdom, helps him to succumb.

Don Fulgencio does not approve of Avito's theories, but neither does he fight them; he does not take even one step to help either the father or the son out of his predicament, because when he ends up opening his heart to Apolodoro—in a sort of *Profession de foi*—all he does is reveal the mystery of Herostratism. And it is here that, according to Sánchez Barbudo, the two problems join in one; being different, they never merge, but there is reciprocal justification, one of them finding its motivation in the other. "Yes, Apolodoro . . . we don't believe in the immortality of the soul and death terrifies us, terrifies all of us, and the prospect of nothingness, of what lies beyond the grave, of the eternal void grieves us all and embitters our hearts." "And since we don't believe in the immortality of the soul, we dream of leaving a name, of being talked about, of living in the memory of others. Poor life!" "Here you see me, Apolodoro, here you see me swallowing my sorrows, trying to attract attention whatever way I can, acting eccentric. You see me here meditating day and night on eternity, on unattainable eternity, and with no children . . . with no children, Apolodoro, with no children . . ."

Don Fulgencio's confession is long and the theme of children, as a yearning for perpetuation, is repeated and remains as a conclusion or a corollary to his long sermon: "Make children, Apolodoro, make children . . ." So that poor Apolodoro was engendered under the prior mandate to be a genius and he failed to become one. Don Fulgencio showed him the foolishness of such a mandate and replaced it with another: "Make children." In Don Fulgencio's mind, or rather in his particular formula, sterility—Herostratism—is the predominant note; he wants to eternalize himself, because he does not want to die, "no, no, I am not resigned to dying, I am not resigned . . . and I will die!" He says, of course, that he wants to live, but he does not prove that, that is, he does not place the image of life before Apolodoro's eyes as though it were the image of his beloved. Life does not enchain him with its charms, enjoying life is not what he wants. With or without the author's intention . . . ? It's difficult to say, but in fact Don Fulgencio does seem not to have known life's enjoyments.

Life, in all of Unamuno's work—perhaps in all work—is represented by woman and the woman assigned to Don Fulgencio is repulsive. She wears a wig—at the time the novel was written, wearing a wig indicated baldness—and her charms are limited to Apolodoro's observations, *in mente*, on his way to their house, where he will see "Doña Edelmira, and what a fine body, even now! So rosy and plump! And what a wig!" In other words, the enjoyment that life has offered Don Fulgencio, rather the enjoyment he has sought, since there's no reason to think that he suffered paternal coercion, consists of delighting in Doña Edelmira's plump flesh. His aspiration to immortality is not—as Diotima made clear, categorically—"a desire to engender" but a fear of what lies beyond the grave, not an *impulse* for eternity, but the adoption of its substitute, continued life in the memory of others; not impregnating them by losing himself in their lives, with the certainty of *touching* eternity in them, but by astonishing them, with the goal of impressing on their memories, in that inferior, degraded form of memory, the recollecting of the eccentric. The strange, the other, the sterile. Poor Apolodoro, who was hardly docile with respect to his father's commands, diligently sets out to comply with what Don Fulgencio asks of him. Although he is not without a flicker of true desire, since he failed to fulfill that desire in a pure way, at a time when it could have been said appropriately that "[h]umanity starts to sing within him . . . eternity is revealed to him live, the world acquires meaning in his eyes, his heart has found its path, without his having to gallop wildly over the field," he obediently makes a child with the servant-girl and then hangs himself.

Naturally, Apolodoro's end greatly affects Don Fulgencio, leaving him with a remorseful conscience and the fear that his explanation of Herostratism precipitated the boy's moral collapse. That remorse on Don Fulgencio's part is not misplaced, since there is no doubt that he precipitated that end, not, however, in the conversation that preceded the confidential and sorrowful conversation, but in the one that began when Apolodoro went to see him to get his opinion about the short story he had published. "'Well, Apolodoro, you got what you deserved,'" Don Fulgencio tells him.

"A failure, a complete failure. But that's no matter. You wanted to be an artist? You got what you deserve. Because don't think that I've failed to realize that your principal concern has been form, execution, style . . ."

"Art consists in form."

"In form? In form, you say? Knowing your craft . . . knowing your craft . . . That's so measly! What counts, as they say, is thinking high and feeling deep and overlooking . . ."

"But that prevents . . ."

"Yes, don't go on, that prevents it, yes, that prevents it. I know what you were going to say, if a lofty thought or a deep feeling loses its loftiness or its depth if it's not well expressed. Isn't that it?"

"I think they're enhanced."

"Then you think poorly, Apolodoro, you think poorly. They lose, they lose their loftiness or depth by being well expressed . . . You tried to be classical . . . A lot of good it's done you! The classical is repugnant; knowledge of craft is repugnant. Shakespeare blended with Racine would be absurd. Art is something inferior, low, despicable, despicable, Apolodoro, despicable," etc.

What happens to the harmless precepts of Apolodoro's father when they meet up with those harebrained maxims, to which are added those of his friend the poet and critic Menaguti, who, on another occasion, waits for him so he can encourage him to take revenge? "'You let that weak-willed wimp steal your girlfriend? And you do nothing about it?'

'So what am I going to do?'

'What? It's clear your genitor has stuffed you with science, that infamous hogwash that, along with religion, is the cause of our ruin. "The wise and the rich are no good for anything but mutually corrupting each other." I've just read that in Rousseau.'" Such is the other long conversation in which poor Apolodoro swallows a strong dose of Rousseauian resentment.

In truth, Apolodoro does succumb because of his failure, but it is not at all clear that his failure was irreparable. A hopeless failure occurs only in a person who lacks the mettle to insist until he "knows his craft," until his loftiness and depth—things so difficult to bring to light—manage to be "well expressed." And Apolodoro does not lack depth—the loftiness that consists in depth is the most laudable—as he shows in a few paragraphs of a soliloquy in which he accuses himself, after having obeyed Don Fulgencio, seducing the servant-girl. "'I'm a vile wretch; I've done something disgraceful. Farewell, my mother, my phantom! I leave you in the world of shadows, I go to the world of forms; you remain among appearances, I will sleep in the bosom of the only everlasting reality . . . Farewell, Clara, my Clara, my Dark One, my dear disenchantment! You were able to rescue a man from pedagogy, make a man from a candidate for genius . . . make men, men of flesh and blood; make them with your life companion, in love, in love and not through pedagogy! Genius, oh, genius! The genius is born, not made, and he is born from an embrace more intimate, more loving, more deeply felt than all the others, he is born from a pure moment of love, of pure love. I'm sure of that; he is born from an impulse, the most unconscious. As they engender a genius, his parents lose consciousness; only those who lose consciousness when they make love, those who make love as if dreaming, without a shade of awareness, engender geniuses.'" Here for a moment Apolodoro assumes his father's spirit, wrapping his plans for suicide in sarcastic self-confidence and surpassing that spirit as he demonstrates his theoretical powers. "'What a pity that my obligation to resign tomorrow does not allow me to develop this luminous theory!'" And he continues: "'As they engender a genius, his parents must lapse into unconsciousness; the person who knows what he's doing as he makes a child will not make him a genius. What might my father have been thinking about as he engendered me? About karyokinesis or something like that, I'm certain; about pedagogy, definitely about pedagogy; my mind tells me that! And so I've turned out . . . I'm a vile wretch, a disgrace, I've done something disgraceful . . . !'"

Clearly there is something missing from the conversations with Don Fulgencio that prepare Apolodoro to die in such an unfortunate way. Before that, though, in the context of the novel, there is an incident that I'm surprised not to find addressed by any of the critics I've read. Unamuno himself seems to deal with it only in passing, but I find it quite important, and it's the death or, rather, the life and death of Don Avito Carrascal and Marina's little girl. Why does this child of poor Avito die before her time, when he has not put his sinful hands on his creation? It isn't because he did not engender her: about that there's no doubt, but he has not tried to create her. "The second child that Marina gave Avito was a girl. He has neither weighed nor measured her, nor opened a file when she was born, what for? A daughter? Carrascal thinks again about the question of feminism, which he has never been able to grasp. A daughter? Deep down inside, the thing, the daughter, that is, vexes him." The after-dinner discussions long ago in the boarding house with his faithful Sinforiano come back to him: "'The purpose of woman is to give birth to men, and for that purpose she must be educated. I think of her, my friend Sinforiano, as soil to receive the seed, soil that will bear fruit, which is why you have to nourish her, just as you have to nourish soil . . . Yes, nourish her: with a lot of air, a lot of sun, a lot of water . . . Consequently, I believe that it is principally the woman who should devote herself to physical education . . .'" All of those precepts Avito inculcates in Marina.

"And the little girl, Rosa—because Avito now permits his wife to be the one who names the child, what does it matter what a woman's name is?—grows up alongside Apolodoro, grows up spoiled, tied to her mother's apron strings. And she starts to walk and to speak earlier than her brother did."

"'I'm surprised by it all, Don Fulgencio; the girl seems more alert than the boy . . .'

'The more inferior the species, my friend Carrascal, the sooner it reaches maturity; the higher up you go on the zoological scale, the slower the development of the offspring.'"

Unamuno does not present that assertion in a humorous vein; he allows Don Fulgencio to formulate his thesis about soil and women, in which the latter seem to be found at an elementary level of the zoological scale, an affirmation that has nothing to do with feminism—neither for nor against—but with the most basic notion of these issues. To say that the female of an animal species is found at a different level of evolution than the male is a blunder that Unamuno comes out with because of his Rousseauian disdain for science, the same way that someone says "by Jupiter!" without the least thought of blasphemy. It doesn't matter that a few lines above he has said that "the purpose of woman is to give birth to men"; now he can say that she's on a lower level of the zoological scale.

When Rosita, a very capricious child, cries, her father says, "'Let her cry, woman; let her cry, that's how her lungs will develop. Let her exercise them by crying. When she wakes up she's full of nervous tension and she needs to release it, which she does by crying.'"

Avito bears no guilt because the precepts that govern the raising of his little girl are quite sensible and quite natural. Also, Marina's loving transports, unhampered by any prohibitions, amply nourish her with tenderness. Thus, time passes—without the timid little child uttering a word of protest—Apolodoro reaches puberty—naturally, the girl as well—Apolodoro struggles with his bad fortune and the young girl begins to die. The reader is not warned because he has not been witness to a life affected by any sort of disease, but from the first time that Rosa's poor health is mentioned he realizes that her illness is fatal. No one knows what that illness is; there's talk of chlorosis, something that has little to do with nourishing the soil, and less with the daughter of a woman who in the bloom of her youth was so beautiful that Avito was *bowled over*. But the fact is, the girl leaves this world, lamented by her mother and brother with sentimental, heart-breaking phrases that, instead of breaking the reader's heart, cause him a rather embarrassing shiver, and in a few pages the sad story ends.

Why does this minimal episode arise among Avito's adventures? It's not like the novels inserted in the *Quixote* because there is no novel surrounding little Rosita. Her brief existence has no purpose other than to prompt sundry explanations of erroneous scientific maxims, with no explanation why they're wrong. Don Avito has turned his attention to his daughter, to Rosita, the "nourished" one, who sweetly and sadly leads a languid life of silence and chlorosis, despite all the nourishing and the exercised lungs. And her father begins to fight with a rebellious temperament, to change it using scientific procedures, because science . . . Oh, science.

"But in spite of science, the little girl deteriorates at full gallop, is confined to her bed, and things take their course. Her father fights desperately, but serenely and calmly, having recovered his former resolve and assisted in his task by Don Antonio, until one day, now convinced that science is impotent in this case, he sees that Death is approaching the young girl's bed."

Marina's little daughter, so much hers, since Avito never contended for her, has fulfilled her mission, providing a reason for so many curses against science, that god or demon in whom Unamuno did not believe. But we have already seen how Unamuno is stalked by the gods in whom he does not believe, we have already seen the triviality of his curses and the depth of his *suspicions*. In Don Fulgencio's last conversation with Apolodoro, the repudiated god outlines a vague revelation. First, as a preamble, we could say in a continual *prophetic* state, Don Fulgencio expounds a poetic theory—poetry, herald of prophecy. He shows Apolodoro the list of famous men, with the number of years lived, an inventory he's made, "'in order,'" he says, "'to find the average and learn how long I'm likely to live.'" He also shows him a drawer filled with papers; the plans for his future work: "'Until I finish all of these projects I will not die,'" he says. "'And can't have faith . . . ,'" he adds, "'can't have faith in my immortality! Why shouldn't I be the first man who doesn't die? Is death really a metaphysical necessity? And I made up that joke about anyone who has faith, robust and absolute faith that he's never going to die, faith without one instant of a spark of doubt, will not die. But woe to him if he has a single moment of doubt, no matter how fleeting!'" (Here Unamuno recalls the sentence of Joseph Glanvill that Poe uses as the epigraph for "Ligeia": "Man doth not yield himself to the angels, nor unto death utterly, save only through the weakness of his feeble will." That's improbable: Unamuno agrees with him because poetry is governed by an exactitude comparable only with that of science.) "'I often played like that, devising those jokes with the terrible specter. You know that nothing gets lost . . .'

'Law of the conservation of energy, transformation of force . . . ,' Apolodoro murmurs.

'Nothing gets lost, not matter, or energy, or movement, or form. Every impression that strikes our brains is registered there and, even though we might forget those impressions, and even if we weren't aware of them as we received them, there they remain. . . . Everything that enters us through our senses remains in us, in the unfathomable sea of our subconscious; there the whole world lives, there all the past, our parents and parents' parents are there, and their parents in an unending series . . .'

'What?'

'Yes, let me dream. Don't we inherit our parents' features, organs, race, species? Because we inherit everything; we carry our fathers within, except that their most insignificant traits, their most personal peculiarities are submerged in the deepest recesses of our subconscious . . . So when the spirit-man emerges within our grandchildren's grandchildren, when he is all consciousness, his whole organism reflects consciousness, when he is conscious of the life of the last one of his cells, and of its spirit, then in those grandchildren his parents and the parents of his parents will rise again, we will all rise again in our descendents . . .'

'How beautiful,' Apolodoro says without thinking.

'Beautiful, yes, but is the beautiful true? And those of us who don't have children, Apolodoro? Here's the problem that has always tortured me. Those of us who don't have children reproduce ourselves in our works, which are our children; our spirit is passed into each one of them and everyone who receives our work receives us whole. And how do I know if when I die and my body decomposes one of my cells won't be freed and, turned into an amoeba, won't propagate with it in my consciousness? Because my consciousness is in me wholly and wholly in each one of my cells. This, Apolodoro, is the mystery of the human Eucharist . . .'"

In those long paragraphs, almost two pages of the novel, ambiguity and sarcasm disappear. Don Fulgencio says, "'I often played like that, devising those jokes with the terrible specter,'" but the game is neither malicious nor deceptive—it's a hopeful game. Don Fulgencio plays, bets on *human power*, because he—Unamuno—hopes that someday, that Eucharist, which *is found* in the cells since the cells *are found there*, here, and anywhere, his consciousness will come to be reflected by the spirit-man, "when he is all consciousness, his whole organism reflects consciousness." Stupendous futurition on the part of a blasphemed god supremely obstinate in his endeavor to *haunt* Unamuno's mind.

From the three studies of Unamuno's work discussed in the preceding paragraphs I've been able to gather several comments, enough to chart my course. It's been hard to select the essential points; not only are the books long and nuanced, in truth, they form a whole and the most important things are scattered throughout all three. Since I agree with them, I don't have anything of my own to add. I do, however, want to add a brief comment that occurred to me as I tried to imagine the echo the three *portraits* might awaken in Don Miguel's mind, because they possess the mysterious reach of the telephoto lens as it reveals a bird's secret nest or the distant battle of two beasts. Unamuno's entire inner jungle is examined in those three books, and Sánchez Barbudo is generally considered to have revealed Unamuno's most fearsome demons. That does seem to be the case; he undoubtedly offers us the most startling secrets. But would his account surprise Unamuno more than the others? I think not. Sánchez Barbudo's book would not tell Unamuno anything new. It might make him exclaim with a bit of ill humor: What an indiscreet fellow! On the other hand...

Marías begins his *Miguel de Unamuno*: "Reading Unamuno, especially working through several of his books, one after the other, creates a strange impression... at every moment we seem to find what we're seeking, or at least the promise that its appearance is imminent. We might not find a single page disappointing, but when we close the last volume we feel thoroughly confused." In "Dispersión y unidad" [Dispersion and Unity], the second section of his first chapter, Marías comes up with a perfect definition, which I cited earlier: "Neither system, then, nor aphorism, but the reiteration of scattered moments. Such is the dynamic and permanent unity of Don Miguel de Unamuno's thought." In the third section, "Preocupación filosófica" [Philosophical Concern], Marías points out how Unamuno approaches philosophical themes and "the other men who have addressed those themes, and who are sometimes religious men, sometimes theologians, but principally philosophers... and thus Unamuno finds himself immersed in the problems of the history of philosophy... and consequently in philosophy itself... and in fact, those references and those citations prove to be a matter of erudition, a simple collection of opinions, and the issue could also be one of intellectual curiosity, of a keen sense of history, of the *voluptuousness* of penetrating the manner of thinking or the biographies of the finest philosophical minds. But Unamuno is a hundred leagues from those two attitudes; the erudition and *delight* of historicism were always equally foreign to him; rather, he stood out because of his profound aversion to the first and something of an incapacity for the second." (The emphasis is mine because those points deserve a long explanation.)

Marías continues with "Literatura y filosofía" [Literature and Philosophy], followed by "El tema de Unamuno" [Unamuno's Theme], the second chapter. There he explains "the sole question," and then addresses "Razón y vida" [Reason and Life]. The currents of thought that precede Unamuno Marías condenses by pointing out that

"Intelligence is characterized by a natural incomprehension of life" (Bergson), and he adds: "[t]his philosophy, based on intuition and on its proximity to vital reality, has been extraordinarily fruitful for contemporary thought, but from its beginnings it has been affected by the danger of irrationalism. In order for intuition to become authentic knowledge, it must be conceptualized and to be reason, in a strict sense; and this Bergsonian thought does not achieve."

"Long before Bergson, though, Kierkegaard had stated the problem, and in a dimension much closer to the center of Unamuno's concern." "The same thing happens with existence as with movement, and it's very difficult to deal with. If I think about them, I annul them, and therefore I don't think about them. So it might seem accurate to say that there is something that cannot be thought about: existence. But that leaves the difficulty of existence and thought occurring at the same time, since one who thinks exists." "The problem," Marías says, "is stated clearly, but it's a long way from being resolved. Unamuno will take it up at this point, but he won't be able to find a metaphysical solution for it either."

"Intelligence is a terrible thing," he [Unamuno] says. "It tends toward death as memory tends toward stability. In the strict sense, any living thing, anything absolutely unstable, anything absolutely individual is unintelligible.... The intellect aspires to identity, which is death. The mind seeks death, but the living thing escapes it; the mind wants to halt the fugitive current in floes, wants to freeze it." "How, then, will reason open to the revelation of life?" To those quotes selected from Unamuno, Marías adds: "It would be hard to find the problem expressed more concisely, densely, and accurately, exactly as it was felt at the time in European philosophy.... Unamuno's work is essentially conditioned, one could say negatively, that is, limited by the state of knowledge when he reached maturity, and he is affected by the temporality of that very specific form."

Consider the angry fright and irritation that those assertions would have caused Unamuno. If we imagine an Unamuno beyond the grave, now purified by contemplating Truth, we can believe that he would receive them calmly, but if we imagine a "flesh and blood" Unamuno, the one who did not want to die, seeing himself detached from— almost an enemy of—that living thought, from revitalized, we could say nourished reason, not threatened by chlorosis, but fighting, full of omnivorous appetite; combined with a dynamic and fertile memory—Mnemosyne, she of heavenly births—and with a loving tutelage that enters through the eyes . . . Too loving? It is never too loving, even if it leads us to die of love. This is what we learn from Unamuno—not in his Don Manuel Bueno, but in his Don Manuel Terrible, the one from *Vida de don Quijote y Sancho*, and who would dare to undertake that study?—but he was not able to know the fruits of the love of reason since birthed by pedagogy.

Marías continues: "It's important to realize that—save exceptional cases—the major characteristics of a thinker's intellectual formation are defined at a particular moment in his life, which can occur between thirty and fifty years of age. After that time, the ideas he acquires are certainly incorporated into his intellectual capital, but now they fall into a different category; rather than living ideas that inform his thought they are things he knows, material he has learned but not effective principles that serve him as a way to understand reality." What Marías says is very true; only exceptional natures are able to incorporate the meaning of a reality and also remain on its margin, its banks. And that ability does not tell us the degree of their genius—assuming that genius is measurable—but reveals the quality or type of the drive that propels them: their futurity. Nor does that ability show us what they might be made of, because the future finds its substance in stones. The only thing we can see in a continual adherence to, or refusal of, the life of thought—as in the fear of a flowing stream that on its banks deposits the mud that will have to fuse with the soil—the only thing we can determine from this is whether the drive that propels those exceptional natures is an *impulse* for eternity or a *longing* to last.

I need to summarize, which is very difficult, less because of the technical difficulty—which is large—than because of the difficult restraint required. Reflecting on what I have noted so far, considering the topic I proposed or, rather, that imposed itself, I find it hard not to keep gleaning down to the last stubble. But I will stop because a little more would add nothing, a great deal more would be unbearable, and everything would be impossible.

To find out why there are so few confessions in Spanish literature, I began by meditating on what confession is, referring to the greatest confessants from the past. But then I searched the outstanding works of Spanish literature and found quite a few confessions by their authors. Nevertheless, in all of those works one senses a sort of reserve, not always voluntary, rather something like an opaqueness that makes certain areas impenetrable. That opaqueness might seem to be caused by an innate modesty—naturally innate, in the way that the Spanish pride commonly called touchy is innate, or acquired through precepts related to morality and religion, or to caste, sex, virility, manliness, etc. Of course all of those elements usually inhibit or strangle confession, but if we focus on the confessional aspects found in my first three examples, that is, if we meditate in earnest on what confession is, essentially, we will be able to glimpse—although only as a phantom—the absence gliding over their visible lives.

In confession, whether spontaneous or reluctant and concealed, there are two categories that occupy the foreground, for observation, and the background, for meditation. Those two categories, which are faith and love, form the starting point of confessions and the drive that propels them. In short, what gives rise to confession is the vital disquiet of both categories, when their uneasiness affects one's personal life and makes it necessary to distance them, banish them so that one's conscience can calm down by reflecting on them. Not in hope of reassurance—rather, so that one's conscience can stabilize, settle, or become fixed—so it will know what to abide by, which can lead it to accuse or sentence itself.

In the preceding paragraphs, I've made a point of stressing that the important thing in confession is not the deeds recounted; nevertheless, in the great confessions we see that the conflictive secret of each of the men whose confession we heard informs his entire life. This relation between inner conflict and real life consists, fundamentally, in something that we could call its qualitative orientation; a tendency that gives color, aroma, and flavor to both deeds done, and those not done. In other words, its imponderable but certain, unchangeable, unmistakable, irreplaceable quality.

Another thing I must point out is that I proposed to search for confession in Spanish literature, and the writers I chose from the past are not novelists, although as writers they are extraordinary. Rousseau is the one who most clearly tried his hand at the novel, but in all three writers we find that a *world* stands out, one whose core seems to be the conflict they confess. With respect to Spanish writers, I believe that the path leading to their phantasmagoric, elusive confession lies in the confrontation between the worlds of their novels and the secret motive or consistency in their lives.

As I've said above, I believe that Cervantes is the only one who truly confessed. Don Quixote bears his world within himself, hermetically sealed. It seems strange to me that Unamuno, basing himself on the *Quixote*'s evident superiority over the rest of Cervantes's work, allows that it might be the chronicle of an external deed, the story written by an Arabian historian and found by Cervantes. Of course Unamuno affirms nothing; he leaves the case in the ambiguous area of what he calls a "historical character." In his *Vida de don Quijote y Sancho* he gets rid of Cervantes and *appropriates* Don Quixote: this was the greatest glory that Cervantes could attain. In my few paragraphs, I too try to appropriate him, since the Unamunian system is highly reliable. But I can't manage to see *my* Don Quixote except within Cervantes. I don't see Don Quixote, Unamuno says, as a knight of the faith, out to conquer faith and glory. It's true that Don Quixote talks to Sancho about Herostratus, but not the way that Don Fulgencio talks to Apolodoro. He doesn't tell him, this is the illness we suffer from; rather, he points to it as the illness from which many, and Sancho himself, suffered, since Don Quixote alludes to Herostratus when Sancho tells him that slander doesn't matter a bit to him: "'But let them say what they want; naked I was born, naked I find myself. I neither lose nor win; even if I see myself placed in books and passing through this world from one hand to another, I don't give a damn if they say whatever they want about me.'" To combat that position, Don Quixote tells the story about the woman who wanted to be included in a poet's satire, even if she was flayed there; her story is followed by that of Herostratus and then a long string of illustrious men who threw themselves into the conquest of fame, concluding that "'we Christians, Catholics, and knights errant must attend more to the glory of future centuries, a glory eternal in the ethereal and heavenly spheres, than to the vanity of such fame as one can achieve in the present and terminable century . . . therefore, oh, Sancho, our works must not exceed the limit placed on us by the Christian religion we profess.'" A list of goals follows: "'We must kill the pride in giants; the envy in generosity and courage; the ire in a calm countenance, etc.'"

Unamuno maintains that Cervantes did not write *Don Quixote* with the objective of improving morality and justice, which is obvious; he did not include those elements because he didn't need them. He included, solely, the image of perfect purity, the purity that can be perfect only in the eternity of an instant. Don Quixote had no existence—permanent, temporal life—other than the power of memory, the deity that keeps alive the flash of a moment like "lightning unceasing." How long was the blaze that was Don Quixote? Who could reckon that? It might have lasted no longer than the flash of the scimitar—or the blunderbuss, I don't have enough information to say—that clipped off Cervantes's hand. But then, in captivity—the first, in Algiers and the second, in Spain, in Valladolid, in the dungeon of abandonment and misery—Don Quixote lived his unfortunate adventures for a long time, holding on like an unfading lily or like a flame against the wind. If there was Herostratism in Don Quixote, we would laugh at him and Unamuno is so right to say that the *Quixote* makes you weep. Of course Unamuno weeps for Herostratus; I don't share that feeling with him. The *Quixote* makes you weep because only crucified truth deserves tears.

I said at the beginning that, Don Quixote being love, as Maeztu noted, is a love that asks only for honor. Unamuno hurls a few insults against the feeling of honor—which does not prevent him from being Calderonian—but the honor for which Don Quixote longs is nothing more than a brotherhood he assumes is found in the sublime, which he grants to all men. It's good—better than good—to dust off our moth-eaten idols, to throw out the ones that today *are* a heap of worm-eaten splinters, but in order to save what they *were*. What they *were* is the only thing that's eternal; there is no past for what truly *is*. If the honor in which we once believed *had never been* anything, it would be better if we had remained discreetly silent. But today we can give only a simple definition of honor. Honor *is*—I mean it *was*, when it *was* and if it doesn't continue *being* that, it *is* nothing—honor *is* the feeling that man has about himself when he realizes that he is "the animal that can make a promise." Don Quixote's honor *consists*, above all, in *fidelity*. Times have changed a great deal, but Don Quixote prevails—because he's a fountain, not a pond—faithful to himself, even though an era might exploit his abundance, sometimes channeling the flow for the most equivocal and inappropriate uses, which is inevitable but in fact unimportant; squander does not diminish the abundance of his truth—about this, Unamuno agrees.

But my aim is not to write one more study of the *Quixote*, which would be an aspiration both excessive and unnecessary. I'm trying to show that the *Quixote* is the only Spanish work that has no blind spot, no opaqueness or rampart, no limit on its being because it is a truth confessed. Theorizing, advocating, or preaching that truth—faith and love, in fidelity and purity—would have been much less efficient (let's not forget that Don Quixote is a symbol of inefficiency, but Cervantes created him, aware that he, his creation, was maximum efficiency), less fertile than *taking the being of that truth*, clothing him in insanity, thus armoring him, leaving him secure, invulnerable, defenseless in his madness, and giving him time, that is, to suffer. His Christian being, as I've said, tied to the post, his human person drubbed and kicked by the world, permanent purveyor of shame and temporal pain.

In Galdós, confession is unattainable because Galdós lacks "the tragic sense of life." That does not mean there is no tragic sense in Galdós's work, what I mean is that in his work you don't glimpse a life—the author's—whose sense is tragic. Both categories, faith and love, whose pressure, as I've said, make the dike of confession overflow, seem to fill Galdós's life no more than moderately. I regret not having access to the sources about the traumas in Galdós's childhood or adolescence that Gullón alludes to in his study, but I believe that the opening paragraph of the chapter titled "El descenso a los infiernos" [Descent into Hell] is appropriate here. "Confessions," Gullón says, "even the most sincere, often conceal the most essential thing. Huge crimes, according to one expert, are confessed with less difficulty than acts of pettiness. It's harder to admit that you're a miser than to say you're a murderer. Some character defects seem to lionize and even enhance the person who suffers from them; others prove diminishing. It's easy to declare yourself guilty of arrogance, anger, harshness, indifference to ordinary laws, an indifference—or pride admitted gladly—as a label that reveals a destiny different from that of everyone else; it's difficult for us to confess that we're obsessed by trifles, destroyed by seeing in our neighbor what's lacking in ourselves."

With that paragraph, Gullón ventures into the blackest abyss in Unamuno's soul—envy, forged by Unamuno, that is, converted into oeuvre, into its own forge. And with those few lines by Gullón, which are as applicable to one of Spain's two great novelists as the other, I have enough to affirm without hesitation that if they did not confess it was because they lived *unconfessable lives*. Very different, those two lives, very different the two absent confessions because absence, in Galdós's life, is total, whereas in Unamuno's it is only like a dark silent point in the violent clamor of an agonic life; a small locked door in the basement, covered by the cobwebs that testify to his uncompromised aloofness. Later, we will try to force that door; for the moment, let's speak again about Galdós.

In Galdós there is a conscious intention not to confess, which is consistent with his unconscious lack of the need to confess. Those two sides, manifest and concealed, of his character provide the key to what is achieved and what is not in his work. In his *Vida y obra de Galdós*, speaking of Galdós's trip to Madrid, Casalduero comments: "It's hard to say good-bye, and good-byes are always unpleasant for someone unaccustomed to making his feelings public, both because he's guarded about himself and because of a natural inclination toward humor." The combination of those two motives forms a compound that we can consider the timbre or consistency of Galdós. One pays no attention to the first, his being "guarded about himself," unless the feelings are expressed in a ridiculous way, or for the explicit or hidden purpose of public show, but if we focus on it solely, it could have a dramatic quality or tension, as the effect of an unyielding pride. Here, though, "the natural inclination toward humor" tempers the atmosphere of that reserve. And it does so as diabolic contact—not by lowering the temperature, but by piercing it through with an icy, recurrent, and sterilizing gust. To that chemical makeup of Galdós's character we can attribute his conscious decision not to confess, but it does not explain the unconscious lack of an *urge*—I use that term here to indicate the vital movement of a spiritual process. Galdós feels no urge to confess because the two categories mentioned above exert no pressure on his soul, which is where confession presses. And of those two categories, the less forceful in the Galdosian formula is Faith. The frequent presence of religious themes in his work gives us the key to his fondness for comfort because, more than being accommodating—although he is that too—he is naturally comfortable. Agonic faith is something that Galdós never experienced.

It might seem risky to accuse works like *Nazarín*, for example, of being lukewarm with respect to religion, since in that novel sacrifice and martyrdom reach a maximum. Sacrifice and martyrdom, however, are perfectly delineated, not a single detail is missing from the extreme situations they attain, in other words, they're perfectly clichéd. Every reaction on the part of Nazarín or his disciples is obvious, every incident or adventure is predictable as soon as it begins. Of course highly dramatic things do happen in the novel, but none of them reveals anything to us, none of them stands out from what's well known in similar cases.

Galdós sees Nazarín in the context of the Semitic type very abundant in Spain, a figure in whom impassivity and misfortune are inseparable. Nazarín is a character—Galdós's mastery of characters is supreme—to whom we would never think of referring as a *person*. Nazarín is a character, a figure with a determined nature who might or might not attain saintliness, being, in any case, the same figure, the same character. He is the same Semitic figure that Galdós places at the door of the church in *Misericordia* [Compassion]: an Arab beggar, covered with sores—though not so docile—as comfortable in Madrid's beggary as a fish in water. In *Nazarín*, above the protagonist's natural—we could say racial—character, spreads a system of ideas or voluntary, adopted or professed inclinations: the quest for poverty, for humiliation through begging, insults, and cruel treatment, exactly like the quest of seraphic Saint Francis as he walked the roadways with his little friars, seeking the *perfetta letizia*. Nazarín is, in my opinion, one of the most external figures in Galdós's work, seen mostly from without.

Bear in mind that Galdós begins his story on Shrove Tuesday, telling about a time that he and a journalist friend, "one of that new breed we refer to with the exotic term *'repórter*,'" visited a rundown boarding house or inn, hoping for some Goyesque revelry. Walking past the house next door, they see the strange priest who lives there at his window; they go in to speak with him and have a long conversation. To their numerous questions Nazarín answers "without giving any indication that he was annoyed by our tedious questioning. Nor did he seem arrogant, as one might naturally feel, finding himself the object of an interrogation or *interview*, as they're called nowadays." That interrogation fills the first part of the book, some thirty pages, and in them Nazarín confides his *Profession de foi* . . . , or so it seems. All of the Savoyard Vicar's denials and voluntary limitations are explained with Franciscan sweetness and Mohammedan impassivity. Nazarín tells them that he has no books; he's given them all away, "'because they have few benefits to offer the soul and the intellect. Things related to Faith are riveted deep in my spirit and neither commentaries nor paraphrases of doctrine have anything to teach me. And what good is everything else? Once you've added a few ideas to the knowledge you're born with, by dealing with people and observing society and Nature, there's no need to consult books for better instruction or new ideas that might confuse and complicate those ones you already have.'"

He ventures then into capricious hypotheses, basing them on the inflated production of print: "'There is so much written and so much published now that humanity will find itself drowning in monstrous amounts of print and have no choice but to abolish its entire past.'" "'Human memory is too small a barn for the fodder of history. Gentlemen, the time is coming when the present will totally take over life, and when the eternal truths acquired through revelation are the only things that man preserves from the past.'" "'At that time,' he added in a tone I don't hesitate to call prophetic, 'the Caesar, or whoever exercises authority, will issue a decree that reads as follows: The entire contents of all libraries, both public and private, are declared ineffectual, useless, and devoid of value except for that of their physical properties. Considering that chemists have found papyraceous substance, seasoned by time, to be the best of all fertilizers for the soil, we hereby command that books both ancient and modern be piled in large commons at the entrance to every town, so that residents of the agricultural community can take their share of precious matter that falls to them, according to the amount of land they have to till.'"

In that markedly ironic paragraph there is something like an involuntary intrusion on the part of the author. Nazarín does not speak ironically again in all the rest of the book. Profoundly serious and simple, he possesses the clearly defined concentration and distance that one reads in the features of an Arab, which is the sign under which Galdós read all of Nazarín. But by attributing that paragraph to him, Galdós confesses his skepticism, reluctantly, not as the result of an urge, but as if it were a game, since he does not believe in that skepticism either; his skepticism is modest—modest enough that he can confess it without feeling the urge. His futuristic caricature is not entirely misguided, since he suspects that, in some way, "'human memory is too small a barn,'" but he finds no solution to the problem except the destruction of the accumulated heritage, staunching the flow of human knowledge with one blow.

Galdós's Savoyard-like denial here is trivial, because it's such a caricature; Unamuno's denials are more caustic. More dramatic in the case of Don Manuel, more sarcastic in that of Don Fulgencio, who, even when he's not denying science he attacks common sense—front man for reason—with equivocal paradoxes not always enriched with poetic spark, as, for example when Don Fulgencio tells Apolodoro on learning that he's studying mathematics: "'Mathematics? It's like arsenic; prescribed sparingly, it fortifies, administered in abundance, it's lethal. And mathematics combined with common sense make a combustible and explosive compound: the *supervulgarine*. Mathematics? One . . . two . . . three . . . everything in a series; study history so you learn to see things in process, in flux. Mathematics and history are poles apart.'" "'I was telling you, my boy, don't spend much time with sensible souls, since anyone who never risks his fate, you can swear to it, is totally stupid. A special syringe for inoculating all our brains with a serum of four paradoxes, three embolisms, and a utopia and we're saved. Flee from their brutish constitution,'" etc. Those topics spring up in the work of both authors and they can seem like momentary outbursts, but they're something more because Unamuno, as I've noted, was obsessed with Galdós, not because he agreed with him—their temperaments are like oil and water—but because in Galdós he gathers the best seeds. Choosing them from the jungly tangle, the inexhaustible proliferation, he gathers and highlights them, isolates them in his hothouse, nourishes them with condensing substances, and subjects them to a high-speed centripetal acceleration before shining a powerful spotlight so as to highlight them on his black backdrop.

Unamuno would be furious if he heard his novels described as products of a hothouse, but, nevertheless, they clearly are. I must be careful, though, that what I'm doing here doesn't seem like literary criticism, because it's not, not at all. This is merely a search for a phenomenon that's almost impossible to grasp but that, like any phenomenon of the spirit—of the mind, the soul—has roots and branches, produces reflections, emits odors, and alters the temperature. One of the iridescent aspects of that phenomenon encompasses and fuses or mixes opposites, so harmoniously that the soldering is not noticeable; it allows tones to change from one to the other like a simple play of lights.

Adopting a minimum of neutral good sense so we aren't dazzled, let's consider the dates. *El amigo Manso* [Our Friend Manso], 1882, begins: "'I do not exist.'" "'I am (I'll phrase it obscurely so you'll understand it better) an artistic condensation, a diabolical creation of human thought (*ximia Dei*), which, if its fingers can get hold of a little style, uses it to start imitating the works in the physical world that God made from matter; I'm a new example of those forgeries of men that ever since time began travel the world, offered on the block by what I call idlers wholly lacking in filial responsibility but what the kindhearted masses call artists, poets, or something similar.'" *Niebla* was published in 1914, the character who declares that he does not exist now having existed for over twenty-five years. *Nazarín* appeared in May of 1895, and I believe it to be the last of Galdós's three novels that we could say shared a concentric composition. *El amigo Manso, Lo prohibido, Nazarín*. Those three novels, in my opinion, are Galdós's most *refined*, I mean they're his most carefully crafted. In *Nazarín*, the most external, craft is limited to focusing on a faithful copy of the model; the other two are much superior with respect to psychological nuance. Setting aside literary superiority—although it's something that cannot be set aside—what makes them superior is the fact that they don't copy the model in every detail, but, rather, that they analyze its dimensions within its own inward curve.

The personal novel begins there, but Galdós did not know that. Unamuno, knowingly or not, cultivated the unsociable plant and surrounded it with a thorny fence, his rigid and complicated style. When we speak about Unamuno, style means a very particular difficulty cubed—a difficulty is a lack, is something negative on which Unamuno bestows the density of a presence, the power and surliness of a fierce mastiff that stops the fearful in their tracks. In that enclosed space, Unamuno tended his seedbed of persons, feeding them all alike with the food of his personal substance. The tragic sense of his life was centered and rooted in the "sole question." Unamuno might have had doubts about himself, felt that he was shipwrecking in insincerity: it doesn't matter, that shipwreck spread his anguish throughout every Unamunian creature. They're all oriented in the direction of the "sole question." Consequently, his confession has the tone of a confidence given sincerely. Needless to say, he was never more sincere than when the secret confided was the drama of insincerity, because sincere confidence—which is what we're looking for here—exists only when confidence involves, in just proportion and perfect fusion, the inner conflict and the reality of life, experienced.

Unamuno's inner conflict invaded every act of his life. As "the sole question," the crux of his spiritual life, it also affected his material life or, more precisely, the materiality of his life affected it like a termite. But that element, "the sole question," by having an impact on spheres of consciousness such as authenticity, the ambiguous personality, and all the crossroads of mind or soul, encouraged them, focused them on themselves, inflated them with truth—even when dealing with doubt. The difficult thing is to see what happens when "the sole question" affected the materiality of life, because there are spheres—of the soul, for instance—in which the idea of materiality is ambiguous, but the idea of life is real, fundamental, essential. I'm referring to the second, although principal, category, love.

Am I designating love as the principal category, placing it before faith? Not exactly. The difficulty that I'm trying to tackle now consists in the fact that love is the ambiguous category informing everything that we can call life; including the category of faith.

I want to finish offering examples because so much quoting is bound to be boring and annoying, although I've used fewer quotations than I would have liked, because my goal in this study is merely to highlight something long evident, something that now is shouting and clamoring without being heard; even so, I can't ignore one pressing example. In the introductory words to "Nicodemo" [Nicodemus], Unamuno says: "When reason tells me that there is no transcendent finality, faith responds that there must be one, and since there must be one there will. Because faith does not consist, dear sirs, of believing what we didn't see, as much as creating what we don't see." Kierkegaard says: "If I had not had faith, I would not have left Regina." The difference lies in the fact that Unamuno needed faith to create, to give life and make visible to others the things that he created without seeing them except in his will to have faith. Kierkegaard needed faith because without it he was not fit for life and, consequently, without faith, life, reality, could not give him the answer his ideal longed for.

That difference helps me to focus, you could say limit, my search because I need to make continual incursions into the conflict of Unamunian faith, and that conflict is studied exhaustively in all its ramifications and import by the authors I draw on. I'm trying to break off a branch, something nearly impossible because the branches are so tangled and because the pith is made of the same substance as the rest, but, in short, my reason for proposing that limitation involves something more extensive than Unamuno's work. I prefer to use Unamuno as an example, because he provides the most intense example. Galdós, on the other hand, can be used as an example of extension and, consequently, in him the question of faith is more or less resolved. Let's see what the question of love comes to in the work of the two of them.

What I find most obvious in both Unamuno and Galdós—it's also worth noting about Spanish literature in the modern age, since here I won't talk about contemporary literature, which is not to say that the problems I address have been surmounted by contemporary literature— is that love "remains immobilized" in such contorted images, in such trite or banal representations. Love never goes so far as to suggest the invitation to a path or a current—being neither alluring nor continuable. To use superlative similes, neither the star of Bethlehem nor the flower of evil.

In short, love, in Spanish literature, gives no one the urge to follow it.

That love so lacking in seduction is best studied not by first observing it in the most clearly amorous scenes, situations, or paragraphs; the best way is to investigate what it is there is of love in each of the personal formulas our two authors offer. We could say, unarguably, that where there is Herostratism there is no love. The distinction I made at the beginning between the *generative impulse* for eternity and the *creative yearning* to last, amounts to this: *impulse*, a drive that propels, *yearning*, an absorbing aspiration. Herostratism confined to that area of will acts centripetally. The concepts of both creation and endurance seem to contradict that, but there is no contradiction because Herostratic yearning strives only to ensure a narrowly defined everlasting *I*—whether creative or destructive makes no difference. Both the furor with which Unamuno destroyed and the passion so infused with suffering as he created are, equally, a burnt sacrifice for his I; and, as we know, the generative impulse to be eternal, takes hold of an individual and makes him lose the eternal, in a conflagration. Here it might seem that I'm not defending the supremacy of the I, as I have at other times, although I am. The generative impulse for eternity does not annul the I, but quite the opposite: it inflames that impulse and sweeps it along until uniting it with eternity itself, until the I gives itself over to eternity, the gift true and real. The I surrenders wholly and what parts from the I is also a whole that leaves to follow its destiny, although the I remains equally whole, nourished by the hope of touching eternity again. That explanation obviously concerns the generative function, but it also concerns the creative function, and no less precisely.

 The reach of love's radius is limitless, which allows it to surpass by far everything usually called love, because certain things are of course called love, but it's not easy to discern what is truly loving about them. Officially, what bears the name of love—and what essentially is love, when it appears as it really is, something not at all frequent—what is most traditionally called and time-sanctioned as love, is charity. Here we find ourselves facing one of the most intricate of knots. In charity, love is not a blind movement, impelled by the genus of the species. Or *is* it? Could it not be an extension of the spirit that springs up the way *personal* enmity is kindled in the face of any destruction, any pain, death, or adversity conveyed verbally, and is therefore, paradoxically, a response that involves both generosity and power? Whatever the case, in charity, the movement of love is spiritual in nature, since it can even lead to self-sacrifice. Even so, what usually inspires that love is, above all, another's pain—pain that most often arises from material causes, illness, or misfortune. It can also be something nonmaterial, for example, bad luck in love, persecution, slander, etc. When charity can help in those situations, it must be with goods of an appropriately spiritual sort, although in cases of material pain, suffering can be relieved only with material goods. Charity in life and work—in the deeds of those who were charity's notable heroes and in the literary creations that offered it, objectified, for our contemplation, charity is well known to be one of love's most seductive forms. I could cite—and will—the great works that spread their spell over our souls, but I prefer to begin by examining some of the Spanish works in which charity is displayed either implicitly or explicitly.

※ ※ ※

In what *people say* about Galdós, *Misericordia* is usually mentioned as an example of divine charity. I don't think it is. I do recognize that divine charity was what Galdós wanted to portray, and he faithfully copied his example from the milieu in which that virtue is often found. As in *Nazarín*, where he dealt with religious practice, in *Misericordia*, where he focuses on mercy, Galdós does not miss a detail. But if we can say that nothing in the book is extra, this is because Galdós's purpose was to put nothing in the work but a single element, which meant that his theme could fill the book from beginning to end; there is nothing that interferes, nothing superfluous or discordant. There is not a single act—since everything in her is action—on the part of Benina, *Misericordia*'s heroine, prompted by a different motive. Nevertheless, like Nazarín's saintliness, her charity is pure cliché. To place a work with the theme of *compassion* in the world of begging, it would have been appropriate to develop the pathos of that prison to the maximum. It would have been worth studying that world so profoundly that the reader is asphyxiated, or startled, or troubled, confronted with everything that can happen there. But to make the reader visit the miserable ensconced in their misery, with their petty picaresque wiles, for the reader to watch a character (here, Benina) move amidst misery so compassionately that compassion seems to be almost habit, even a natural inclination, but without the reader learning what hell her soul went through to become what that reader sees before him . . . Benina is not, like Nazarín, a character observed and understood in her totality; her past is alluded to briefly, but it's not clear how that past leads to her present. Benina's charitable impulse is clearly deep and permanent. This is certainly incontestable, but why is she not more captivating? Principally because of the environment that provides the framework for her. Undeniably, Galdós describes very precisely the formation of the emotional tie that binds Benina to the family in whose house she works as a servant and that explains why she remains loyal to them to the point of abject poverty, but his same precision highlights the imponderable stupidity of the people involved. The characters who make up that family are so stupid that it's impossible to imagine how anyone could feel any affection for them, unless that someone shared equally in their stupidity. What's more, Benina's choice among the beggars is Almudena, the blind Arab.

Galdós says in his preface: "In *Misericordia* I proposed to descend into the infamous levels of Madrid society, describing and presenting the most humble people, the greatest poverty, professional mendicity, vicious vagrancy, and misery, which is almost always painful, in some cases picaresque, criminal, and deserving of correction. In order to do that I needed to spend long months of study and personal contact, visiting the dens of the miserable or malicious souls found in the populous neighborhoods south of Madrid. Accompanied by policemen, I scrutinized the 'Sleeping Houses' on Medio Grande and del Bastero streets, and I had to disguise myself as a doctor from the municipal health department so I could enter the repulsive dwellings where the most debased proselytes of Bacchus and Venus celebrate their nauseating rites." "The Moor Almudena, 'Mordejai,' who has such an important role in *Misericordia*'s plot, was snatched from his natural habitat by a happy coincidence. A friend who, like me, is a habitual flâneur on the streets of Madrid, observing events and people, told me about a ragged blind man who begged in the Oratorio del Caballero de Gracia and who looked and spoke as if he might be of Muslim descent. I went to see him and was amazed by the uncouth, coarse, and unhappy soul who promised, in Arabized Spanish punctuated continually by horrific curses, to tell me his romantic tale in exchange for a few alms." "*Seña Benina*, the philanthropic servant with the purest of Evangelical natures, is a specimen drawn from the documentation that I laboriously gathered in order to write the four volumes of *Fortunata y Jacinta*. Doña Paca and her daughter, two examples of the ruined bourgeoisie, and the elegant but needy Frasquito Ponte are from the same source."

Here, with laudable sincerity—naïveté of an age unfamiliar with the holy inquisition of our present—Galdós gives us the chemical formula for his characters, albeit unnecessarily, because the book itself is enough for the reader to know how and of what they were made. At the end of his description of Almudena the Moor, he also notes: "In this way I acquired the interesting specimen that readers of *Misericordia* have found so real." Something incomprehensible that can only be explained by the mediocre level of the intelligence attributable to Galdós's readers in his own time—since Almudena's reality is soon bastardized by Galdós's virtuosity. In the case of *Nazarín*, he takes nothing from the specimen but the specimen, assuming that Nazarín is fully explained as a particular type; but Almudena he tries to enrich with details, with displays of his knowledge about Almudena's situation. He makes him express himself continually in his Arabized gibberish, with caricaturist exaggeration, and ends up mixing his thousand-and-one-nights daydreams with plans to return to Jerusalem, allusions to the synagogue, and invocations to Adonai: "He was still reciting Hebraic prayers in fifteenth-century Spanish, which he had retained in his memory since childhood." The hodgepodge leaves us not knowing if Almudena is an Arab or a Sephardic Jew. But that information is not overly important for the theme of compassion.

Almudena's trivial and inconsistent behavior, however, is important. When Benina meets him, Almudena is living with a rather young woman who was once beautiful; he lets it be understood—very discreetly—that they're lovers. He tires of her, though, because she drinks heavily and has bad habits, and he falls in love with Benina. Since he can't see her, he imagines that she's wonderful: "You be like the leely . . . jazmeen and roses your mouth," etc. The Moor is young or, at least not old, but there is no mention of his relations with Benina, not even about his intentions, the supposition being that they don't go beyond intentions because she opposes them. He ends up wanting to marry Benina, and what does go beyond intentions are the couple of blows he deals her when he assumes that she's betrayed him with the *preety* gentleman. To top it all, we're left to surmise that Almudena is rather repulsive and the adjective very appropriate at the end when he's covered with a rash that—to the fearful nouveau riche, or reestablished rich—looks like leprosy. A detail or accident introduced so as to round out the composition. Here the ingratitude of the clan—the clan of imbeciles, in a perfect union of putrid nobility and plebeian distaste—becomes evident as they refuse lodging to Benina when she arrives with her Moor covered with sores and lice—or so we assume, since they've come from the jail. After the finale, Galdós introduces a melodic motif, which closes the book like an inspired moral. The most plebeian member of the clan—a young woman, the picture of health—is attacked by a malady, apparently hysteria, that makes her afraid that her children are going to die. The children enjoy perfect health, but she lives in torment because of her terror and the only way she finds consolation is by going to see Benina, for Benina to assure her that the children are in no danger. Benina grants her that assurance and the story ends.

Such is the monument that Galdós erects to charity, the love most sacred. With notes taken from his conversations with Madrid's inhabitants, he forges this episode of love in the sphere of suffering matter, a sphere that, with or without faith, is religious terrain. I've already stated my belief that Galdós must be analyzed without pity, and I don't believe that the pious tone of *Misericordia* can be taken seriously by people of my generation—and future generations, which are those that count the most. That analysis won't diminish the literary value of Galdós's work an iota, and to argue that there are other moral or cultural values in his work leads nowhere. New generations can learn from Galdós only by passing what there is and is not of value through a very fine sieve. Anything else, a different, undiscriminating panegyric, can only serve, as they say here in Brazil, "for the English to see."

Of course, the theme of charity—pity, according to Scheler, feeling for the other, in sympathy—does not appear only in this encounter. I've transcribed above the paragraphs in which Juanito Santa Cruz pours all of his vileness on the unfortunate Ido del Sagrario. On that basis, we infer that Galdós paints abominable scenes for the purpose of excavating them, but in other books, for example *El doctor Centeno* [Doctor Centeno], an estimable character like the student Miquis takes in the little boy Celipe and speaks to him in terms so derogatory the reader feels embarrassed. The behavior of people who take in a starving boy, invite him to their home, and leave him in the hallway while they calmly proceed to have dinner, is difficult to understand, and it differs little from Santa Cruz's despicable behavior. I won't discuss Galdós's kindly male characters, such as Orozco and Manolo Moreno. Their crafty and unbearable natures have already been mentioned, and that commentary is enough to summarize briefly the Galdosian sphere in which love shows its sacred face of compassion.

Let's look at what Unamuno does with this love. But how to delimit it? In Unamuno nothing is either exempt or defined, less than nothing in the case of things that by their very nature consist of finalities. What could I add to the unsurpassable studies of *Paz en la guerra* developed in the books that I've been citing since the beginning? My point of view differs not a bit from theirs. Perhaps following the path they trace from his first work until his last novel will enable us to see what compassion is for Unamuno. But there is much to discuss before addressing that topic.

In the first place, eros for Unamuno was governed or oriented by the sign of the mother. *All loving movement* within him was marked by that stamp, and it's difficult to delimit eros even partially, because all possibilities of its highly complex nature are joined by their roots in that original attachment. Would it be going too far to say that Unamuno never knew any other sort of love? I believe that statement can be proved, and I also believe that Unamuno's most transcendent intuitions and his most impregnable limitations were based in that love.

One very evident and, apparently, very simple thing is the sentimental side of his religious anxieties in the first years of his youth. The play of doubts and Chateaubriandesque conversions has been well studied by Sánchez Barbudo. Strictly speaking, we could call that sentimental facet of Unamuno his amorous side. But eros is not confined to things related to sentiment.

Unamuno's crises, in which his heart struggled with his reason, were not the most important thing in either his life or his work. Rather, the sudden perceptions that overcame him—the first time as he was contemplating Nature—were what planted him, as it were, in the proper soil, what gave his thinking the anguished accent of a prisoner and, consequently, the yearning for freedom—although the yearning within Unamuno that struggled to break out of its jail bore a different name.

"The first time," Sánchez Barbudo says, "then, before he was sixteen, Unamuno had something like a revelation of the void, since 'the mystery of life' undoubtedly consisted in that doubt—an instantaneous certainty that the world had no finality, a conviction that he held deep within until his last days." I believe, however, that the revelation did not occur at that moment, but that it fused gradually with his intuition of mystery, attained throughout his life, as an inner explanation, an *unconscious rationalization*, just as a newborn gradually interprets the use of his limbs in a rational way. And clearly, at the end of his life, all that remained of that colossal perception was the image of the void, rationalized. When he was an adolescent, though, something different was decisive for his senses.

As an attempt at a minimal psychoanalytic evaluation, we can begin by bearing in mind that at sixteen Unamuno attended a wedding. He took a small trip, an excursion, that is, and found himself far from home. He was alone, he peered over "the wooden balcony of the country house" (the evocation of a wooden balcony on a country house in northern Spain can paralyze the thoughts of any *distanced* person for hours, but I must continue), and the country silently whispered a secret to him, his own secret—the mystery of his life. At that moment, led by eros, traveling within himself, as if within his own veins, to his home, his first refuge, where he sensed the beat of the absolute love that created him—absolute because it had made him exist—Unamuno went to those nuptials, in which what was two became one, and there he burned his bridges. Unamuno never left that intuited mystery; that mystery was his adored prison, to be away from it was exile. Although not exactly, because his heart demanded the intimate and profound tenderness of infancy, but because in the flash of that instant he understood—lived—the supreme love, that of life, and he began to weep. Weeping, in the method I've adopted here to study this deep, difficult passage, is an ambivalent phenomenon—simultaneously a spasmatic explosion that relieves tension and a protest against that violent sensation, like the first cry of one entering the world, of the newly born.

I don't believe there's a single word in either Unamuno's work or his life that does not speak of that *critical circumstance* when *he put down roots*. Therein lies his essential paradox. Marías says that Unamuno's "sole question" is *meditatio mortis*, he evidently spent his life thinking that living is *spending* life toward death. Consequently, he decided—his life itself decided for him—not to "undie," in Unamunian language: in ordinary language, *not to be born*. Unamuno never *breathed* life. Does that affirmation seem risky? It's not as risky as it seems; all it lacks is a little hypothetical solidity.

The problem of personality and the sense of nothingness, of death itself, Sánchez Barbudo defines very accurately: "Unamuno joins in one, two problems that have little to do with each other, but that in truth had much in common in him." Here—in that critical circumstance—or happenstance or mischance—is where he decided or, more precisely, where he rooted himself in his indecision. Unamuno launched then one or several of his personalities to live in the world; he launched them in order to play a role and fulfill the mission of immortalizing his name. Why such bitterness, such dissatisfaction, and such boredom in his earthly excursion, and such passion, such violence, and such agony in his creative cell? Because Unamuno could draw only within the walls of his cave, he could create only there where he did not see. As soon as he emerged into the light, he doubted, disbelieved and, most importantly, he doubted what he created, because his figures, his personas, had truth for him only in the realm of his love. His love was the prisoner, the one that never emerged into the light.

To justify that hypothesis, I will study several trivial passages and several characteristics that could be called supreme, several unsurpassable immersions in mystery. First, though, I will employ simple psychoanalytic tactics, adhering to the basic tenets of psychoanalysis, as understood by the general public.

Unamuno experienced his second perception of mystery—invincible anguish and explosion of tears—not while contemplating Nature but at midnight, in bed, with his wife. Something decisive happened there; at that moment Unamuno was sunk in his personal abyss—today it's easy to diagnose that immersion in mystery as a prenatal memory, in other words, *we know wherein lies* the mystery—and suddenly reality spoke to him in his own language. His wife took him in her arms and said: "What's the matter, my son?" For the first—and I believe the only—time those two worlds communicated with each other. It's not that Unamuno took his wife into his world, but that he saw the extension, the concavity, the reality of the mystery within her. He saw—deep in the darkness—that only *in* her could he continue *in* his cell; that she—the wife, the cell—was the only thing livable in the world of the living. (There is a detail, more than difficult to understand, difficult to admit because it's dissonant. Unamuno lavishly tended that moment—I would prefer not to call it an episode—frequently throughout his work, sometimes as an insistent, obsessive presence in his memory—a "reiteration," his system—it also appears a few times as a cliché, something unusual for him. As a result, that phrase spoken by his wife—the one in which that moment is summarized—appears so often in his work that its value is somewhat diminished. This can be understood only by thinking that solely at that moment could Unamuno feel reality speaking his language, but that afterward, as time gained control of that voice, it gradually became included in reality, in external reality, and eventually Unamuno no longer distinguished it or inscribed it in one or another particular role of those representable outside his cell.)

It was at that second moment when Unamuno believed that he now saw clearly, and he named his darkness "void." The first one, before he turned sixteen, was dazzlement and plenitude. At that first moment he touched unquestionable truth and curled up in it, but from there he perceived lying in wait for him the question he adopted as his sole question because it was the fatal exit, and he did not want to leave. That entire agonic game—which at the beginning I called a battle, because a man could never find himself more naked and defenseless— is developed in Unamuno's texts, and in those of his commentators, about faith, the longing for immortality, the dualism or pluralism of personality. In my opinion, the true crux of that conflict is eros.

In *Vida de don Quijote y Sancho, Del sentimiento trágico de la vida, La agonía del Cristianismo*, and many other, not to say all, of Unamuno's works, it's possible to see how immeasurably far his perception of the generative mystery reached. By following the specific and datable facts, however, we can find an initial and simple indication. Sánchez Barbudo, attempting to see how unsociability and socialism could both be present in Unamuno, refers to a letter in which Unamuno says that before 1891 he had been very close to suicide. Unamuno mentioned the letter in the prologue he wrote for José Asunción Silva's *Poesías*: "Through his verses you can see so clearly in Silva what happened to me! And I was spared his end by getting married in time." Having married at the beginning of 1891, Unamuno enjoyed a period of peace and work that lasted for several years. That period continued until 1897, year of the great crisis and the publication of *Paz en la guerra*. Quite clearly, in that long space of six years his creativity and his erotic—more precisely generative—consummation closed a cycle of energies, a process that a mystic as well as a neurologist could verify. If I fluctuate between those two terms, *erotic* and *generative*, thousands of details make it possible to see how the depression that prompted his crisis was not only an exhaustion of energies, but at the same time it was a yearning to return to his supreme refuge, something like a thirst for a spring whose water has a more intense taste, which the insipidness of his life had managed to erase. He showed openly that he wanted to recover the faith of his early childhood, that he sought to awaken memories in order for them to fan the extinguished flame, but he was unable to revive what he had lived naturally. In truth, what he really wanted was to go beyond his own beginning, to reach the sancta sanctorum of life, and it would be too much to say that he was successful, although we can certainly say that he never gave up trying; moreover, he wove around himself a cocoon in the image and likeness of the unattainable cell.

Unamuno's encapsulation is obvious, but it did not prevent him from either taking action from within it or absorbing the attention people paid to him. He himself explained quite explicitly the game of appropriation and surrender that might seem like egotism. In *Del sentimiento* there's a paragraph that encompasses mercy and enjoyment, the two principal currents of eros, which I refer to as currents in order to indicate their effects: "There is true love only in pain," Unamuno says, "and in this world one must choose love, which is pain, or happiness. And love leads us to no happiness other than the happinesses of love itself and love's tragic consolation of uncertain hope. From the moment that love becomes happy, becomes satisfied, it no longer desires and is no longer love. The satisfied, the happy, don't love, they doze off by habit, which verges on annihilation. To become habituated is to begin not to be. Man is all the more man, that is, all the more divine, the greater his capacity for suffering or, better, for anguish."

That paragraph indicates the conjunction of love and pain that is one of the concepts bifurcating constantly in Unamuno's mind. In the case of love and pain, that concept embarks throughout his entire life on the riskiest course. The indescribable—"indescribable" is not necessarily a negative descriptor—pages about war in *Del sentimiento* and *Vida de don Quijote*, the complexity of Unamuno's concept of power, of the spirit of conquest, etc. that led him to drift from the most violent spiritual terrorism to the most *stultifying* Pascalian precaution, is at the heart of his story as a man of action. (This part of Unamuno's story has been studied by Sánchez Barbudo, whose remarkable incisiveness and discretion suggest that he knows but withholds the cause, from respect for Unamuno's memory.)

However, in that same paragraph there is a reference to another of love's qualities, the most decisive one, since on it depends love's existence. "From the moment that love becomes happy, it is satisfied, it no longer desires and is no longer love." In 1912 Unamuno formulated that idea of love; he was clearly speaking there about the generative impulse, although that did not cause him to abandon the idea of immortality in which love has its seat. "Because from the carnal and primitive love that I've been speaking about, from the love of the entire body and all its senses that is the animal origin of human society, from that infatuation arises spiritual and painful love." But it was the perceptible death of love, of love that when satisfied is no longer love for the cessation of life, desire, that Unamuno experienced at the moment of his second crisis and was what made him go in search of the water in that eternal spring—the eternity of prenatal, pretemporal peace, absolute darkness in which nothingness is discernible and all—the All—is perceptible.

Unamuno sought refuge in a convent because only in a sacred place could he revive, revive himself as he was when all as all was mystery. Except at that decisive moment he could cry, flee, make his person into whatever he wanted but he could not say, *love has died*. He could not say that because presumably, and I believe that it was sufficiently proved, love had not died entirely. He placed it, enthroned it, one would have to say, since the formula is one of exultation, in the maternal environment. Not in the mother's generative cell, but in her compassionate refuge. "Woman's love, above all, is always compassionate in essence, is maternal, as I've said. Woman always yields to her lover because she feels him suffering from desire." Consequently, Unamuno did not publicize the death of love, did not speak further of its mortality: compassion remained on its altar and he suffered love's periodic annihilating deaths in silence. The fact—and it is a fact—of his suffering that persistently appearing death created a longing to find revitalizing resources. But what resources would have been legitimate for Unamuno's internal law?

It was in the letter to his friend Juan Arzadun, in which Unamuno announced his upcoming wedding, that he wrote: "This unsociability is incurable . . . I, firm in my Quaker ideal, disdainful of etiquette, cut out for home life, with her determined to domesticate me . . . There is no question that she has civilized me; but even though the bear is susceptible to refinement, he will forever remain a bear and I always a Quaker." We can assume that climate in which Unamuno and his fiancée shared their intimate moments would best be described as puritan. How well a young Catholic Spanish girl could truly understand that climate is something that only those who knew her personally could judge. The important thing, though, is that the restlessness caused by the death of desire ("he tossed and turned uneasily in the marriage bed," Corominas explains as he describes Unamuno's great crisis) made Unamuno *yearn for adultery*. One can commit adultery not only without yearning for it, but while hating it; it can be merely the effect of a passion that assaults the sufferer and interferes in his life without the effect, which is produced blindly, being avoidable. But in Unamuno's life that was not at all what occurred: what occurred was that the temptation of adultery stimulated him to overcome love's lethargy. And since love in Unamuno was one and the same as faith, like the two categories faith and love, they formed in him a very tight cord—the umbilical cord of his soul; he sought the stimulus in the thing that could give him the illusion of freedom without breaking that cord. With the clandestineness characteristic of illicit love—but at the same time with the vain ostentation that usually accompanies that sort of affair—he maintained a dialectical *liaison* with Protestantism at the margin of his Catholic faith.

Reducing Unamuno's world to a few such meager lines causes a perturbing dissatisfaction and uneasiness, because the disproportion between what one manages to say and what one has been pondering for many years is so great that it leaves room for nothing but the fear of not having said the most important things. The only consoling thought is that in this terrain, everything, no matter how scanty, is important.

Rather than linger more on the study of what Galdós and Unamuno said about love, I will move to a meditation on the result: the love that their works prompted in their readers.

In the context of the parcel of literature allotted to the novel and the subject indicated above, literature has two effects, at times independent of each other, at times merged into only one. The most fruitful of the two is the one that adopts, tacitly, the ruling heart of an era. "Love" as they say, "is a literary style," there has also been discussion about *fashion* and there have been efforts to grant that word the seriousness it merits. The word *manner* is less equivocal, and it designates one of the two effects more precisely. Readers of novels, who are the most vital, least intellectual readers—although many intellectual readers also read novels—allow themselves to be led or infected through sympathy, the most intimate contact, by their authors' *manner* of love. *Their* authors are their most beloved authors, because literature's second effect is that love gives back to the sources from which it flows. And that *manner* of love, learned by a few—the readers of novels—is the love imposed by those readers on their contemporaries; not on all of them, not on those who don't read novels, but on those who don't read because they don't know how to read; on the most simple and uneducated, far from the city or secluded in their poverty, in other words, passive spectators of all the luxuries of life. Spread above them all is the influence of *fashion*, all of them working and feeling, which is the most important, in the *manner* of their age, and this *manner* is decreed by a few, a very few, sometimes by only one of the *creators of love*.

 I won't allude here, even slightly, to cinema, the medium of our age, because I've spoken enough about it elsewhere and because, for the purposes of my search, I need to stick to the three generations that began the century; grandfathers, fathers, and sons, who drank in the great novels—the fluent "image of life," the *roman fleuve*.

 My generation, which I can place in the second of the two indicated above, did not learn how to love from Spain's great novelists (something very serious they learned from a few very poor writers; which meant they learned very poorly). That statement really refers to Galdós—bear in mind that when I speak about loving I'm not speaking only about love affairs, when I allude to eros I'm speaking about both generative and compassionate love. Young people of my generation, I among them, rejected Galdós categorically. On the other hand, we adored Unamuno, but not as a novelist. Unamuno accomplished his grand invasion of our hearts with his essays, *Del sentimiento trágico de la vida*, *Vida de don Quijote y Sancho*, *La agonía del Cristianismo*, etc. Unamuno's novels we needed to reach a certain maturity to *endure*, because what happened with Galdós's novels never happened with Unamuno's; we never rejected them, but *swallowing* them was hard on our gullets. The extraordinary thing is that, harsh and irritating as they *went down*, they were easy to digest. They were a nourishing but hardly delightful food. As Marías has noted, Unamuno possessed a "certain incapacity" for delight, for both feeling it and producing it. His books of theory, which we adored, did not delight either: they intoxicated (to the point of someone succumbing to *delirium tremens*, but there's no need to speak about that).

Would even the most hermetic of regimens have been able to prevent us Spaniards from devouring the novels written in the rest of Europe? France, Russia, the Scandinavian countries, passions and climates oozing with human content. We used that content so we could mature and acquire skills, have tastes and preferences. We also used it to see what we lacked and, above all, to intuit what we lacked. Therein lay the timidity of our love. We were so censured for anything foreign, there was so much talk about the *snobbish* mania for pursuing the exotic. What distanced us from our writers was our perception that they were concealing something from us. We sensed that what in Galdós seemed to be discretion, "self-respect," and in Unamuno Quakerish sobriety, economy without delight, was undoubtedly concealment. But falsehood? Hypocrisy? No, none of that, but the most serious concealment of all: they concealed from us what they concealed from themselves. For that reason, the absence, the blind or opaque spot, the ugliness, at times, the muteness of the phantom disappearing in their work can be summarized by saying that what we found lacking in them was confession.

At the beginning of these pages, I referred to the greatest confessants, calling them pugilists of the will because, blow to blow with will—with blows of will—they either wanted to awaken will, inspirit it, even spiritize it, as if to lift life's spirits, or they wanted to censure it—with a hair shirt of will—to dampen its nerve and prune its arborescence so "desirous" of life. Those three warriors were not hermits when it came to meditation, which is why their confessions included the landscape that framed their adventures, although that doesn't mean their deeds were placed in relief. No, what those confessants placed in relief was themselves, their persons against the world from which they drew their coloration, like insects in relief against the plants on which they grow. (Once again the memory of Cervantes's silent confession leaps to mind, bearing the landscape around it as the most consubstantial element of its secret. Because there is a difference; the outer landscape is described, the inner landscape—no less of a landscape, that is, no less of an authentic landscape, and not the coloration or the climate of the meditations themselves, a landscape seen and absorbed as nourishment, the landscape of which one's very being is a loving copy—is not described, it develops on its own from an allusion and follows the person in his wandering. The entire landscape of *Don Quixote* is summoned in the novel's opening line, in the dynamic vagueness of the first sentence, because a *place* can be a town, but it can also be any point in *la Mancha*, a noun or name that like its meaning of stain or spot, spread on its own and *was placed* in memory; if it went unnamed, that was because there was no desire to name it. The vague location was allowed to hold until Garcilaso's aura covered it with trees and streams, then it become parched again and gradually hardened until it reached the rocky Sierra Morena, which darkened beneath the name of Beltenebros. This is the landscape confessed, never described, by Cervantes. Of course I can provide a more conclusive example. Who is not familiar with the landscape of the Gospel, "a divine novel" in which heaven and earth accompany the Errant, the Living, with palms or with lightning flashes and thunder while the Gospel confides in us with its supreme news?)

If I noted that in great confessions we see around their persons the world in which the confessions were produced, like testimonies of their very real struggles, like a *boxing ring* in which they exchanged blows with themselves, it was so that I could try to explain one of the details that reveals concealment. Spain's two great novelists either have no landscape—Unamuno—or the one they describe—Galdós— is a landscape devoid of secrets (another idea comes to mind here that can exemplify what I mean, without my having to explain it. Baroja's landscape—above all, a Madrid landscape—has a climate, an intimacy absent from that of Galdós. I won't try to explain it because the only thing I want to point out is that it has *a certain something*. I could have used Baroja's work instead of Galdós's for this study. Because Baroja also conceals a secret, but I preferred to analyze Galdós because his linkage with Unamuno is more evident, and the continuity between them interests me particularly. But, I repeat, there is a climate in Baroja, a landscape that at a particular moment we loved and accepted because it was a landscape of *youth and egotism*, in the end, something that could be communicated.)

Why is there no secret in Galdós's landscape? Because it's a landscape described, undoubtedly very well described, but *not claimed*. For example, the best landscape in Galdós, that is, the description of a place as intimate for a person as its shell is for a mollusk, is Camila's kitchen, because there the character is at her peak in the most intimate harmony possible with her surroundings. Fortunata has a landscape at the moment she makes her appearance, but she does not retain it, she does not carry it with her in her dramatic and ever-changing adventures. Irene, in *El amigo Manso*, has no landscape either, despite the perfect construction of her character because that character, although very lively, is a generalization of a certain type of personality.

But why select those three female characters? Because the great concealment, the *unconfessable life* is what governs the relations between men and women. Of the entire Galdosian world of incalculable love affairs, in such a colossal novelistic oeuvre, which character redeems itself as most authentic? That of Camila, the woman most loved, the one who represents the love of the flesh, desire's agonic struggle with the impossible. And Camila has her landscape, her kitchen is her shell. In Camila, the Galdosian Aphrodite emerges pure and naked, and never again, in no other environment, does she reemerge.

If at issue here were the methods of one writer, there would be no reason to feel shocked; this discussion, however, involves more than one, and they include the most representative. Even so, the fact that there are several is no cause for concern, but what we should find alarming is Unamuno's presence among them. The alarming thing is that reading his work, one senses that the supreme intuitions of mystery, and the violent passions of his person in agony, have their fullest presence in the hothouse, cavern, or camera obscura of Unamuno himself. There, his being, so decidedly "of flesh and blood," attains its obscure truth, in which even such infernal monsters as envy are exalted to the highest level of creation. Suddenly, though, a small character, barely a person, springs up or, rather, is pressed into service because he's something near at hand in earthly reality, and he reveals the inconfessable life of the flesh, its sad *necessity*. I mean that he reveals or unveils how Spain's ancestors lived the life of the body. Only the writers? No, the Spanish people as a whole. That sad defect Spain's writers don't confess, although at times they do allow a glimpse of it, in a careless slip or a gloss on what they hope to show as lofty and pious serenity but is in fact the most awkward, passive, and mercenary resignation. Examples, since epithets are useless.

A few lines above, I cited a paragraph from *Del sentimiento trágico de la vida*, but I did not cite all of it. It reads: "Woman yields to her lover because she feels him suffering from desire"—and it continues—"Isabella felt sorry for Lorenzo, Juliet for Romeo, Francesca for Paolo. Woman seems to say, 'come, poor thing, and don't suffer so much on my account.' For this reason her love is more loving and more pure than man's, as well as more courageous and more long lasting." Such a crass error about loving heroines would be excusable because, as I've said, eros for Unamuno was governed by the maternal sign, and love has the right to err. However, there is another passage, in *Vida de don Quijote y Sancho*, in which the situation glossed is not shackled to sentiment; it's explained, I could say theorized, freely. The gloss burns its incense before Maritornes: "Believe that the generous Asturian maiden sought to give pleasure more than to receive it and, if she yielded, it was, *as happens to not a few Maritornes* (emphasis mine) so she would not see men suffer and waste away. She wanted to purify the muleteers and the clumsy desires that fouled their imaginations and to leave them clean for their work." I won't stop to analyze the contradictory nature of this theory because what's important for my investigation is what we can glimpse in *not a few Maritornes*.

In *Amor y pedagogía*, in *La tía Tula*, in *Nada menos que todo un hombre*, the *servant woman* is there, not the serf woman—that is something entirely different. The serf does not submit to pleasure, but to Omnipotent Will—the servant-girl is at hand, a jill-of-all trades who can be used for all of the *señorito*'s base needs, and he knows that he uses her, senses that what he imposes on her is a base need. He disdains her before, during, and after the act to which she lends herself. I can't expand on the infinite psychological causes, and it's no exaggeration to say *infinite*, because the question involves *combinations*. Who could calculate the factors at play in those submissions? Those women lend themselves to such a service for as many reasons and with intentions as highly varied as the color of their eyes, hair, skin, and coming from every one of Spain's forty-nine provinces, etc. What makes them the same is the result. If there is no result, the matter is unimportant, but if there is a result, a wretched soul—a man or a woman, a human being either deplorable or perfect—is thrown into the infinite game of chance combinations.

That unsavory domestic chore has marked the amorous initiation of 80 percent of Spanish males. Yes, yes, I know that arrogant Goethe also had a predilection for such practices and was responsible for immortalizing a couple of jocular remarks about young girls in domestic service. But the dramatic predicament of the humble seduced maiden marks his most transcendent work. There the class difference is decidedly stressed: the girl is so humble that she can't be seen in public on the arm of a *señor*. The gentleman is enraptured by the pure and poor dwelling of the maiden and the maiden allows herself to be seduced, not only by the gentleman's charms but also by a small box of jewels. And in the end, there's a child thrown into the river. In the subsoil of sublime drama lies a clumsy history of abuse, seduction—corruption, rather, because when there are jewels in the picture, the one in charge is not Aphrodite but vanity and ambition—double or triple crime, mother, son, brother. It's definitely an unsavory story, elevated to the highest possible category. Goethe grafted it onto the trunk of a secular condition, covered it with poetic splendor, and ended it in heaven. You can't go higher than that. And Tolstoy developed *Resurrection*'s grand scale from the outline of a similar tale.

Is it some fatal movement of will that leads a man to literally lord himself over the submissive woman? Lord himself, deify himself? Is possessing the serf woman magnifying his own power? There must definitely be something of that, but the only thing certain is that, whatever it is, it occurs in that ultimate place we can call the shrine of life. From the depths of this unsavory story, those two great creators from wise Germany and saintly Russia drew everlasting will, sacred essence, immaculate beneath carnal mud. The Iberians have no divers capable of such depths.

Well, it's not exactly that. It's not that Spain's great creators don't go to such depths: quite the contrary, in unattainable depth, they move with complete ease. What happens, though, is that they don't want to—don't dare . . . can't?—connect depth with real life. They can't or they don't dare because they sense the "fouling" of matter. Semitic, or rather Mohammedan, inheritance? The Arab does not accept the notion that God can engender because engendering seems something indecent and dirty to him. He sees in it only what he sees. He does not realize that *only God engenders because engendering is a fiat*. But in the end, no matter how much we blame the Moors, Christians are not exonerated.

❊ ❊ ❊

It's in *La agonía del Cristianismo* where Unamuno gives full rein to his imagination in a sort of apologue about the Shunammite Abishag's burning passion for old King David. A beautiful name can symbolize whatever one wishes, and the same is true in the case of a king, so it does not seem preposterous to make an allegorical figure from the beautiful maiden in love with the great king. Things don't stop there, though. Unamuno begins by acknowledging that he cannot verify the information: "The Biblical text does not tell us this," he warns, "but David must have died in the arms of Abishag the Shunammite, his last wife, who clasped him in his agony, passionately kissing and embracing him, perhaps also cradling his last dream with motherly rocking. Because Abishag, the virgin, the one whom David did not know and who knew David only through desire, was the last mother of the great king." This chapter of *La agonía del Cristianismo* is a brief digression with references to Petronius, Leon Chestov (Les Shestov), Alfred de Vigny, don Nicolás Salmerón, and other important men, but the leitmotiv of the beautiful maiden in love—the soul in agony that, as I understand it, longs to be known by God—is repeated throughout the twelve pages, always with an emphasis on her insatiable kisses and embraces. Of course, "motherly rocking" also appears frequently, since Unamuno is speaking about love. From that lofty vantage point, he does not see how repulsive the image is, a young maiden smothering an old man with kisses. Am I cruel to stress that caricature? No more so than is merited, because bear in mind that to make his allegory as vigorous as possible, Unamuno speculates that Abishag "knew David only in *desire*." Unamuno imagines that desire exists in that ghostly girl, something he did not admit about Juliet or Francesca.

La agonía del Cristianismo was written in 1924, in exile. Unamuno is *born*, placed naked in the *ville lumière*, and he cries out, he bellows in his abandonment. Everything in this book is a clamoring to reach, if only mentally, the refuge of his sacred cell. That explains why he prolongs the discussion of Père Hyacinthe's strange and equivocal history. As early as chapter 6 ("La virilidad de la fe" [The Virility of Faith]), Unamuno refers to the priest's *Diary*, which he had to have found disturbing. "The thinker affirms or denies. Renan's intellectual power did not exceed his doubt, he lacked virility." The entire chapter deals with that sentence, the last in Père Hyacinthe's diary; then at the end of the book, Unamuno considers the case at length, saying that he read it, "or rather devoured it, with growing anguish." He quotes numerous paragraphs from the *Diary*, in which the Friar speaks of his first temptations of the flesh. "The faithful and enthusiastic practice of celibacy had led me to a false and unhealthy state. . . . I'm in love, not with a woman but with woman." There Unamuno amends his page; he speaks of the mystical alliance that forms between Père Hyacinthe and Mrs. Merriman, whom he ends up marrying, and says that the alliance was not like "Saint Francis of Assisi's with Saint Claire or Saint Francis de Sales's with Saint Joan of Chantal, or Saint Theresa's with Saint John of the Cross. *Nor was there sexuality* in Hyacinthe's love either. There was *furious paternity*, the desire to ensure the resurrection of the flesh" (emphasis added). He continues to speak about the overwhelming force pushing him toward marriage: "To try to destroy it would be suicide," Père Hyacinthe says.

What a leap of thirty-three years Unamuno's memory must have made! So that now at eighty, the Friar writes: "[t]he grand vision of God and of eternal vision, always present in my consciousness and more so in my *subconsciousness* has been MY JOY as well as my strength." "He was unaware," Unamuno adds, "that the subconscious was the genus of the species Schopenhauer talked about, the pessimistic bachelor, the genus of the species that sought faith in the resurrection of the flesh. He needed the son." But the one unaware of the crux of that highly abstruse case was Unamuno. Even with the typographical alert. He criticized italics; they seemed pedantic to him, he thought the reader sufficiently intelligent not to need them, when intelligent is something that no one is sufficiently. In Père Hyacinthe's text, MY JOY is more than italicized, it's superlativized by those capitals. Should we assume that Père Hyacinthe wants to tell us about the degree of his joy? No, the magnitude he indicates is of another sort. What he means is that *his joy* has been what granted him the vision of God and of the eternal, because joy—delight, to use a Biblical term—is the *word* of eternity. I would dare say that Père Hyacinthe's intuition here, because of its extraordinary gravity, unbalances any and all of his rational processes;

I don't mean that it annuls them, but that it produces a feverish reverberation, which sends him zigzagging across the sand shifting beneath his feet. Unamuno considers such instability a form of agony; in my view, it's something very different.

Kierkegaard, the most agonic soul that has ever existed, had a clear mind, an implacable rational capacity; which is why his blows hit their mark. Unamuno did not share that extraordinary faculty because Kierkegaard *walked the streets with it* and what fascinated Unamuno about Père Hyacinthe was that his debating all occurred *within the CHURCH*. I use capitals because if I capitalized only the first letter, the allusion would be to the congregation of the faithful; if I used no capitals, the allusion would be to the church as a sanctuary or chapel, and what I want to suggest is that for Unamuno, the Church was, above all, chapel, cell. In it, beneath its nave or, rather, in its crypt, he lived with his grand visions "of flesh and blood," he took them out on the street and they often stumbled.

The genus of the species did not speak to Unamuno with the word *joy*; it tormented him, in his youth, until he was almost at the point of suicide, but he resolved the issue in the nick of time by marrying and rationalizing his grand intuition about the mystery of life with the idea of the resurrection of the flesh. There is unarguably something of a Herostratic cast to the notion of living on in one's son. Letter to Juan Arzadun, 3 August 1892: "This morning Concha gave me my first son . . . I'm working more than ever and more fruitfully on my spiritual son. As one was struggling to emerge, I was laboring mentally on the gestation of the other . . ." Isn't this moment in Unamuno's work the embryo of Avito Carrascal? Rather, it's the egg not incubated, which remained frozen in his subconscious until the time came for the deadly practice. With his first spiritual child, *Paz en la guerra*, now wandering about in the world, and fatigue, lack of desire, the death of love led Unamuno—Cervantinely—to give life to that fruit of his rancor. He placed the child he had gestated in the world of suffering while the other one "was struggling to emerge." By making Avito Carrascal a cruelly sarcastic character, he thought he was purging his Herostratism, but the character got out of hand because Avito is less Herostratic than Unamuno intended. Avito wants to make a son for the future and he wants the future—in which he believes blindly, blinded by the light of reason for his son. He wants to make him fit for what he will come to be, so that he, the son, will be. Not so that he himself will continue being in the son, since that task is incumbent on the genus of the species. Attending to life corresponds to love, to the destiny of the one who will continue. But if Unamuno was not contemplating the son who was struggling to emerge, abandoning himself to the contemplation of mere life, real, material life, it was because the source of his grand intuitions lay elsewhere. He knew desire, which took him to within two steps of death, but he did not know how to contemplate the *joy* he obtained. The person in whom he most *personified himself*, although ironically, agonically, is Don Fulgencio, and look at what Don Fulgencio's *joy* is based on.

Such ambiguities and equivocations on Unamuno's part leave us asking will he be, will he not be? Because Edelmira's "plump flesh is sterile." Does that suggest—or reveal—that for Unamuno delight is sterile? Does it suggest that the pleasure Don Fulgencio habitually finds capped with a blond wig—feminine baldness adding a most derogatory note—is the tribute paid by the thinker, who longs to live forever; a despicable tribute that fails to satisfy his hunger for paternity? And isn't that hunger for paternity, formulated categorically in the imperative—Make a son—a painful yearning to live on forever but with no regard for the pleasure that contemplating the future—the future of one's own son, in *his* world, in *his* tomorrow—can provide to the loving imagination (boundless rather than hungry, or half one, half the other) that's the formula of eros? Isn't it obvious that in Unamuno's work there is never a glimpse of desirous daydreaming about that pleasure? It's obvious because a future subsequent to Unamuno's existence inspired no confidence in him. He *did not see* the outline of that future, or perhaps he did see it and found it unsatisfying; he wanted to impose his own plan on it. His powers of deduction were more than plentiful enough to do that and he had more than enough material—spiritual material—to carry it out, but in a shower, a downpour, forcefully, harshly, roiling the flow without focusing the current, becoming lost in dispersion. In the end, beginning to feel the lack of vitality, the image of that future increasingly closed to his love, rather, his desire, nothing inspired him but the compassionate impulse to cover it with consoling fog.

Could that brief excavation of Don Fulgencio's *joy* have uncovered a veiled confession of *unconfessable life*? There are many reasons to assume that it has. Commenting on the time of Unamuno's marriage,

Gullón refers to "chaste Unamuno." It's the only point in his excellent book with which I disagree. Not only is there no chastity in Unamuno, there is—despite, or beneath, his puritanism—an unconfessable lasciviousness. Before going any further, though, I need to explain what I mean by chastity. In my view, chastity is literally an abstention from the generative function, which has value only as a sacrifice. Whether that sacrifice is to God or to a human being, its value is indisputable: maintaining it is virtue. Chastity, as a way of being, can manifest itself physically, in which case it has no value, but it can also be manifested psychophysically, which may not occur as an act of denial but which gives every deed—act, movement, intention—of one's erotic life a fullness and harmony free of triviality and superfluous lust. Lust is, first and foremost, heaviness, stupid insistence. Lasciviousness is something different; above all, it's a surreptitious urge not present until it finds a way to appear in situations where it's very hard to detect.

And it's in *Vida de don Quijote*, about the *purest*—*chaste* is a very weak term for Don Quixote—*purest knight*—consider those two words redundant—that a late lasciviousness appears like a vapor escaping from tiny cracks or clefts in Unamuno's interpretation, rather, his *appropriation*, thanks to imperfections in the novel's composition. Why consider some descriptions lascivious when they aren't truly obscene? Because they're unnecessary, because they become detached from the actual situation and the character to whom they're attributed, because they have no reason to exist other than their having found the occasion to appear.

"Confidence" and *appropriation* are two forms of closeness that are constants in Unamuno. In *Vida de don Quijote y Sancho*, there's a paragraph in which their energies meet and merge, vibrating with intimate truth, "Tell me, only me, my Don Quixote, tell me: the intrepid courage that led to all of your heroic feats, wasn't it perhaps an outburst of the longing for the love you could not bring yourself to confess to Aldonza Lorenzo?" Unamuno wheedles Don Quixote's secret out of him in such a way that in the sentence quoted above, when he says "*my* Don Quixote," the possessive indicates not loving appropriation but proprietorship. Unamuno gives us the secret of *his* Don Quixote. He repeatedly stresses Don Quixote's repressed love, his longing for the perpetuation of the flesh, and the struggle between that longing and the yearning for glory. Time after time, he repeats that beneath Don Quixote's struggle lies the love suffocated for a dozen years and he presses him, speaking in intimate terms: "I believe that you're still wrapped in melancholy sorrow, thinking about how it's no longer possible for you to receive either Aldonza's embrace on your breast or her kiss on your lips, the kiss that died without being born." "How many poor mortal immortals whose memory blooms in human memory would give the immortality of their name and their renown for a full-mouth kiss, for only one kiss of which they dreamed throughout their whole mortal lives?"

How superfluous that image. Why, thinking about Don Quixote, speak about "full-mouth kisses"? Of course it seemed even more offensive and repulsive speaking in relation to the death agony of King David. In both cases, what offends is the fact that the allusion is unnecessary. It's that surreptitious superfluity that I call lascivious.

But deep within the confidence Unamuno wheedled out of Don Quixote there is another, strangely bitter secret. It concerns a seldom-discussed, exceptionally clear, and well-structured passage in chapter 6 of the second part of the *Quixote*, to which Unamuno calls special attention—a little more than four pages of dense prose, with no ambiguities and no detours. Its title reads: "About what happened to Don Quixote with his niece and his housekeeper; one of the most important chapters in the entire history." "And truly important it is," Unamuno exclaims. Because while Sancho was quarreling with his wife, Don Quixote was arguing with his niece and his housekeeper about the domestic disturbances caused by his heroism.

"And the good knight had to listen to a young girl like his niece who barely knew how to manipulate two bobbins."

"And to think that this girl Antonia Quijana is the person who today subdues and leads the men of Spain. Yes, it's this young girl, this small, unimaginative, gossipy barnyard hen is the one who snuffs out any budding heroism . . ." "And even though she's a simpleton and a homebody with a heart as empty as her head, she might be impudent with you, her uncle, but she probably won't be impudent with the men who court her as suitors or who possess her as husband . . ." "There's a common sense, and along with it also a common sentiment; along with the coarseness of our minds, the coarseness of our hearts dampens and dulls us. And you, Antonia Quijana, my lady reader, are the guardian and warden of that coarseness . . ." "And you, my Don Quixote, it's sad to think that when you withdraw to your house, to the love of your home, as to a castle built atop the rocks that keeps you far from the world's poisoned arrows, and protects you from hearing the voices of people talking without ever shutting up, it's sad to think that your ears are still being worn out by echoes of those same troublesome voices. It's sad to think that your home does not permit your spirit and the environment that formed you to expand, but is instead an exact copy of the outside world. Aldonza would certainly not have told you such things, she would not have told you such things."

A quick glance might suggest that in his mature dreams Unamuno yearns for some unrealized love. But it can also be something else—something similar, but not the same thing—it's possible to yearn not for *a* woman, but *woman, pleasure*. It's also possible that by mentioning "domestic disturbances caused by his heroism" he was not alluding to the disturbances in his own home—although around the time of his second crisis he uses some very similar sentences in reference to himself—but to the general climate of Spanish domestic life which, at that moment, was weighing on his conscience, because he had not "stirred it up" more violently at the opportune time, not freed it from the right-minded mediocrity to which he himself contributed with his puritanism. If in 1905, the date of *Vida de don Quijote y Sancho*, when Unamuno was forty-two, he suffered some inner uprising, it proved to be an aborted revolution. His puritanism emerged triumphant, and the rich flow of violence and rebellion that sprang from him was channeled into the areas of intrahistory and intralife. Life of the spirit, conflicts of faith and survival. Life of the soul; novelizable passions, which he believed he had *incarnated*, but which he had *personated*, in all the ungraspable complexity of that term. The definitive result of that total internalization of soul and spirit was "the sole question, *meditatio mortis*."

Having taken this long journey, do we have at least a partial inkling of where we're going to end up? I will allow myself a few more words of explanation.

The concealment of which I accuse Spain's great creators can be symbolized, outside of the novel, by Velázquez, the most Cervantinely silent revealer of secrets, and one of the most authentic—free of any ambiguity—creators in the history of the Spanish people—so equivocal a word as "people" I use not without hesitation, but any other I might substitute for it is today corrupted by the same evil.

I want it to be very clear that if I attack Unamuno's concealments so *shamelessly*, it's because I esteem him so highly and have long adhered to the inspiring spring that flows from him. To explain him vaguely and metaphorically, then, I will place his Christological Christ of Velázquez before the meta-erotic Venus who turns her back on us in the National Gallery.

Why did Ortega not speak about her, since he analyzed Velázquez's silence so profoundly and rigorously? The only explanation, I imagine, is that he would have had to say too much. Well, that's certainly one reason, but it's not the only one. To be able—or have the right—to affirm something about a topic that such an impeccably coherent author did not address, it's necessary to consider that topic within the system governing the study in which we notice its lack. In his *Velázquez*, Ortega shows that it's impossible to understand a creator without studying the historical climate in which he developed. In doing so, he suggests very precisely the principal aspects of the intellectual and moral process occurring during sixteenth- and seventeenth- century Europe and Spain, in particular. The various phases of the intellectual and artistic process—*stylism, realism, formalism*—are outlined in a highly nuanced way. The same is true for the moral process, which culminates in the *form* that—supreme insight—Ortega symbolizes with the elegance displayed by "Don Rodrigo on the scaffold."

Another of Ortega's premises is that to understand an artist, it is necessary to study not only what he did but also what he did not do. In the case of Velázquez, the *prevailing weariness* of Raphaelesque beauty gave rise to a unanimous preference for ugliness, and that general current—what it held of a general nature is what matters—led Velázquez *to produce hardly any* religious or mythological paintings. He did produce some, however. In the religious paintings, he refrained from disseminating ugliness, maintaining a discreet and noble prosaism. In the mythological paintings, his *de-idealization* savages the gods represented. I mentioned earlier that it's very easy to blaspheme the gods in which you don't believe; Velázquez wraps Bacchus and Vulcan in ugliness, but if he had attacked Venus in the same way he would have blasphemed common sense. His Venus is devoid of ugliness, but she shows as little of her beauty as possible. Ortega provides enough information in his study for us to understand why Velázquez shunned beauty, and that same information allows us to understand why Ortega avoided speaking about a painting that, pictorially speaking, is marvelous. The question bifurcates, then, in the restraint shown by Velázquez and that shown by Ortega.

According to Ortega's theory, cultural and moral processes or movements have authentic value when they involve almost every area of an age and when the creator—the artist, poet, or thinker—speaks knowing that he will be understood, which does not mean that he will be well received—the dissonant creator is also understood. In 1947, when Ortega gave his lectures in San Sebastián, the intellectual and moral climate did not offer the grand guarantees of understanding needed to speak about Aphrodite. Curiously, however, Ortega did not refrain from burning a small bit of incense on her altar, although so discreetly and, above all, so in tune with the *climate* that his allusions to woman's beauty, to her walk, her eyes, etc., etc. . . . can seem clever, delightful remarks. But if, on the other hand, he had addressed the topic, he would have needed to trace the entire history, from its remote beginnings until the time he spoke, of the single process begun earlier than any other in humanity's past. An in-depth study of Aphrodite must reach from the ant—no, from the amoeba—to Eve, from Eve to Aspasia, and that's not enough; from Aspasia to Saint Theresa. If Ortega had spoken of that, he would not have been understood.

But, if he did not speak, was that the only reason? I've already noted that Ortega did not want to confess, and that he had no hesitation about saying so. It did not occur to me to blame him as violently as I've blamed the other great figures because, aside from one's customary right to privacy about oneself and other topics not usually discussed, for my purpose *it's not important* that Ortega avoided the topic because *it was not his concern*, not being an effective action. That statement seems absurd in the case of a thinker whose *irremissible vocation* was to be a leader of generations. Accordingly, nothing fell outside of his *theoretical* concern: as his essays about love prove quite clearly. But *what's effective, in regard to this subject*, is not something theoretical—don't contradict me by saying that no one has surpassed Plato as a leader of generations, because Plato did not doubt for a moment that he could be misunderstood (whether he was or not is another question). The best suggestions offered by thinkers in this our age both realist (ambiguous adjective) and democratic (even more ambiguous adjective)—lie in the area of thought, where few living people venture. Only novelists can make themselves understood by even the illiterate. Consequently, according to Ortega, just as the painting speaks silently and everyone understands it, beneath the verbal—or mixed with it, or enlivened by its energy—the novel has the power of silent presence. The novel's *presences*, its *persons*, are what govern in terms of the style—fashion or fashioning—of an age. Therefore, leading generations along the path of things most vital to humanity *is principally the concern* of novelists. Of course, this refers not to novelists whose work bears messages or morals but to those who birthed—onto the page—silent presences that do not stop talking.

That word play is not excessive because silent pictorial presences have, like few presences, the ability to speak in all languages and in all times; like the Bible when it's opened at random, they have the ability to answer any question. For example, if we ask the Spanish Velazquian Venus why she doesn't let us see the softest and most delightful side of her body, she will answer us—she won't answer us and that's the problem!—but her silence will reveal the narcissistic monodialogue she addresses to her veiled, impersonal—but not ideal—image in the cloudy mirror. Would it be a lot to say that between that mirror and the soft, pictorially carnal side of her back—I'm trying to suggest, but I don't know if I'm successful, the pictorial reality embodied in the painting, and not the *painted* image of living flesh—in that silent space is Aphrodite's meta-erotic body (here I prefer to use the Greek name, less popular but more suggestive of her heavenly powers). It's not a lot to say that, it's very little! So little that it's better to say nothing more.

In short, what I proposed to do in this meditation was look for something almost nonexistent and to ascertain, solely on the basis of information I've gathered tenaciously, that it exists. The information seems irrefutable, but there is something much more certain: what one suspects, what one senses with a sense that never deceives (the crook's under cover and won't come out, but the sleuth is sure he's there).

Since I knew that something had been denied to Spaniards when it was greatly needed, my search lacks the serenity of a critically rational researcher. Its tone seems laden with reproaches, jealousy, lovers' laments. It's not a question of seeming that way; it is that way. What's reproachable is the malnutrition we suffered from during our intellectual formation as adolescents, even those of us who had the good fortune to receive an excellent preparation: that preparation was reduced to the principal points of *El buen Juanito*. When the time came to enter the labyrinth, we had to confront it alone—because our parents had negotiated it blindly. I'm referring here to the labyrinth of life and mind, in which it's necessary to have silent companionship as one moves from familiar precepts to magisterial theories: companionship embodied, as ideals, in archetypal forms. I see no need for me to say that I'm not pining for moralizing examples, in the sense of good Juanitos for adults. What I long for is a cast of *types*, fraternally *typical*, whose footprints on Spanish soil spur us to follow or to shun them: the paradigm of a retinue of Spanish humanity. And this is the province of novelists, because thinkers—teachers—must tell us how they are and how things should be, but writers—novelists—must show us that they can be. The true precursor—the prophetic creator—is the one who sets us before the evidence of something that might never have been yet, but that by simply appearing shows that it's possible.

I believe that Dostoyevsky is the clearest example of what I want to suggest; the people in his novels embodied the vanguard; for fifty years one generation after another were hot on his heels. I believe that Galdós is the clearest example of the opposite: long before his death, his characters already formed a wax museum, because they had neither what it takes to belong to a living reality nor the air of timeless grandeur needed for a museum filled with timeless figures. There was something *suranné* about them, an air not devoid of charm but definitely devoid of effectiveness. What can I believe with respect to Unamuno? His creatures possess enough dimension to claim timelessness, it's true; also enough dimension to move us with their dramatic essence, but their drama offers no companionship, it sheds no light for the Spanish people—speaking here in a geographical sense—their darkness is not the one that at times has surrounded us, oppressed, or terrified us in the life we experienced: they are visible, evident, but impenetrable. They are in their world, not in ours; they appear through the misty glass. Yes, there's no doubt that Unamuno's mirror is misted, a narcissan confidant, before which he sits enraptured, his back turned to everything else—blasphemy? Not a bit; rather, simple and sincere regret—enclosing between him and himself a space inhabited not by supreme eros but by the supreme shadow, *meditatio mortis*.

Of course a lot of water has flowed under the bridge. If only it had been water! But that doesn't make life colorless. On the contrary, every day it's more tempting to meditate on life, contemplate it, snap its picture, fill our mental dwellings with its portraits.

—Rio de Janeiro, 1968

Afterword
Pieces of a Scattered Puzzle

Carol Maier

Translators realize that no ultimate solutions to translation's challenges lie hidden in information about a writer's life; they are also aware, however, that the more intimate and comprehensive their acquaintance with a writer's work, the better their chances of re-creating it appropriately and affectingly. This is particularly the case when the work in question has resulted from an inseparability of self and circumstance as complex and absolute as that found in *Two Confessions*. One could hardly expect otherwise, since both Rosa Chacel and María Zambrano internalized (albeit in different ways and with differing responses) Ortega y Gasset's insistence on precisely that inseparability. What is more, toward the end of their lives, Chacel explained in a long open letter to Zambrano ("Rosa mística" [Mystic Rose]), written for a homage volume in her honor, that even the relationship they shared must be understood in terms of a context as much, if not more, historical than personal.

"[O]n top of—I'm not thinking of height but ostensible surface—the serious issues involved in our close personal friendship," Chacel wrote in "Rosa mística," "there is now the *business* of our lives, the public event that marks us as specimens of a particular world, rather, as pieces of a scattered puzzle" (526).[1] Chacel's words are provocative, especially when one recalls the "conversation" between the two *Confessions* that Noël refers to in the introduction, and several of them merit comment. "Ostensible," for example, a literal translation of the Spanish *ostensible*, indicates visibility but also hints that surface comprises more than patina. Consequently, when she refers to the "business" of their lives (and to her choice of a "business letter" for her essay in the homage volume), she does so having reminded her reader that public incorporates private. The "public event" (*hecho público*) Chacel had in mind might have been the open, rather than private letter, but was most likely the Spanish Civil War—*hecho* can mean fact or deed as well as event. "Specimen" seems to support that reading. Chacel's word here is *ejemplar*, which, in addition to prototype, indicates an example not necessarily exemplary, and, particularly intriguing in the case of *Two Confessions*, a (copy of a) book. The two of us, she seems to be reminding Zambrano, as writers, represent a world in a special way: by virtue of writing about it, in effect we ourselves have become public(ations) and at times it is through words that our most intimate exchanges have occurred, and will continue to occur. As proof of that she describes their numerous "always epistolary, always intimate and hermetic pages... launched furiously" over the years, often born in response to each other (526).

Chacel's comment and more is borne out by the juxtaposition of the essays in *Two Confessions*. Not only has it led to the close "double" reading found in Noël's introduction, it prompted the recognition that the nearly lifelong interaction between Chacel and Zambrano merits study well beyond the few discussions now available.[2] Such a study presents definite challenges because much of the primary documentation is in fact the very lines of their published writing, as Chacel notes in "Rosa mística," and thus depends to an unusual extent on the reader's preparation and receptivity. Chacel and Zambrano maintained a sporadic correspondence and occasionally one of them referred to the other in an essay, but only a few of their letters have survived. A full discussion of their affectionate but also at times conflicted relationship surpasses the bounds of my comments here, but a brief look at their letters and references to each other in their work demonstrates, as Noël's remarks also suggest, that there is much to be learned by considering the two *Confessions* and their authors, two pieces of Chacel's scattered puzzle, together.

Zambrano

Zambrano and Chacel became acquainted in Madrid in the late 1920s. Reminiscing in "Rosa," a brief essay written in 1988 for a special issue of the journal *Un Ángel Más* devoted to Chacel, Zambrano describes the situation in some detail but does not give an exact date. She writes in the second person, addressing Chacel, as Chacel had done in her open letter a few years earlier. Zambrano recalls that, as a young woman in Segovia, she had learned of a beautiful girl about her own age who gave a talk in Madrid about Nietzsche and was already quite accomplished as a thinker. Philosophy was the field that absorbed Zambrano's own thoughts and in which she too wanted to excel. She felt overjoyed and hoped the two would meet, but admits that the news about Chacel also left her feeling a bit disquieted. Eventually she went to Madrid, where Chacel invited her to a meeting in her home. She remembers feeling nervous, and she tells Chacel that she must have made a bad impression because Chacel impressed her as unapproachable and unforgettable (12). The two became friends, or at least colleagues, nevertheless, and were in contact during the first months of the war. They were both strong supporters of the Republican government, although their support took different forms. Zambrano was intensely involved in politics and she remained in Spain until the end of the war. Chacel defined herself as a writer and intellectual, not an activist. She was also a mother, and she left Spain early in 1937. Her departure and the differences between the two women's commitment to the Republican cause evidently prompted harsh feelings, if not a rift between them. They did not meet again until sometime after Zambrano returned to Spain in 1981, Chacel having resettled there permanently in 1974. During their years away, they corresponded occasionally, although apparently only seven of their letters were saved. Six of them were written by Zambrano.

The first of Zambrano's letters was sent from Barcelona in 1938; at that time Chacel was in Paris. The next was mailed from Puerto Rico in 1941; by then Chacel was in South America, where she lived in both Buenos Aires and Rio de Janeiro, and Zambrano had spent time in Mexico and Cuba in addition to Puerto Rico. Zambrano's remaining letters were sent from Rome in the 1950s; it seems that she did not write to Chacel again, except for the epistolary homage essay in 1988. Few though they are, the letters are rich with information and emotion. Zambrano's affection for Chacel and admiration for her work are clear. She writes intimately about the suffering of friends and family after the war; about her husband and her divorce.[3] She tells Chacel about her work in some detail, and in a particularly poignant passage of the letter written on 1 April 1956, recounts what she has learned about the death of Ortega, who was so important in the life and work of them both. Her thinking gradually diverged from his over the years, and she was openly at odds with him over his sympathies for the Nationalists in the civil war—leaving behind all of her notes from his courses when she left Spain—but Zambrano says that Ortega's concept of vital reason was the point of departure for her. She has developed it in her own way, but she will always be his disciple (53).[4]

A not dissimilar simultaneous distancing and affinity can also be seen in Zambrano's comments to Chacel about their relationship. On the one hand, she seems to have considered Chacel something of a mentor, or "a supreme witness," to use her words in "Rosa" (12). This might have been partly because Chacel was several years older than Zambrano. Evidently, it was also because she consistently found Chacel a person on whom she could count for "revelation" rather than "rumors," as she wrote on 31 August 1953 (43), a person to whom "I confess"—as she tells her in the same letter (46). "I've always believed," she explains, "that you knew me better than I knew myself, and not 'psychologically'" (46). Although Chacel has apparently not written to her for several years, she (Zambrano) has read the few examples of her work she could get and she has repeatedly asked about her of anyone who might have news, becoming annoyed when her interest was met with surprise by persons who recalled that they had disagreed during the war (43). On the other hand, in neither her letters nor in the homage essay of 1988 does Zambrano hesitate to refer candidly to that disagreement and the differences that made their friendship "faithful but not constant" (*Un Ángel Más* 11). The faithful nature of that friendship has been easy enough to demonstrate above; its inconstancy stemmed from reasons difficult to explain concisely without oversimplifying them, in particular because that inconstancy was embedded in the interrelation of the two women's temperaments and the complex circumstances prior to, during, and following the war. Fortunately, Zambrano's two earliest letters to Chacel are illuminating in that regard.

The first of those letters, written 26 June 1938, as the war continued to rage, differs significantly from the others. It begins not "Dear Rosa" but "Friend Rosa Chacel," and the tone, although hardly unfeeling, is decidedly harsh, Zambrano's feelings raw. Nearly a year has passed since Zambrano heard from Chacel, and part or parts of Chacel's last letter had clearly been angry and argumentative. A reader infers that its contents concerned the nature of what Zambrano defines as the two women's love for Spain, in particular as that love was reflected in their differing—at times incompatible—ways of supporting (or even expressing support) for the Republican cause. The same is true of their position with respect to Ortega's defection and Unamuno's individualist and, in the eyes of many, elitist understanding of the *pueblo*—the people or the "popular." Zambrano tells Chacel that she has not responded sooner to her letter because she did not want to answer in kind, nor is she writing to argue now. Seeing that the war is not going well for the Republicans and that she does not intend to leave Spain unless absolutely necessary—the difference between her location (Barcelona was a war zone) and that of Chacel (now safely in Paris) is stressed—this letter could be the last contact she has with Chacel and she wants to make contact, to tell her that what matters are not their past differences, that what counts is one's very existence; and it is to Chacel's existence, she says, that she writes. Although she emphasizes her adherence to the Republic, her current writing projects, and her decision to stay in Spain, she also encourages Chacel to write, albeit in her own (implicitly, overly) Ortegan and Unamunian way of countering Ortega and Unamuno (38).[5] The letter's final word is "Adiós"; the signature, "María Zambrano."

Apparently three years passed before Zambrano wrote again to Chacel in 1941, telling her that she has often thought, even needed, to write, although she has not done so. However, noting that it was Chacel's saint's day, she was prompted to begin a letter, thinking that Chacel was also aware of the day and that in this way their thoughts crossed, as it were, since saints' days return one to one's childhood, one's past—in this case, a shared past now distant in space as well as time. Feeling very alone, the intense solidarity of shared struggle in Barcelona long over, Zambrano takes comfort, she says, thinking about and in this way finding other Spaniards who had scattered at the end of the war, "without a common faith, without a faith . . . being Spaniards as we are" (39). The defeat is still very immediate for Zambrano and her letter is poignant, her words a mix of bitterness, anger, concern, and affection. The tone, then, of this second letter differs greatly from that of the first. She tells Chacel about her travels, her husband, who had served in the Republican army but had survived the war and is well; and she inquires about Chacel's husband, Timoteo Pérez Rubio (1896–1977), a painter, who had remained in Spain until the war ended, presiding over the Committee for Artistic Treasures (*Junta de Defensa del Tesoro Artístico*) responsible for protecting and saving Spain's artistic heritage.

Zambrano also tells Chacel that she has immersed herself in her work. "I'm writing," she says, "about things I see so clearly that I believe everyone already knows them, but when I look around me I see they don't, although perhaps that's because they will never know them, since they don't want to" (40). Zambrano does not refer by name to whatever she's working on, but her *Confession* dates from the same year as this letter, and it's hard not to have the essay in mind as one reads about the thirst for vengeance that leads her to write, as does the need to recall "what I have lost" (42). And should a reader of her *Confession* wonder about the absence there of a specific mention of Spain, Zambrano's second letter, with comments such as the following, indicates that Spain is present in every word: "I've taken refuge in history, in a history I dream, a sort of memory, of things that have not happened to me since, I would have to believe in reincarnation, but in some way they *have* happened to me; I go back to my homeland, which is not only Spain, Spain is the most recent, but to the Mediterranean, and in it Alexandria, and the Greek world [. . .] since you and I lost contact I have discovered . . . the Mediterranean, and there I live" (40). Years after writing the second letter to Chacel, Zambrano would tell Juan Fernando Ortega Muñoz that the *Confession* was both the most sorrowful of all her publications and also the one closest to her heart (Ortega Muñoz 81).

That Zambrano would come to have that feeling about the *Confession* is clearly anticipated in her words to Chacel and the desire for rapprochement they indicate. This time her letter closes with love as well as with "Adiós," and it is signed only "María." Zambrano tells Chacel that she would be grateful, that it would make her happy if Chacel would write to her. And she mentions a letter from Chacel that she had found very hurtful, one she had received in Valencia, where she lived for some time before moving to Barcelona. The tenor of her comments, and the fact that Chacel has apparently not written since she herself last wrote, suggest that here she refers to the letter she discussed in 1938. Now, though, her comments are more specific, and they suggest that Zambrano's disagreement with Chacel concerned some writing, apparently about a topic or an individual, that Chacel had sent her and to which she (Zambrano) had responded negatively, prompting Chacel's angry response. Chacel had misunderstood the object of her remarks, Zambarno tells her, saying (although without providing specifics) that something she has published in the interim makes this clear. Moreover, she explains that she had agreed with Chacel about the "positive things, that is, the poetics," which were marvelous, and about which Chacel was right. She too was right, though, and there *had* been agreement between them, at least in some way.[6]

Chacel

The sole surviving letter from Chacel to Zambrano (now living in Rome) was written more than a decade after those comments (1 July 1954), and Chacel makes no reference to their disagreements.[7] Writing from Buenos Aires, she commiserates with Zambrano about the vicissitudes of life in exile, the constant economic difficulties, in particular. In the last letter she received from Zambrano, Zambrano lamented her need to write short articles "that pay" because they prevent her from writing—she used the same verb for both activities—and at times they leave her feeling "asphyxiated by 'material life'" (50). Chacel tells her that she herself refuses to write articles, a practice that can make anyone "inarticulate." Instead, she has been doing translations, of T. S. Eliot's *Family Reunion*, for example. Although she never studied English, she has become something of a specialist in the translation of "difficult works of English poetry," which she describes as "a sort of delirium tremens in verse" (1). The translations steal from the time that she would much rather spend writing, but they "slip through one's mind without leaving a trace."[8] She also urges Zambrano to find a way to "accomplish the impossible" and write, saying that she liked very much the short pieces included with Zambrano's last letter, asking her to send more things as soon as they're published, and telling her that she has "the absolute obligation" to continue her work (3).[9]

In response to a request from Zambrano, Chacel encloses some of her own publications, telling Zambrano that she would gladly have some of her work published in a collection that Zambrano mentioned. Zambrano is now living in Rome, where Chacel and her husband spent the first half of the 1920s and where Chacel wrote *Estación. Ida y vuelta* [Station. Departure and Return], her first novel. In a very poignant passage, she asks Zambrano: "And what's Rome up to?" Mentioning several places, in particular, their studio, she asks Zambrano to look at everything for her, and tells Zambrano that she cannot let herself recall those days anymore, that when she does, it feels like "I'm dying. Because once dead, one is comfortable, what's hard is the actual dying, and when I think that at one time I was alive I feel as though there's something like a tail sticking out of my grave, a mysterious, wagging something, and in that something my agony recurs continually."

Given Zambrano's comments in subsequent letters, one can only assume that Chacel's later letters, if indeed there were more letters, contained similar remarks about life in exile and words of encouragement. In the absence of such letters, however, several published pieces and a reference to Zambrano in the last volume of Chacel's diary provide evidence of her feelings; they also provide insight into the aesthetic and political differences that vexed the women's friendship. The first of those pieces, a group of six essays published in 1937, precedes all of the two women's letters. The essays contain no mention of Zambrano. One of them, however, probably bears directly on Zambrano's letters to Chacel in 1938 and 1941, and Zambrano commented about two of the others in print. All of the essays appeared in the first issues of *Hora de España*, a journal devoted to intellectual and creative material published during the civil war by writers and intellectuals in support of the Republic. Zambrano also contributed to the journal, almost from its inception, and she was involved in its editing.[10] She clearly read Chacel's pieces closely, at times approvingly, at times not. One of those pieces, "Epístola moral a Sérpula" [Moral Epistle to Sérpula], was a long poem dedicated to Concha Albornoz, a friend of both women to whom Chacel would later dedicate her *Confession*. The other pieces were in prose: "Carta a José Bergamín sobre anarquía y cristianismo" [Letter to José Bergamín about Anarchy and Christianity], an open letter to Spanish (and Catholic) poet Bergamín, about recognition of the "anarchic principle" inherent in both Spanish philosophy and Christianity as crucial to the success of the revolution that was occurring in Spain; and essays about Galdós (discussed in Noël's introduction) and nineteenth-century Spanish essayist Mariano José de Larra—"Un nombre al frente: Galdós" [One Name Out in Front: Galdós] and "La primera palabra sobre la vida: En el primer centenario de Larra (1837–1937)" [The First Word about Life: On Larra's First Centenary (1837–1937)], respectively. Zambrano refers briefly but positively to the last two articles in *Los intelectuales en el drama de España*—"two names more alive than ever in the revolution as experienced today" (115); but with two of Chacel's essays she apparently took issue.

One of those two essays focused on the dynamic between culture and pueblo, an issue that Zambrano defines in *Intelectuales* as "central, decisive" (115), and in "Hora de España, XXIII" explains that "never before in Spain's history, nor in the history of any other Western nation ... has it been so evident that the destiny of thought is linked to the *pueblo*" (278). Chacel, in her comments, does not disagree about the importance of that bond, but she cautions against the paternalism and "mirage of pseudo-culture" on the part of well-meaning poets and intellectuals, implicitly those (among them Zambrano) involved in the Pedagogical Missions devoted to teaching the Spanish *pueblo* about Spanish history and culture.[11] Not surprisingly, Zambrano referred to Chacel's essay as a "harsh look" at her topic (*Los intelectuales* 115). The essay's dense, highly nuanced discussion, as Johannes Lechner has noted, is still pertinent today (181), and Zambrano's brief evaluation could itself be considered harsh. Its harshness is hardly surprising, however, not so much because of Zambrano's participation in the Pedagogical Missions as because Chacel's comments exemplify well the difference between the nature of her support of the Republic—or any specific political position—and Zambrano's. That difference is also manifest in Chacel's essay about Ortega y Gasset that appeared in *Hora de España* ("La nueva vida de *El viviente*"). Zambrano made no comment in print about the essay, but it's hard to imagine that she would have shared Chacel's willingness to separate Ortega's philosophy from his politics, and Chacel seems to do just that (366, 367). Explaining that Ortega "never spoke about politics" and that now was not the appropriate time to "combat" that aspect of his work (as others were doing), she focuses on what she defines as his real contribution—a "luminous and brutal" truth that demanded continual, rigorous contemplation, a mix of "living and standing aside" that is the "essence of the good life" (367).

The words in Chacel's essay, written early in 1937 and published after she had left for Paris, could not have pleased Zambrano, and they could well have given rise to the argument mentioned in her letters of 1938 and 1941. Not only did they address the work of a figure who had inspired but also prompted dissent on the part of the two friends, they spoke to a fundamental difference in their understanding of aesthetics, ethics, and commitment. As Chacel herself once replied when asked about her moment of awakening with respect to politics, she never had such a moment; rather, she was "'normally' engagée," her world "could only be that of the left . . . the progressive left," which she said was "a set of morals, a way of life" (Porlán 33). With respect to the civil war, that way of life included signing manifestos in support of the Republic, her essays for *Hora de España*, and several months of volunteer service with the Red Cross in a Madrid hospital.[12] However, throughout her life she explained that her engagement was that of a thinker and writer, that she would seek to affect the thinking and actions of others through her words, involving herself in the war "with all my soul," but in "an elegiac key" ("*Sendas*" 248).[13] Zambrano's involvement was quite different. As a student and young philosopher, she had struggled throughout the 1920s—also her twenties—to reconcile the philosopher's necessarily detached observation with an activist's participation. She defined her involvement as "moderate" but "intense, implacable, as had also been true of my philosophical activity, which was doubtless behind my activity in the war, sustaining me" (quoted in Ortega Muñoz 64).

Re-encounter (1)

After apparently almost three decades without either written or personal contact, in the 1980s Chacel and Zambrano met again in both print and person. The first of those re-encounters occurred in 1981, in "Pentagrama" [Stave], an essay about *Claros del bosque* [Clearings in the Wood] included in Chacel's collection *Los títulos* [The Titles]. She had read the book and discussed it with her friend, the Spanish poet Clara Janés, as Janés explains in her collection of essays about Zambrano (127). Janés recounts one of their conversations with great fondness;

also present was the writer Rafael Martínez Nadal, well-known for his friendship with García Lorca (25-30). Chacel too found the conversation enjoyable, describing it the following day in her diary as *"magnífico"* (*Vuelta* 442). It was the night of 31 March 1981; the topic was Zambrano's *Claros del bosque*. Janés had long heard about Zambrano and her work, but she had not yet met her—Zambrano was still in exile—and the exchange of memories between Chacel and Martínez Nadal brought Zambrano to life for her as a person. Recalling the Madrid that she and Zambrano knew before the war, Chacel described a passionate mix of love and politics and she spoke about the impact that Ortega y Gasset had on their lives. Her brief portrait of Zambrano was complex and vivid; along with her two essays about Zambrano that date from the same time, it shows that over the years Chacel's memories of Zambrano had not faded. Indeed, she refers to a sonnet she dedicated to Zambrano before the war and the veiled allusions it contains to Zambrano's relationship—intellectual "and something more"—with Xavier Zubiri, philosopher, professor, and fellow disciple of Ortega a few years older than Zambrano.

"Pentagrama" offers further proof of Chacel's enduring feelings about Zambrano and interest in her work. Like all of Chacel's writing, the essay defies summarization, given the extent to which digression and qualification are integral to her thinking, and it is clear that she thought deeply about Zambrano's book. Also clear is her admiration, in particular, of Zambrano's anguished and moving development of the heart metaphor at its center. However, even as she praises Zambrano's achievement—the "perfect music" of her language (her "word")—Chacel explains that the "pure mysticism" that works as the book's driving force differs from her own "natural inclination" (523). The "stave" in her title is suggestive of that inclination and of a measured, Apollonian song. Zambrano's song, on the other hand, springs from a "certainty" that Chacel's does not, even cannot share. Nevertheless, in her admittedly Apollonian way, Chacel expresses enthusiasm for Zambrano's work, finding her certainty hard-won against so many years of "adversity's continual avalanche" and worthy of enthusiasm, sung with or without notation (524).[14]

The second re-encounter, "Rosa mística," occurred in Chacel's open letter to Zambrano mentioned above. A delicate balancing of intimacy and distance, the essay offers an explanation for her lack of response to Zambrano's letters and a meditation on the relationship between the two women. Taking responsibility for the cessation of their correspondence, Chacel stresses that it was not conflict that prevented her from writing. Rather, it was the enormity of the task of keeping in touch in a truly meaningful way. Given all that was happening to them and the differences in their respective natures, what they needed was the person-to-person contact impossible in letters. For the purpose of a vital interchange of ideas and thoughts about experiences, letters were dead on arrival, if in fact they did arrive, seeing that their senders and recipients moved frequently over the years. Consequently, Chacel explains, the divergence between the paths of the two friends occurred harmoniously, even though the paradoxical consonance between their respective "cantinelas" was played on different instruments, and remained undocumented (for themselves and for others) (526). The same was true of the bond itself between the two women.

To describe that bond and affirm her loyalty to it over the years, Chacel recalls its beginning. Evoking the inherent difference between the two women's natures and talents that she had discussed in "Pentagrama," Chacel says that Zambrano always seemed at once younger (even more than the slight difference in their ages would suggest) and more advanced than she was, in her vision as a thinker, a teacher. Perhaps it was that combination of youth and maturity—"a soul, or a being supremely settled in its self"—that prompted the acceptance and respect enjoyed by Zambrano, when Chacel was "always tolerated" (527).[15] Seeking to portray both Zambrano as she was at the time and the difference between Zambrano and herself, Chacel cites Zambrano's question about a sonnet that Chacel had dedicated to her in the mid-1930s: "Am I the eburnean rose?" Chacel's response to that question, although magnificently wrought, is labyrinthine, and to analyze it would require an essay in itself. What's important here, however, is her return to the sonnet she had mentioned in her conversation with Janés and Martínez Nadal, discussed in both instances as a way to demonstrate the confluence of present and past as lived—and living—experience. The sonnet in question belongs to a group of thirty sonnets, *A la orilla del pozo* [At the well's edge], published in 1936. As Chacel explained in her preface to the second edition of the book (1985), the poems were an attempt to write portraits of various friends by marrying the "inextricable freedom" granted by surrealism with the implacable rigor of the sonnet form. Highly cryptic, they alluded to "confidential secrets" related to the friends portrayed. In one of the lines of the sonnet dedicated to Zambrano, an eburnean rose appears, alongside a black lily, "the young philosopher Zubiri," as she explained in her conversation with Janés and Martínez Nadal (27). Hence, Zambrano's question. Chacel's answer in "Rosa mística" is affirmative and she explains why, probing deeply the image of the pure, white rose, relating it to the fairy tale about Beauty and the Beast, and telling Zambrano that her goal in the open letter—an ecstatic, not static, portrait—was to evoke her "exactly as you really were when you were really part of a time easily caught in fourteen lines" (529, 531).

One cannot but note a decided irony here and a mix of critique, praise, and perhaps also pain in Chacel's use of the sonnet. Making it the focus of her comments allows Chacel to stress her long friendship with Zambrano and to praise Zambrano's accomplishments, but at the same time to sing the other woman's praise in her own, more measured way, as she had in "Pentagrama." Although she defines that way as incapable of reaching Zambrano's heights, she displays brilliantly its potential and her ability to realize it. Brilliantly, but not without a hint of bitterness, because even though Chacel admits that she has chosen, not merely followed, her own path, reading her diaries one learns how much suffering her choice often seemed to cause her and the harshness with which she notes the apparent recognition enjoyed by others. Zambrano is mentioned only once in those diaries and, curiously, that mention occurs in relation to "Rosa mística." In June of 1982, when Chacel was evidently writing the open letter, she noted in *Estación Termini* that "I need to finish the hodgepodge about María Zambrano I'm putting together because *Cuadernos* [*Hispanoamericanos*] asked for something" (*Estación Termini* 41). The contrast between that comment and the words in "Rosa mística" is marked, even if one keeps in mind their convincing words of praise. However, the comment is consistent with the ambivalence and nuanced qualification in which that praise is couched in both "Rosa mística" and "Pentagrama." Given such constant equivocation and the complex mix of conviction and questioning throughout Chacel's oeuvre, her relationship with a person as simultaneously like and unlike her can only have brought not only pleasure but pain. How conflicted she must have felt when in 1988 Zambrano was awarded the Cervantes prize, probably the most prestigious award a writer in Castilian can receive, other than the Nobel. Although she names few names, and Zambrano's is not among them, the entries in Chacel's diary around the time the prize was announced indicate the hope that in this, "my ninetieth year," the prize might fall to her (322).[16]

And if Chacel had won that prize, would Zambrano have experienced a similar disappointment? Without documentation it's of course impossible to know, and to my knowledge, the last published pieces in which one of them mentions the other are the entry in Chacel's diary and Zambrano's brief homage to Chacel in *Un Ángel Más*. However, there is documentation that the two women met in person at least once after Zambrano returned from exile. It was Zambrano who initiated the meeting, by asking Clara Janés, a friend of them both, to "Bring me Rosa" (48). Janés did as Zambrano asked and more, "traversing half of Madrid" with Chacel "until we found white roses . . . the symbolism had not only lasted, it had become a tradition" (28). As Janés tells it, the encounter was more than cordial, the conversation "very lively," Chacel and Zambrano laughing as they exchanged comments about where they would be buried, both of them saying—albeit not without qualifications—they were Catholic. They also reminisced about Zambrano's marriage and her husband's reluctance to divorce, despite their long separation. Chacel's comment was that she had expected him, being Basque and "so strong, such a brute," to have provided her with a real mainstay. "He was not a brute, if only he had been," Zambrano replied—quite likely alluding to Chacel's explanation in "Rosa mística" of the white rose and its ties to Beauty and the Beast. Their friendship, then, seemed to have come full circle. About how they felt as they talked, however, all one can do is speculate. If only, as Janés comments, describing Zambrano as "reflective" and Chacel as "impulsive," we could "see . . . the secret intention of each word spoken" (48–9).

Re-encounter (2)

The encounter between Chacel and Zambrano in the form of *Two Confessions* was prompted by an email exchange in which Noël and I learned that we had each conceived of the same book project. The many associations between the two essays and the friendship—often noted but never much studied—between their highly accomplished authors intrigued us both. Each of us had even planned to give the book the same title. Playing in our thoughts, the name of a magazine for women highly popular in the 1930s and early 1940s evoked the distance between the truth confessed in the magazine's stories of romance and the virtual impossibility of truth implicit in the very effort of confession.[17] As Chacel noted in her diary about the time she was writing her *Confession*, "There is an ambiguity or falseness intrinsic to this genre—diaries, memoirs, confessions . . . one silences what one would most want to have revealed" (*Vuelta* 83).

The coincidence of our plans encouraged us to collaborate. Because each of the two authors approached confession in her respective way, we wanted to honor and convey their differences as well as their similarities; consequently, each of us translated one of the essays. However, we each edited and critiqued the other's translation; the same is true for the introduction and the afterword. Considering the length of Chacel's essay with respect to Zambrano's, Noël offered to do the preliminary translations of the excerpts from Rousseau and Mauriac used by Chacel, to locate the passages Chacel refers to or includes in her essay, and to prepare the list of annotations. I then made alterations to the French as appropriate, noted additional citations, and suggested additional annotations as I worked on the translation. Although we prepared our respective translations independently, we consulted with each other when we had questions, at times making joint decisions, especially about issues that pertained to both essays.

Of those issues, the one that stands out most vividly concerns the two authors' "thinking through the question of confession" that Noël identifies as one of "the most fascinating features of their use of the essay" (10). The ways that Chacel and Zambrano put that thinking into written words—their style, as it were—differ, but they both make it possible for the reader to "see," as Noël notes, their thinking occur. Having translated Chacel's essay and worked with Zambrano's, I would suggest "experience" instead of "see" or, even better perhaps, "feel." I say that because Noël and I both remarked on traces of orality as we prepared the translations. Neither of the essays derived from a spoken text—indeed, the dense, intellectually challenging nature of their prose would not lend itself well to an oral presentation, and in neither essay is there an indication of a confessor, or reason to believe that the narrator is speaking, not composing. In both essays, however, there is a tentativeness and, consequently, also at times a lack of clarity, at least the sort of clarity that accompanies a well-plotted argument. Rather, the register is often mixed, there are incomplete sentences and apparently uncompleted ideas. In addition, the distinction between narration and citation is not always apparent. "Chacel moves from one of her writers to the next," I once wrote to Noël, ". . . at times with little or no transition or identifying reference." She noted that they "both internalize the writers they comment on, as though there were a permeability between the two of them and the object of their meditations . . . finding parts of themselves in all three." Also, I would add, between the two of them and their respective confessor-readers in whose thoughts they speak silently aloud.

Writing those last sentences, I am reminded of Noël's response to a question I asked about the challenges she might have encountered as she worked with Zambrano's prose, remarking that at times I had felt that translating both Zambrano and Chacel could be "tortuous," and that I've often spent as much or more time thinking about and taking notes about how Chacel thinks as I have translating. Noël observed that she too had spent "hours and hours [feeling frustrated]" but then "suddenly grasping how utterly original Zambrano was in interpreting Aristotle's dictum [for example] that the soul is 'like a hand.' The way she took hold of (so to speak) that hand and made it her hand, her thought, her image, was actually quite beautiful and moving. And exhilarating. And then of course suddenly I understood better how to translate that passage."

Noël's response was striking to me because it described well my own experience with Zambrano, as reader, translator, and in the present instance, reader-translator. Not only that, Noël's description of her work had prompted precisely the sort of certainty that Zambrano discusses as the culmination of her method, her understanding of how truth can be known, how one can be certain—with an inner certainty of which one might have neither tangible proof nor reasoned explanation. Zambrano's term for this certainty is "evidencia," a term that on my first reading of her *Confession* I found challenging, especially as I thought about its translation.[18] Noël reported having a similar

Afterword ❊ 221

feeling but at the same time following a process not unlike the one she had followed with Aristotle's *De anima*: "'Evidence' and 'proof' didn't seem right in English," she wrote, "so in most cases I opted for 'certainty,' since it seemed to me that it was what she was really aiming for. Also, the [dictionary of Spain's] Real Academia notes that 'evidencia' in Spanish is 'certeza clara.' The problem is, 'evidencia' is also a moral, theological, rhetorical, and philosophical term, and Zambrano's condensed thinking does not indicate what she means. So we have 'certeza' but one not necessarily 'clara.'"

A certainty or evidence sure but not clear. Noël's comments about Zambrano's work impressed me strongly in yet another way, because they reminded me of Chacel's discussion in "Pentagrama" and "Rosa mística" of Zambrano's thought and writing. Even more strongly in this context, they reminded me of Chacel's discussion in those essays of her own thinking and writing, of how it differed from Zambrano's, explaining Zambrano's sphere as that of Dionysius, as opposed to her (Chacel's) long avowed adherence to Apollo's law ("Pentagrama" 523). Noël's comments about translating Zambrano's essay bear out that distinction, I realized, especially when I thought about the notes I took as I worked with Chacel's prose. Just as "certainty," even though not clear, seems apt for Zambrano, the term that played in my thoughts as I worked—and thought about the translation while doing other things—is "arborescence." Chacel herself suggests that term early in her *Confession*, in her explanation of eros "as arborescent in structure" (94).

Chacel's statement stopped me when I first read it. Of all the terms dearest to her, I would suggest that "eros" is the most dear, the closest to Chacel's understanding of (and preferred way of referring to) the force that prompts, propels, and sustains life. Here I can note only that the word appears continually throughout her oeuvre and stress the importance of Chacel's representing it as an unceasing, organic, living, branching out. Consequently, in both form and nature, as Chacel indicates in her essay, her comments are inevitably digressive, but in a patterned—or structured—way. Her prose moves slowly, clottedly, but it does move, the narrative dense and elegant but with fits and starts of passages marked by occasional spurts of, or allusions to, a lower register, which in places, despite the conceptual complexity, it seems best to translate using contractions so as to convey rather than conceal the seemingly spontaneous reflections and asides on Chacel's part, the sporadic accelerations in pace. To cite just one example: in her analysis of Cervantes's continual mistreatment of Don Quixote as a punishment for his (Cervantes's) own weakness, his self-deception, Chacel devises a complex discussion of a coarse Spanish expression for telling someone that he's worthless, that is, by "shitting on him" (101). She never uses that vulgar verb, though. Rather, she alludes to it and explains its use in this context as particularly Spanish. Consequently, even if a reader quickly grasps her conceit, a full recognition and appreciation of its dimension grows slowly with respect to the *Quixote*—the novel, not merely its protagonist—as a humorous but painful self-deprecating confession on the part of Cervantes.

Thinking about my work with that conceit and reading Noël's translation of Zambrano's "evidencia," I cannot but note an ironic contrast between the two authors' masterful discussions of confession and the profound sense of failure that marks their essays. No doubt that contrast is inevitable, however, given their topic, the moment of their composition with respect to the civil war, and their place in the work of their respective authors. Although both Chacel and Zambrano were living and working in situations directly related to the outcome of the war, those situations differed greatly.[19] In Zambrano's case, the war had ended only recently and the experience of defeat was raw, as her letters to Chacel poignantly reveal and as she explained later in detail in *Delirio y destino: Veinte años de una española* [Delirium and Destiny: A Spaniard in Her Twenties]. Chacel, writing more than two decades later—three, when she wrote the preamble—had been living with its consequences for a long time. Not surprisingly, then, the interests and concerns registered through and throughout her work as a whole, her confession speaks to the role of writers and intellectuals with respect to Spanish literature and culture as a whole. Seeking to explain the absence of confession in the past, she makes—if not a confession—a stunning admission of the failure on the part of herself and the writers and intellectuals of her generation to "do something overwhelming. Something seductive, tempting, which is the only thing that counts" (70). As she noted in her homage to Zambrano, the pieces of the Spanish puzzle have been, and remain, scattered. For that dispersion, Chacel believes, the good bear as much guilt as the evil.

Re-encounter (3)

Years ago, as Spanish majors at Douglass College, Noël and I learned about the historical and cultural heritage of Spain from three extraordinary teachers. Micaela Misiego, translator of *The Red Badge of Courage*, taught a memorably animated course on the civilization of Spain; Marina Romero, a widely published poet and essayist, showed us that language, literature, and culture are inevitably and integrally interrelated; Leonardo Santamarina, who had been an artillery captain in the Republican army, spent time in a French refugee camp, and, on his release, studied in Havana before arriving in New Brunswick, instilled in many Douglass students an appreciation of both the humor and the pathos of *Don Quixote*. With great respect and heartfelt thanks, we dedicate our work in *Two Confessions* to their memory.

Notes

1. All references to Chacel's essays will be to their publication in the *Obra completa* and included parenthetically in the text.

2. There are several excellent introductory discussions of both Chacel's and Zambrano's work (see, for example, Mangini and de la Fuente), but little attention has been paid to the interaction between the two writers, their thought, or their styles; notable exceptions are Clavo Sebastián, Janés, Johnson, Paraíso de Leal, and Rodríguez-Fischer (in her introductory essays in the two volumes of articles in Chacel's *Obra completa* and in *Cartas a Rosa Chacel*). I am grateful to Anna Caballé for corresponding with me about this issue.

3. In 1936, Zambrano was married to Alfonso Rodríguez Aldave (1911–2008), who served the Republican government during the war as secretary to the Spanish ambassador in Santiago de Chile, and then in the Republican army. Zambrano writes movingly in *Delirio y destino* of their departure from Spain at the end of the war. They separated in 1948 and divorced some years later.

4. All references to Zambrano's letters to Chacel will be to *Cartas a Rosa Chacel* and noted parenthetically in the text.

5. Clavo Sebastián explains quite succinctly the differences between the "reasons" of Chacel and Zambrano, the former adhering more closely

to Ortega's "razón vital" [vital reason], since Zambrano developed her own "razón poética" [poetic reason]. Caution is in order, however: if one considers narrative as poesis, as Chacel certainly did, it is clear that Chacel exposes the limits of Ortega's reason poetically through the first-person protagonist of *La sinrazón*.

6. Considering the probable date of Chacel's letter, the nature of her comments about Ortega in "La nueva vida de *El viviente*," and Zambrano's close involvement with *Hora de España*, where the article appeared, it seems likely that the disagreement occurred over that piece.

7. My thanks to the Fundación María Zambrano for granting me permission to cite from the letter, to Madeline Cámara for making it possible for me to have a photocopy of it, and to Roberta Johnson for sharing her notes from a visit to the Fundación and her thoughts about both Chacel and Zambrano. The letter comprises three typewritten pages; the signature is written in longhand: "I look forward to your letter and embrace you warmly. Rosa."

8. Several passages in Chacel's diaries belie this remark and suggest that the translations did indeed leave a trace. For example, her comments about a "zone of prayer" (zona de oración) and the presence (as scent) of the Eumenides in T. S. Eliot's *Family Reunion* reveal more than a passing acquaintance between her thoughts and his (*Ida* 33, 385; *Vuelta* 35, 401). Similarly, Chacel's intimate knowledge of Racine's *Phèdre* was clearly important when she wrote the passages in *La sinrazón* about Herminia's crisis. Equally telling are the comments in *Estación Termini*, the third volume of her diary, about a performance of her translation ("my *Fedra*") she attended in Madrid in 1986. Although she found the play well done overall, she was chagrined to find herself listed as a member of the Spanish Real Academia (Royal Academy), an honor she never received but one she certainly deserved, as she herself knew all too well (260).

9. "El cáliz" [The Chalice] and "La condenación de Aristóteles" [Aristotle's Sentence], the pieces to which Chacel refers, were later revised slightly and included in *Delirio y destino*.

10. In "*Hora de España*. XXIII," Zambrano says that when she left Barcelona, she took with her a few page proofs from the journal's last issue, which had been printed but did not see distribution until long after the war had ended (275).

11. For a discussion of Zambrano's work with the Pedagogical Missions and her political activity during the 1920s and 1930s, see Johnson's essay in *Delirium and Destiny* (215–35).

12. Many years after the war, Chacel reflected on that period of service and the Red Cross itself in "Evocar la Cruz Roja" [Recalling the Red Cross].

13. Throughout her life, Chacel spoke openly and frequently in her essays and interviews about her minimal participation in the war, often using the verb "confesar" (which can be translated as either "confess" or "admit") to stress the very limited nature of her role. At the same time, however, she usually explained, as in "Invitación a la escuela" [Invitation to a New Semester], for example, that she "enlisted in literature," feeling confident that from there would spring the truly essential contribution, "precisely because of its [literature's] purity" (329). That Chacel believed "literature" had failed, perhaps utterly, and that its failure anguished, even tormented her, is clear in both "Invitación" and her *Confession*.

14. Chacel's comments about the years of struggle that made possible the "clearings" in *Claros del bosque* remind one of the difference that separates the much later book from the anguished fragmentation of the *Confession*. Her comments are also reminiscent of the affectionate words that in the same year she inscribed in a copy of her *Ofrenda a una virgen loca* now found in the Fundación María Zambrano, urging Zambrano to "work some miracle" and return to Spain, where there are people who love her, she herself among them.

15. Chacel's remark here echoes her frequent references in her diaries and interviews to unhappiness with her physical appearance and her awkwardness in social situations.

16. The title refers to Stazione di Roma Termini, the main train station in Rome. The title Chacel chose for the last volume of her diary and the reference to her advanced age call to mind the dedication to Zambrano she inscribed (1988) in a copy of *Ciencias naturales* now in the Fundación María Zambrano. She affirms her admiration and affection for Zambrano, telling her that no distance will ever come between them, although she sees Zambrano now in her dawn and she herself is approaching twilight.

17. *True Confessions* was published between 1919 and 1979 but was at its most popular during the 1930s and early 1940s.

18. My thanks to Maryanne Bertram for helping me think through this passage philosophically, in particular Zambrano's use of "evidencia."

19. The shift in perspective in Chacel's *Confession* with respect to Zambrano's is no doubt indicative of a general evolution in the work of the Spanish writers in exile as a whole. As Sebastiaan Faber has explained, thinking about the war became more reflective and nuanced as the experience of the war and the defeat of the Republic grew less immediate; that change was inevitably registered in the writing (345–46).

Works Cited

Chacel, Rosa. *A la orilla de un pozo. Poesía (1931–1991).* Ed. Antoni Marí. Barcelona: Tusquets, 1992. (Orig. 1936).

———. *Alcancía. Ida.* Barcelona: Seix Barral, 1982.

———. *Alcancía. Vuelta.* Barcelona: Seix Barral, 1982.

———. *Alcancía. Estación Termini.* Ed. Carlos Pérez Chacel and Antonio Piedra. Salamanca: Junta de Castilla y León, Consejería de Educación y Cultura, 1998.

———. *Artículos.* Vols. II and III of *Obra completa.* Ed. Ana Rodríguez-Fischer. Valladolid: Excma. Diputación Provincial de Madrid, Centro de Estudios, Fundación Jorge Guillén, 1993.

———. "Carta a José Bergamín sobre anarquía y cristianismo." *Artículos* II. 377–89. (Orig. *Hora de España* 7 [July 1937]: 13–26).

———. "Cultura y pueblo." *Artículos* II. 369–76. (Orig. *Hora de España* 1 [Jan. 1937]: 13–22).

———. *De mar a mar. Epistolario Rosa Chacel-Ana María Moix.* Ed. Ana Rodríguez-Fischer. Barcelona: Ediciones Península, 1998.

———. "Epístola moral a Sérpula." *A la orilla de un pozo. Poesía (1931–1991).* 45–49. (Orig. *Hora de España* 6 [June 1937]: 45–49).

———. *Estación ida y vuelta.* Madrid: CVS Ediciones, 1974.

———. "Evocar a la Cruz Roja." *Artículos* II. 357–60. (Orig. *Cruz Roja* [1987]).

———. "Invitación a la escuela." *Artículos* I. 319–31.

———. "La nueva vida de *El viviente* (sobre las *Obras completas* de José Ortega y Gasset)." *Artículos* I. 365–68. (Orig. *Hora de España* 4 [Apr. 1937]: 47–50).

———. "Un nombre al frente: Galdós." *Artículos* I. 75–79. (Orig. *Hora de España* 2 [Feb. 1937]: 47–50).

———. "Pentagrama." *Artículos* I. 521–24. (Orig. *Los títulos.* Ed. Clara Janés. Barcelona: Edhasa, 1981. 73–77).

———. "La primera palabra sobre la vida. En el primer centenario de Larra (1837–1937)." *Artículos* II. 71–74. (Orig. *Hora de España* 3 [Mar. 1937]: 54–56).

———. "Rosa mística." *Artículos* I. 525–31. (Orig. *Cuadernos Hispanoamericanos* 413 [1984]: 5–9).

———. *La sinrazón.* Buenos Aires: Losada, 1960. (*Dream of Reason.* Trans. Carol Maier. Lincoln: U of Nebraska P, 2009).

———. Unpublished letter to María Zambrano. 1 July 1954. Fundación María Zambrano. 3 pp.

Clavo Sebastián, María José. "Rosa Chacel y María Zambrano: *La confesión.*" *Actas del Congreso en Homenaje a Rosa Chacel. Ponencias y comunicaciones.* Ed. María Pilar Martínez Latre. Logroño: Universidad de la Rioja, 1994. 121-32.

Faber, Sebastiaan. "The Exile's Dilemma: Writing the Civil War from Elsewhere." *Teaching Representations of the Spanish Civil War.* Ed. Noël Valis. New York: Modern Language Association, 2007. 341-51.

Fuente, Inmaculada de la. *Mujeres de la posguerra. De Carmen Laforet a Rosa Chacel. Historia de una generación.* Madrid: Planeta, 2002.

Janés, Clara. *María Zambrano. Desde la sombra llameante.* Madrid: Siruela, 2010.

Johnson, Roberta. "The Context and Achievement of *Delirium and Destiny*." *Delirium and Destiny,* trans. Carol Maier. Commentary by Roberta Johnson. Trans. of María Zambrano, *Delirio y destino.* 1989. Albany: SUNY P, 1999. 215-35.

———. "'Self'-Consciousness in Rosa Chacel and María Zambrano." *The Bucknell Review* 39.2 (1996): 54-72.

Lechner, Johannes. *El compromiso en la poesía española del siglo XX. Parte Primera. De la generación de 1898 a 1939.* Leiden: Universitaire Pers Leiden, 1968.

Mangini, Shirley. *Las modernas de Madrid: Las grandes intelectuales españolas de la vanguardia.* Barcelona: Península, 2001.

Ortega Muñoz, Juan Fernando. *Biografía de María Zambrano.* Málaga: Arguval, 2006.

Paraíso de Leal, Isabel. "Lo apolíneo y lo dionisíaco en la poesía de Rosa Chacel." *Actas del Congreso en Homenaje a Rosa Chacel: ponencias y comunicaciones.* Logroño: Universidad de la Rioja, 1994. 31-50.

Porlán, Alberto. *La sinrazón de Rosa Chacel.* Madrid: Anjana, 1984.

Rodríguez-Fischer, Ana, ed. *Cartas a Rosa Chacel.* Madrid: Versal, 1992.

———. "Introducción." *Artículos. Obra completa de Rosa Chacel.* I. 11-30.

Zambrano, María. *Claros del bosque.* Barcelona: Seix Barral, 1977.

———. *Delirio y destino: los veinte años de una española.* Madrid: Mondadori, 1989. (*Delirium and Destiny: A Spaniard in Her Twenties.* Trans. Carol Maier. Albany: SUNY P, 1999).

———. "'Hora de España,' XXIII." María Zambrano. *Los intelectuales en el drama de España y escritos de la Guerra Civil.* Ed. Jesús Moreno Sanz. Madrid: Trotta, 1998. 275-92. (Orig. 1973. Introduction to the facsimile edition of *Hora de España.* Vaduz-Barcelona: Topos-Laia, 1977. iii-xix).

———. "Los intelectuales en el drama de España." *Los intelectuales en el drama de España y escritos de la Guerra Civil.* Ed. Jesús Moreno Sanz. Madrid: Trotta, 1998. 75-127. (Orig. Santiago de Chile: Panorama, 1937).

———. "Rosa." *Un Ángel Más* 3-4 (Winter-Spring 1988): 11-12.

Annotations

Confession
María Zambrano

Title Page

Zambrano's essay was originally published under the title, *La confesión: género literario y método* [Confession: A Literary Genre and Method], in the Mexican journal *Luminar*, in two parts (1941 and 1943), and then in book form (Mexico City: Ediciones Luminar, 1943). This translation is based on the 1995 edition (Madrid: Ediciones Siruela), which incorporates Zambrano's manuscript corrections from 1965. We have not included the separate essay, "La soledad enamorada" [Solitude in Love] (1939), which appears as an appendix in the Mondadori edition (Madrid, 1988). All translations are our own; when published translations were available, however, we consulted them, in some instances slightly modifying our versions. Biblical quotations are taken from the King James Version.

page 20. Anacreon (582 BC–485 BC): A Greek lyric poet, much imitated for his hymns and bacchanalian and love poetry.

page 29. "I do not wish to argue": Zambrano mistakenly replaced Augustine's "iniquity" (orig. "iniquitas") in the phrase, "lest my own iniquity be deceived," with "disquietude" ("inquietud").

page 30. "firmness and clarity": "And I fixed my gaze on other things that are below you, and I saw that they neither altogether are, nor altogether are not" (Book VII, 17). [Author's note]

230 ❋ Annotations

page 33. Tschuang-Tse, or Zhuangzi (4th century BC): A Chinese philosopher with a skeptical turn of mind, considered a precursor of relativism.

page 38. "foundations of Stoicism": In her revisions of 1965, Zambrano substituted "Stoicism" for "Scholasticism," leaving a question mark in the margins. [Editor's note, 1995 ed.]

page 40. "It is not a question of identity": In her revisions of 1965, Zambrano underlined this apparent contradiction [between "not a question of identity" and "a question of identity" in the previous paragraph] without resolving it. [Editor's note, 1995 ed.]

page 41. John of Ruysbroeck (1293/94–1381): A Flemish mystic, author of *The Spiritual Espousals* and *The Seven Steps of the Ladder of Spiritual Love*.

page 45. Abenarabí, or Ibn Arabi (1165–1240): A Sufi mystic and philosopher of Al-Andalus, known for *The Revelations of Mecca*.

page 48. "That love so honest": Lines from "Unos conjuros de amor" [Love Spells], by the fifteenth-century *cancionero* poet Costana.

page 50. Madame d'Houdetot: Rousseau recounted his novelesque encounter with Sophie d'Houdetot (1730–1813), a French noblewoman, in Book 9 of his *Confessions*.

page 59. "Antigone, buried alive": In Sophocles's play, Creon sentences Antigone to be buried alive, but she kills herself first.

page 61. "the soul is like a hand" and "the soul is, in some sense, all things": Both quotations are from Aristotle's *De anima*. Aristotle explains the first image in this way: "as the hand is the instrument of all instruments, so is the intellect the form of forms." What follows is Zambrano's rich elaboration on the soul's *potentia*, embedded in the second citation, beginning with the soul as a "particular place, or seat, or power."

page 63. "Posthumous works": Soren Kierkegaard, *Either/Or* (1843).

Confession
Rosa Chacel

Title page

Originally published in 1971 by Edhasa, in Barcelona. This translation is based on the second edition (1980), which includes a Preamble written in 1979. We have also consulted the edition published in Chacel's *Obra completa* [Complete Work], which contains a few minor corrections (Valladolid: Excma. Diputación Provincial de Madrid, Centro de Estudios, Fundación Jorge Guillén, 1989). All translations are our own; when published translations were available, however, we consulted them, in some instances slightly modifying our versions.

Dedication

Concha de Albornoz: Daughter of Republican politician Álvaro de Albornoz, student, with Chacel, at the San Fernando School of Fine Arts, and writer; died in 1972, three months after *La confesión* was published.

Preamble

page 69. "The event is sufficiently explained in my autobiography": Chacel refers here to *Desde el amanecer: Autobiografía de mis primeros diez años* [Since Daybreak: Autobiography of My First Ten Years] (Madrid: Revista de Occidente, 1972). Although this is the only specific reference that Chacel makes to her own work in her *Confession*, she clearly alludes to it in other passages of the essay. The incident in the La Plata zoo, for example, and the failure to "tempt with the good," both of them found in the Preamble, are strongly reminiscent of her novel *La sinrazón*, which was published shortly before she began to work on *Confession* (1960; *Dream of Reason*, trans. Carol Maier [Lincoln: U of Nebraska P, 2009]).

page 71. José Ortega y Gasset (1883-1955): The most influential Spanish thinker of the period, whose philosophy centered on the dictum, "I am myself and my circumstance, and if I do not save it, I cannot save myself." Chacel refers to his essay, "Sobre unas 'Memorias'" (1927), and the prologue to the first edition of his *Obras completas* [Complete Works] (1932).

page 66. "To dare to be completely oneself": Kierkegaard, *The Sickness Unto Death* (1849).

page 67. "The fleeting winged halo": Line from the poem, "A la rosa," by Francisco de Rioja (1583–1659).

page 68. *Un chien andalou* [An Andalusian Dog] (1929): Iconic silent surrealist film by Luis Buñuel and Salvador Dalí.

page 69. *Les Chants de Maldoror* [Maldoror] (1869; 1874) (Spanish trans. by Julio Gómez de la Serna, 1927), by the Comte de Lautréamont, a source of inspiration for symbolism, dada, and surrealism.

page 72. "the more will there is": Kierkegaard, *The Sickness Unto Death*.

page 75. Manuel Durán, "El sentido del tiempo en Quevedo": Published in *Cuadernos Americanos* 13.1 (Feb. 1954): 273–88.

page 76. Astete: A popular catechism text (1599), composed by the Jesuit Gaspar Astete.

page 76. Julián Marías, *Miguel de Unamuno* (Madrid: Espasa-Calpe, 1943).

page 76. Ricardo Gullón, *Autobiografías de Unamuno* (Madrid: Gredos, 1964).

page 78. Alphonse Daudet (1840–1897): Author of *Lettres de mon moulin* [Letters from My Mill] (1869) and *Sappho* (1884); Théophile Gautier (1811–1872): author of *Mademoiselle de Maupin* (1835) and *Le roman de la momie* [The Story of the Mummy] (1858).

page 79. "it's repulsive that someone would have said": In Chacel, *Estación. Ida y vuelta* (1930).

Annotations   ✳   233

page 80. François Mauriac (1885–1970): French Catholic novelist and author of *Thérèse Desqueyroux* (1927) and *Noeud de vipères* [Knot of Vipers] (1932).

page 83. Jacques Bénigne Bossuet (1627–1704): French bishop and theologian.

page 84. "She made every effort": Saint Augustine, *Confessions*, Book I, 17.

page 85. Françoise Louise de Warens (1699–1762): Patroness and mistress of Rousseau; Thérèse Le Vasseur: Seamstress and companion of Rousseau.

page 87. Madame de Dupin de Francueil (Marie-Aurore de Saxe) (1748–1821): The Lady of Chenonceaux Manor House, a freethinker and admirer of Rousseau.

page 88. "When he uttered the word 'reality'": In 1842, Kierkegaard heard Schelling lecture in Berlin and was overjoyed with his second lecture, as he wrote in his journal (III A 179).

page 89. Regine Olsen: Kierkegaard broke off his engagement with Regine Olsen (1822–1904) twice, in August and then in October 1841.

page 98. Ramiro de Maeztu (1875–1936): Member of the literary Generation of 1898 and author of the essay, *Don Quijote, Don Juan y La Celestina* (1926).

page 98. *Fêlure*: Jules Buisson, a friend and painter, first spoke of Baudelaire's *fêlure* [crack or fissure]; Sartre enlarged the notion as the experience of separation and solitariness.

page 101. Cambronne: When asked to surrender at Waterloo (1815), the French general Cambronne was said to have replied, "Merde!"

page 103. Juan de Mairena: An apocryphal writer with a philosophical, ironic voice, invented by poet Antonio Machado (1875–1939).

page 107. Pío Baroja (1872–1956) and Ramón María del Valle-Inclán (1866–1936): Stylistically innovative, modernist writers of the Generation of 1898.

page 107. *Esperpento*: A ferociously ironic literary style created by Ramón María del Valle-Inclán, which is based on the critical and often grotesque distortion of reality.

page 110. Salvador Monsalud: The gallant protagonist of Galdós's second series of *Episodios nacionales* (1875–79); Juanito Santa Cruz: The bourgeois Don Juan of *Fortunata y Jacinta* (1886–87); José María Bueno de Guzmán: The abulic and cultivated first person narrator-protagonist of *Lo prohibido* [The Forbidden] (1884–85).

page 110. Joaquín Casalduero, *Vida y obra de Galdós* (Buenos Aires: Losada, 1942; 2nd ed., 1961), the first serious book-length study to reevaluate the then-neglected novelist.

page 111. Gabriel Araceli: Youthful protagonist of Galdós's first series of *Episodios nacionales* (1873–75); Manuel Moreno Isla (Manolo Moreno): Inveterate bachelor and Anglophile in *Fortunata y Jacinta*; Federico Viera, who appears in *La incógnita* [The Unknown] (1889) and *Realidad* [Reality] (1889), is another Galdosian example of a wasted life, like Moreno Isla and Juanito Santa Cruz.

page 113. *El equipaje del rey José* [King Joseph's Luggage] (1875): The first novel of the second series of Galdós's *Episodios nacionales,* recounts the French defeat at the battle of Vitoria (1813) during the War of Independence, after which King Joseph I (Bonaparte) abdicated the Spanish throne.

page 113. Resistance: The World War II French Resistance Movement during the German Occupation of France.

page 114. *Los cien mil hijos de San Luis* (1877): The sixth novel of the second series of Galdós's *Episodios nacionales*, narrates the invasion of the French "Hundred Thousand Sons of Saint Louis" (also known as the Spanish Expedition) in 1823 to reimpose Fernando VII's absolute monarchy over the liberal government.

Annotations   ❊   235

page 114. Frenchified: *Afrancesado*, referring to Spanish liberals who espoused Enlightenment ideas and, in some cases, supported the French occupation of Spain (1808–14), hence the analogy to World War II Nazi collaborationists.

page 115. Fernando VII (1784–1833): Remembered for his despotic misrule of Spain.

page 116. Cádiz: The Cádiz Cortes (1810–12) established the first liberal constitution of Spain.

page 116. Fortunata: Mistress of Juanito Santa Cruz, the wild working-class protagonist of *Fortunata y Jacinta*; Benina (or Nina): The servant protagonist of *Misericordia* [Compassion] (1897); Nazarín: The Quixotic, unconventional priest from the eponymous novel (1895).

page 117. Pipaón (Juan Bragas): Friend and confidant of Salvador Monsalud, from the first three series of *Episodios nacionales*.

page 118. *La segunda casaca* [The Second Turncoat] (1876): Third novel of the second series of Galdosian *Episodios nacionales,* narrates the events leading to the Liberal Triennium government (1820–23).

page 119. Jacinta: Wife of Juanito Santa Cruz, the other female protagonist of *Fortunata y Jacinta*.

page 122. Camila Bueno de Guzmán: One of three cousins the protagonist-narrator woos in *Lo prohibido*.

page 123. José Ido del Sagrario: One of Galdós's most memorable secondary characters, a mentally unbalanced writer of trashy serial novels, appears in *Fortunata y Jacinta* and three other novels.

page 124. Guillermina Pacheco: A strong-willed woman of charity; Mauricia la Dura: An alcoholic, occasional prostitute. Both appear in *Fortunata y Jacinta*.

page 125. Pepe Carrillo: Husband of Eloísa, cuckolded by his best friend, protagonist José María de Guzmán, in *Lo prohibido*.

page 125. Tomás Orozco: Honorable if passionless character who appears in *La incógnita* and *Realidad.*

page 131. Joseph Schraibman, "Onirología galdosiana": Published in *El Museo Canario* 75-76 (1960): 347-66.

page 133. Antonio Sánchez Barbudo, *Estudios sobre Unamuno y Machado* (Madrid: Ediciones Guadarrama, 1959).

page 133. Pedro Jiménez Ilundain: A Basque businessman and friend, with whom Unamuno corresponded on the subject of his religious crisis, literature, and other matters.

page 133. *Amor y pedagogía* [Love and Pedagogy] (1902): Unamuno's story of a misguided father, Don Avito Carrascal, whose failed positivistic upbringing of his son Apolodoro ends in the son's suicide.

page 134. *Paz en la guerra* [Peace in War] (1895): Unamuno's first novel, set during the last major Carlist War (1872-76).

page 135. Don Fulgencio: Philosopher friend of Don Avito, in *Amor y pedagogía.*

page 135. Geoffrey Ribbans, "The Development of Unamuno's Novels: *Amor y pedagogía* and *Niebla.*" *Hispanic Studies in Honour of I. González Llubera.* Ed. Frank Pierce (Oxford: Dolphin Book Co., 1959), 269-85.

page 135. *Sainete:* One-act comic vignette, performed between acts or at the end of a play (18-20 c.).

page 135. Carlos Arniches (1866-1943): Popular playwright celebrated for his rich colloquial style.

page 135. Enrique García Álvarez (1873-1931): Playwright who specialized in puns and side-splitting jokes.

page 136. Clarín: Pseudonym of Leopoldo Alas (1852-1901), master of realism and author of the novel, *La Regenta* [*La Regenta* (The Judge's Wife)] (1884-85); see Adolfo Alas, ed., *Epistolario a Clarín: Menéndez y Pelayo, Unamuno, Palacio Valdés* (Madrid: Escorial, 1941), for Unamuno's soul-baring correspondence with Alas.

page 137. Federico de Onís (1885–1966): Spanish literary critic and professor at Columbia University.

page 139. *Obermann* (1804): Epistolary novel by Étienne Pivert de Senancour, exemplifying the *mal du siècle*.

page 140. *Sartor Resartus* (1836): Thomas Carlyle's satire critiquing materialism and utilitarianism while advocating spiritual reform.

page 140. *San Manuel Bueno, mártir* [Saint Manuel Bueno, Martyr] (1931; 1933, definitive ed.): Unamuno's classic novella about the anguish of a secretly nonbelieving priest who inspires faith in his parishioners.

page 141. *Recuerdos de niñez y de mocedad* [Memories of Childhood and Adolescence] (1908): Unamuno's effort to capture "the soul of childhood."

page 143. Herostratism: A term coined by Nietzsche in *Human, All Too Human* (1878) and taken up again by Unamuno; from Herostratus, who set fire to the temple of Diana in Ephesus, to gain immortality.

page 144. Unamuno, *Ensayos* (Madrid: Aguilar, 1945).

page 145. Unamuno, *La enormidad de España* (Mexico: Séneca, 1945).

page 150. *The Potting Shed* (1957): A play by Graham Greene. Father Callifer says: "'Let him live, God. I love him. Let him live. I will give you anything if you will let him live.' But what had I got to give him? I was a poor man. I said 'Take away what I love most. Take—take—,'" to which his nephew James replies: "'Take away my faith but let him live?'"

page 150. "I cite here without having the text": Chacel's comment here about citation hints tellingly at the conditions under which she wrote *Confession*, and to which she refers poignantly in her diary. Living in Rio, she found herself frustrated by the lack of access both to materials she would have liked to read again and to current publications, in particular work done in Spain. She was limited, however, to her memory of things read in the past, to books she either owned or could obtain from Buenos Aires, and to whatever she could read in Brazil's national library. In the library, she could spend an entire day, but there she had to read furiously and take notes (*Alcancía. Ida* [Coin Bank], Barcelona: Seix Barral, 1982).

Those notes, it goes without saying, were taken in longhand and then recopied to a typewritten page. Consequently, it is not surprising that there are frequent minor errors in the passages she transcribed; the same is true for those she cited from memory. We have located, confirmed, and compared each of Chacel's sources, but rather than reproduce her errors in our translation, we have consistently made silent corrections.

page 150. "You don't have me fooled": Spoken by the protagonist, Santiago Hernández, in Chacel's *La sinrazón* [*Dream of Reason*, 1960; trans. Carol Maier]: "The truth that lies deep in the well of my conscience can be expressed with the most provocative of sentences: 'You don't have me fooled!'"

page 159. "Man doth not yield himself": The epigraph Poe uses for his story of death and resurrection, "Ligeia" (1838), is attributed to Joseph Glanvill (1636–1680), English clergyman and philosopher.

page 163. *Vida de don Quijote y Sancho* [Our Lord Don Quixote: The Life of Don Quixote and Sancho] (1905): Unamuno's sui generis rewriting of Cervantes's novel.

page 166. "lightning unceasing": The title of a book of love poetry, *El rayo que no cesa* (1936), by Miguel Hernández.

page 167. "tragic sense of life": The title of one of Unamuno's most celebrated philosophical essays, *Del sentimiento trágico de la vida* (1913).

page 172. *El amigo Manso* [Our Friend Manso] (1882): Galdós's comic metafiction on a philosopher-teacher's unrequited love.

Annotations ❊ 239

page 172. *Niebla* [Mist] (1914): Unamuno's metafictional, antirealist *nivola*.

page 173. "Nicodemo": "Nicodemo el fariseo," an essay first delivered by Unamuno at the Madrid Ateneo in 1899 and published in *Revista Nueva* 29 (25 Nov. 1899), 241-75.

page 179. "for the English to see": A nineteenth-century Brazilian expression meaning "just for the sake of appearances," referring to Brazil's camouflage of the continuing maritime slave trade outlawed by the Anglo-Portuguese treaty.

page 179. Max Scheler (1874-1928): German philosopher and author of *The Nature of Sympathy* (1913).

page 179. Celipín Centeno, who dreams of becoming a doctor and gentleman, and his friend and protector Alejandro Miquis, the eternal student and dreamer, appear in the Galdós novel, *El doctor Centeno* [Doctor Centeno] (1883).

page 183. *La agonía del Cristianismo* [The Agony of Christianity] (1925 [French trans.]; 1931): Written in exile and against the backdrop of the Primo de Rivera military dictatorship in Spain, focuses on Unamuno's exploration of spiritual struggle.

page 183. José Asunción Silva (1865-1896): Colombian *modernista* poet; the edition of *Poesías*, with Unamuno's prologue, was published by Maucci in Barcelona (1918?).

page 185. Arzadun: Unamuno wrote a prologue for his friend Juan Arzadun's *Poesía* in 1897.

page 186. Pedro Corominas (Pere Coromines) (1870-1939): Catalan writer, politician, and economist; see his article, "El trágico fin de Miguel de Unamuno," *Atenea* (Santiago de Chile) 53, No. 157 (July 1938), 101-14.

page 189. Garcilaso de la Vega (1501-1536): Spanish lyric poet, celebrated for his eclogues, sonnets, and elegies.

240 ❈ Annotations

page 191. *La tía Tula* [Aunt Tula] (1921): Unamuno's novel on the theme of maternity; *Nada menos que todo un hombre* [Nothing Less Than a Man] (1920), from his *Three Exemplary Novels,* a novella on the struggle of being.

page 193. Petronius (ca. 22–66 AD): Author of *The Satyricon*; Lev Shestov (Leon Chestov) (1866–1938): Ukrainian religious existentialist; Alfred de Vigny (1797–1863): French Romantic poet, playwright, and novelist; Nicolás Salmerón (1838–1908): Spanish philosopher and, briefly, president of the First Republic in 1873.

page 193. Père Hyacinthe (Hyacinthe Loyson) (1827–1912): A Carmelite friar who left the Church, married the widowed Mrs. Merriman, and established a "Catholic Gallican Church."

page 200. "*Shamelessly*": I've italicized that term because of its long history in my discipular adherence to Unamuno. I can't explain that here, but neither can I let it pass unremarked. [Author's note]

page 200. Don Rodrigo: Rodrigo Calderón, Count of Oliva (1580s–1621), whose dramatic downfall in the Spanish Court led to the scaffold.

page 203. *El buen Juanito*: A possible reference to *Juanito. Obra elemental de educación* [Juanito. An Elementary Educational Work], by Luigi Alessandro Parravicini (Spanish trans. by Genaro del Valle, 1861), a religious-didactic work for children that Unamuno discusses in his *Recuerdos de niñez y de mocedad.*

Printed in Great Britain
by Amazon